In a world connected globally by the internet and increasingly affected by virtual reality, Bock and Armstrong help us—whether we receive the help eagerly or with apprehension—to understand the brave new world in which we find ourselves. The authors observe accurately the place of innovation in the history of evangelicalism, as evangelicals seized new technologies for the sake of the gospel. They provide a useful history of the rise of technology from newspapers in the day of Whitefield, to radio, to controversial televangelists, to D.J. Soto's recent VR Church. Their assessment of both helpful and harmful aspects of the new technologies available to the church will help every church leader think through the ramifications of technology. This is a topic every Christian leader post-2020 needs to understand, and *Virtual Reality Church* boldly goes to where few in the church have gone before.

ED STETZER
Dean of the School of Mission, Ministry, and Leadership, Wheaton College, and Executive Director of the Wheaton College Billy Graham Center

Scholars and practitioners Bock and Armstrong offer their knowledgeable insights on Christianity's current and future engagement with virtual reality. Grounded in their academic backgrounds of New Testament and church history, they provide a foundational overview of virtual reality, a biblical analysis of how the technology could be incorporated by Christians and the church, and a glimpse of a hopeful future. To me as a university leader and member of a church, their vision of how the gospel could go forth through virtual reality is compelling. Chapter 4 alone provides a practical starting point for organizational leaders. I would highly recommend this book to anyone interested in the intersection of virtual reality and the church.

WENDY LIDDELL
President of Great Northern U...

What a great contribution to
balance of history, tradition,
tions that all churches need to
ogy in evangelism.

WALKER TZENG
Executive Director, World Evangelical Theological Institute Association

The church today rarely discusses with substance its greatest available missions tool. Read *Virtual Reality Church* and catch a vision for what God can do. The VR harvest is plentiful, but the workers are few!

DOUGLAS ESTES
Author of *SimChurch* and *Braving the Future*

Informed by history and shaped by solid biblical commitments, *Virtual Reality Church* raises the important questions about the application of virtual and augmented reality for ministry, Christian living, worship, and the formation of Christian community. Exploring the theological meaning of church, including the practice of baptism and the Lord's Supper, Jonathan Armstrong and Darrell Bock reach across the denominational spectrum to offer thoughtful and pastoral guidance on these pressing issues, always with the goal of advancing the gospel message in our rapidly changing world. While readers will likely yearn for more answers and additional guidance to these perplexing challenges, *Virtual Reality Church* is the best introduction available on this subject. Moreover, this volume will become an essential prerequisite for those wishing to engage these issues in the days to come. Highly recommended!

DAVID S. DOCKERY
President of International Alliance for Christian Education

The most robust book on understanding virtual reality for the church. You get a great historical overview of all the ways the church has creatively embraced the newest tech along with a solid theological framework for embracing VR and whatever else comes online down the road.

JAY KRANDA
Online Campus Pastor at Saddleback Church

Technology is evolving at a rapid pace and many church leaders find themselves unprepared. How are new digital realities affecting our ecclesiology? What does it mean to be the church in the internet age? Are online and digital connections real connections? These questions are complex, nuanced, and require critical engagement on multiple levels. In this book, Darrell Bock and Jonathan Armstrong offer us several tremendous and timely gifts—deep and thoughtful reflections, thorough surveys of the current and potential future landscape, and maybe most importantly, a confident reassurance in knowing that "the one who created the universe will supply His church with sufficient creativity and guidance" to navigate this and any forthcoming technological changes we may encounter. This book is a must-read for any and all who are serving and leading the local church in the digital age.

JAY Y. KIM
Pastor and author of *Analog Church*

Bock and Armstrong describe in this well-researched volume the fascinating and at times mind-boggling possibilities of virtual reality technology. They explore through a biblical lens the opportunities and challenges it holds for the church. Be informed and be prepared for the future by reading *Virtual Reality Church*.

CRAIG OTT
Professor of Mission and Intercultural Studies, Trinity Evangelical Divinity School

Two of the main reasons Jesus sent the disciples out two by two (Mark 6:7) was to create a trustworthy account of the spreading of the Word, and garner a great reward that could be shared and validated throughout history. It is clear that Jesus did the same in the inspirational writing of *Virtual Reality Church*. He sent Darrell Bock and Jonathan Armstrong to share the credible and trustworthy witness that God is not offended by advanced technologies but will use them prudently and wisely to reach, teach, and preach to a global society in a pandemic world. If you invest the time and hear the voice of these two witnesses, you will be part of the great reward—as God spreads the knowledge of His glory around the world (Hab. 2:14). It is completely plausible God is using Bock and Armstrong to fulfill Habakkuk 2:4 and digitally run like heralds with His vision that is awaiting the appointed time. The outcome of this book will affect billions of people as it inspires every educator and minister to move forward with every means possible to carry out their mission, and the Great Commission, in unique and exciting methods.

MICHAEL L. MATHEWS
Vice President of Technology and Innovation, Oral Roberts University

Just over twenty years ago, I cofounded the Internet Telephony Consortium with one of the fathers of the internet at MIT, and people scoffed at the idea that most of our voice and video communication would be over the internet. History has proved them wrong, and in a pandemic for many churches, Zoom is their main way to stay connected. Today many people scoff at the idea that virtual reality will ever go mainstream, but in a few decades the world will likely spend more time in VR than it does in church. Armstrong and Bock show the importance of how, in the future, being sent out to where the people are is likely to mean being sent out into VR worlds as future missions fields. The effectiveness of the church in VR will depend on God and our cultural fluency in VR.

ANDREW SEARS
President of City Vision University

A foundational book! *Virtual Reality Church* addresses head-on the identity issues for the body of Christ in our increasingly digital and virtual world. The historical survey, the analysis of the medium, and the theological response will help you see where we are and where we might go as the people of God.

CLYDE TABER
Founder/Director of Visual Story Network

Armstrong and Bock connect the dots from the past to the present concerning the gospel and technology. Understanding this journey is essential because it honors the past and cultivates courage for the future as Christianity pioneers into new technology.

D.J. SOTO
Bishop of Virtual Reality Church

Wow! It may seem odd that two scholars committed to the study of the ancient texts of Holy Scripture would be our best guides for engaging the new world of virtual reality. But they are! This book charts a clear and exciting path, enabling the church to embrace new technology in the effective service of and true to the historic faith. Much needed and much appreciated!

FRED DURHAM
City Director, C. S. Lewis Institute, Dallas

Just as the global pandemic of the COVID-19 virus has created a major disruption in the way we do church, this timely book seeks to encourage and equip the church to explore the use of digital technology, particularly virtual reality (VR), for ministry. Drawing on personal experiences of teaching via virtual reality, as well as many interviews with thinkers, practitioners, and visionaries, the authors model a sound approach to assessing the potential changes—good and bad—that using new technology might bring to the church. They also provide a fascinating historical overview of the use of communications technology for evangelism and the development of online church, and look onwards to how it might develop, including a thorough exploration of the vexed question of online communion. The authors provide a strong theological exploration of how our understanding of God and the digital world might shape each other, always placing God and the gospel at the center of their exploration. There is much to learn from this book for anyone considering the use of VR for online church or evangelism, for those who are thinking through the adoption of new technology for ministry for the first time, and for more experienced practitioners.

PAM SMITH
i-church.org

New situations often require new tools, but new tools always require new wisdom. Armstrong and Bock bring much needed theological reflection paired with real-world VR experience, and whether you see VR as a problem or an opportunity, they are steady and helpful guides.

JOHN DYER
Dean and Professor, Dallas Theological Seminary and author of *From the Garden to the City: The Redeeming and Corrupting Power of Technology*

If your life has been shaped by Paul, John, and other New Testament authors you never met face-to-face, you have already experienced the power of technology to bring people together across time, distance, and culture. In their timely Virtual Reality Church, Darrell Bock and Jonathan Armstrong address critical ideas that will shape our beliefs about what it means to be the body of Christ for years to come.

KEN COCHRUM
Vice President of Global Digital Strategies, Cru

So timely! If you'd like to understand digital media's potential, be inspired to imagine new ways to communicate, and to be informed of the challenges of technology and our calling, then *Virtual Reality Church* is your book. Don't think it through by yourself. Bock and Armstrong have set the table.

JEFF BAXTER
Producer at Our Daily Bread Ministries

VIRTUAL REALITY CHURCH

PITFALLS AND POSSIBILITIES

DARRELL L. BOCK AND
JONATHAN J. ARMSTRONG

MOODY PUBLISHERS
CHICAGO

Interior Design: Ragont Design
Cover Design: Darren Welch Design
Cover illustration of hand on the right copyright © 2009 by Wojtkowski Cezary / Alamy Stock Photo (R6E69H). All rights reserved.
Cover illustration of hand on the left copyright © 2019 by portokalis / 123rf (45317277). All rights reserved.

Library of Congress Cataloging-in-Publication Data

Names: Bock, Darrell L., author. | Armstrong, Jonathan J., 1980- author.
Title: Virtual reality church : pitfalls and possibilities (or how to think biblically about church in your pajamas, vr baptisms, Jesus avatars, and whatever else is coming next) / Darrell Bock and Jonathan Armstrong.
Description: Chicago : Moody Publishers, 2021. | Includes bibliographical references. | Summary: "In Virtual Reality Church, theologians Darrell Bock and Jonathan Armstrong present a systematic reflection on how to faithfully apply virtual reality for ministry purposes. They examine the risks-like compromising the meaning of tangible worship-and opportunities-like safely reaching persecuted churches-of integrating revolutionary technologies into the Christian life"-- Provided by publisher.
Identifiers: LCCN 2020042545 | ISBN 9780802420800 | ISBN 9780802499080 (ebook)
Subjects: LCSH: Religious broadcasting--Christianity. | Church. | Virtual reality--Religious aspects--Christianity.
Classification: LCC BV655 .B63 2021 | DDC 250.285/68--dc23
LC record available at https://lccn.loc.gov/2020042545

Originally delivered by fleets of horse-drawn wagons, the affordable paperbacks from D. L. Moody's publishing house resourced the church and served everyday people. Now, after more than 125 years of publishing and ministry, Moody Publishers' mission remains the same—even if our delivery systems have changed a bit. For more information on other books (and resources) created from a biblical perspective, go to www .moodypublishers.com or write to:

Moody Publishers
820 N. LaSalle Boulevard
Chicago, IL 60610

1b 3 5 7 9 10 8 6 4 2

Printed in the United States of America

*To those behind-the-scenes people at many organizations
who work in institutional technology and media,
making us all more efficient in the process*

To Marie Armstrong and Sally Bock

CONTENTS

TECHNOLOGY: A SURPRISING CORONAVIRUS SUBSTITUTE

I t was March 2020. In the blink of an eye at the end of spring break, I (Darrell) was told as a faculty member that all my classes would not meet in a traditional classroom. "Social distancing" had become a stock phrase, students returning from who knows where to meet in the proximity of a classroom had become dangerous, and anyone could have been a hidden carrier. What would be the solution? All classes would go online. Teaching would be by livestream, in a limited virtual environment. Professors could choose from a number of technology platforms: Zoom, Canvas, or Moodle. In the last few months, I have used each of these and more. Our workspace would follow the same rules. Suddenly, colleagues who were used to spending hours together collaborating side by side would do so only from a safe distance. Learning and work would go on, just in a fresh, desperately needed way.

When Jonathan and I first envisioned this book, the above scenario requiring online teaching was nowhere in our thinking. A global pandemic that shut down the world was a plotline for movies and science fiction. It sprung on us like Pandora's box. Yet suddenly, thousands of professors and teachers, and millions of students—some of whom had never even stepped into a video-conferencing platform of any sort, much less ever donned VR goggles—had to discover a new way of teaching and learning with or (in the vast majority of cases) without goggles! Instruction, which is as old as humanity itself, had to take on a different form. Fortunately, an alternative was available. The same story was replayed in churches worldwide. All of a sudden, I found myself preaching or discussing theology online from Dallas to places like Cape Town in South Africa and Chennai in India. My ministry literally changed overnight.

Virtual platforms for telecommunication run along a spectrum. A plethora of VR (virtual reality) and AR (augmented reality) products have debuted over the past several years. However, the beginning of that spectrum is basic livestreaming and video conferencing. Most class chatroom environments do not work at the level of sophistication of VR, but they are related in some important ways. All these environments share some level of interactivity. Depending on the size of the group, they also vary in levels of intimacy. Any of them can provide social distance in the face of threatening viruses, something made painfully but gratefully evident during the unprecedented global coronavirus pandemic of 2020. In this book, we will discuss the potential in such engagement, as well as its limits, and I (Darrell) will share what pushed me to think more positively about all forms of online engagement. I will also discuss from a ministry perspective the issues that administrators think through in order to decide what the medium of instruction should be, and what we decided to offer or cancel when the virus necessitated changes in the way we did ministry.

Lessons from Australia

When I was growing up, we as a society communicated differently from how we do now. We had rotary dial phones, typewriters, and Xerox machines. There was no satellite communication between nations that could send video until I was eight years old (in 1962, the Telstar satellite made live transatlantic television broadcasts possible for the first time). I have had to grow into technology. Many of you reading this have lived with it your whole life. These different experiences have produced different responses to technology's presence and near omnipresence.

My change of heart toward certain forms of the use of technology for teaching, the church, and theological instruction came in 2012. I was always open to technology and appreciated it but had thought that when it came to learning, face-to-face was always best. I still think this, but what I experienced was that the definition of "face-to-face" was being altered by technology. In 2012, I was invited to teach a New Testament Introduction (NTI) class in Perth, Australia. I had been teaching for thirty years, always face-to-face in a classroom. NTI is a class loaded with detailed information about the setting and context of the books and study of the New Testament. It is information heavy.

My class was to be a hybrid: six weeks communicating online and then a final week in Perth with my students. In the six weeks before my trip to Perth, I submitted questions related to some topics in NTI for students to respond to online. They did the assignments faithfully. All I had to identify my students was a picture of their face with their response. Today, one can interact live, face-to-face, with others in a variety of effective ways: Skype (initially released in 2003), FaceTime (2010), Zoom (2011), or Google Hangouts (2013). Get in line and take your pick. But my interactions with students were based on a question-and-answer format and involved a less technical, less visual chat interface. Still, I was able to learn about these students without ever seeing them. As they responded to my questions over the six weeks, I saw how they thought and reasoned, what sources they sought out, and how clearly they could express the ideas they grappled with.

When I finally went to Perth to teach in the classroom there, names and photos became faces and complete persons. Yet I knew more about each of those students and what they needed teaching-wise than I had known about any of my students in thirty years of previous teaching. By interacting with them one-on-one, back and forth in the chat interface, I discovered what each student had in terms of background, strengths to reinforce, and weaknesses to work on.

The whole experience revealed to me what was possible because of technology. Through that class, distance learning became real to me, and I immediately saw its value. This does not mean there were not limitations. Communication is complicated and even tedious when one is only writing and cannot see another's face, but even some of those limitations have been overcome with improved technology that now exists and with even more enhancements to come. During the pandemic, others would experience some of what I had earlier. Still, questions remain about outcomes, "Zoom fatigue," and ultimate effectiveness. We will explore such questions, yet with a view to what might be possible and effective for the church.

Two lessons emerged from this experience for me. First, I cannot fully assess what I have not experienced. Some discuss, and criticize, new forms of technology without trying it out to see what it does and what it can and cannot do. That is not how one rightly assesses capability. Second, each medium has its own strengths and weaknesses. Each enhancement can bring changes to what is possible. With this experience, I stepped onto the live and distance spectrum—baby steps for sure, but now driving on the technological highway. In that light, this book has two core goals: (1) to encourage educators and ministers to think about the history of the church's use of tech and so to be disciplined and flexible in their approach to future use, and (2) to think critically about which processes in education and church life can be improved by increased use of virtual telecommunication and which processes should be kept on campus or conducted in person in the church building.

Lessons from Department Meetings and Board Work

My first computer was a Kaypro. It predated Apple and arrived in the 1980s. It was a metal box, with no thoughts given to its ascetics; the pixelated screen brought text to me in green letters. But it changed my professional career. I could write and edit on the fly. No longer did footnotes have to be measured to fit on the bottom of a page via typewriter and carbon Xerox paper. It used floppy disks and had barely enough memory to do much beyond write the text, but it opened up new options for me as a writer. Gone were notes on three-by-five cards. I could edit fluidly, moving sentences and paragraphs around at will. Editing no longer required rewriting each page with a fresh layout.

About a decade later, many resources became available online. My trips to the library decreased. I could write anywhere, including on an airplane, and still do research. Most importantly, the two suitcases of books that used to travel with me as I was writing and researching disappeared as those resources came online. I even led a team that produced the precursor to Logos Bible Software as we worked with a CD-ROM based program that made standard resources available in a digital format (CD Word Library in the late 80s, which Logos purchased and used to make a far better product). All this is now part of technological history, as we have progressed significantly in many of these areas, but the spectrum of opportunity remains, just enhanced in its capabilities.

Technology grew even as aspects of what I did as a professor remained the same. I still had content to teach. I still had to engage with students whom we cared about, not only because of what we wanted them to know but also because of who they needed to be in ministry. As these technological changes came to my world decade by decade, our seminary was also considering how to reach people who would likely never come to the Dallas campus for a seminary education. There were many reasons why that might be the case. By the 1980s, electronic resources for biblical research became available for the first time to the consumer market, and more reliable and sophisticated versions of these resources were released in the 1990s. Suddenly, by the late 2000s, speaking to and interacting with people online by video call became possible. By the 2010s, numerous platforms for videoconferencing had emerged, mimicking classroom instruction and dialogue. The nature of face-to-face communication was changing.

So did the new debates.

Could we teach classes online and provide the relational aspects needed to prepare someone for ministry? Could mentoring take place online? Could you really get to know someone hundreds or thousands of miles away? These were the questions that swirled and, to some degree, still swirl in the faculty meetings and board meetings that I am part of, as someone who has taught for almost four decades and who has served as a board member at Wheaton College for a decade. Will teaching online compromise the nature of the teaching-learning experience, a tradition with a centuries-old track record? I sometimes hear "we have never done it that way before" echoing in these conversations.

When these issues come up in these contexts, I ask another series of questions: What do we gain and lose when we apply a new technology or process? What can the new medium do for us that we otherwise could not do and why? What might be possible that was not possible before? I am wired to look ahead not just back. Technology was no exception. I had learned since the age of eight that it opened interesting doors and provided links that otherwise could not be contemplated. It was a matter of new vistas, but it takes thinking through them with care, not with an all-or-nothing attitude. Also, there is the reverse question. What can we *not* do when we apply a new technology or process and why? Is there any way to adjust for what is lost? If we take a moment to think outside the box, what might we find? It is the call of our schools, colleges, universities, seminaries, and churches to reach and train people and to nurture them in the faith. So a core question is: Can the use of technology help us to get there? Once someone steps onto the technological spectrum, these questions arise and remain, regardless of the specific medium under view. These are the kinds of questions that must be asked and reviewed in order to utilize the resources effectively.

I have watched two campuses transition in their use of such resources. I have watched them wrestle with such questions. I have heard those who were gung-ho speak up and have listened as those who were skeptical raised their concerns. I have seen successes and failures. In many cases, you learn by doing. Seeing and engaging produces understanding in how something works, both well and poorly. And then sometimes something comes along that alters circumstances, whether it be a technological enhancement or a change in the setting that causes one to ask even harder questions, sometimes out of necessity.

That is what the coronavirus crisis did for countless educational institutions, ministries, and churches. All of a sudden, technology was not just optional but a necessity. IT (Institutional Technology) or AIT (Academic Institutional Technology) became one of the most important departments on campus. Even faculty who had hardly touched technology beyond using email had to learn a new way to teach classes. A new world with its possibilities and limitations opened up and—simply for the school to operate—the technology had to work. It was a brave new world as students quarantined around the globe were still able to attend and participate in classes.

Lessons from Recent Ministry

Faculty meetings were different in the wake of the coronavirus crisis. Due to social distancing, we met to pray and to plan how we would bring seminary to students scattered across the globe as seventy-five faces on a screen. No one was going to be able to walk into traditional classrooms and teach as we used to. New issues had to be faced: How best to position the computer so that the instructor could be seen? What was the best technique for lighting? Could students access the PowerPoint presentations along with video recordings of the professors' lectures? How could professors create and distribute video clips for their classes? All of this could be done; one just had to learn a new way of doing things. Church also changed. My wife and I sat in our living room and caught a sermon preached from miles away with a music team on video recording. It was strange at first.

When my class finally reconvened online after the initial shifts from the pandemic, I created what I called "The Open Hour." No lecture or new material, as we had not met for a month—just time to adjust to the new teaching environment, ask questions, and reconnect in a new way. Not everything lost could be replaced, but it surely was a blessing that we had technology to help us deal with the situation.

About the same time all this was going on, I purchased my first personal virtual reality headset. It was not for class but as preparation for this book project. Previously, I had visited a church in virtual reality and had roamed around AltspaceVR, the platform on which one VR church commonly convenes. Now it was my chance to connect more directly with a full sense of the new environment VR creates. At first, it was awkward to have a few pounds dangling from my head. Upon trying the headset on, I waved to my wife to see what it was like. Being able to see our photos of the Sydney Opera House laid out in 360 degrees was an unexpected pleasure. Stepping into a race car and getting an up-close feel of that experience was something I'd be unlikely to do in real life. The real revelation was stumbling on a website about opera and watching Tosca up close and personal through VR, selecting where to place myself on the stage and seeing the singer's eyes and all the characters' actions, the joy, the tragedy, while hearing the beautiful harmonies. That was far different from what my wife and I could do when we attended the opera in an auditorium both in Dallas and in Europe years ago. A traditional form of entertainment had been recast in a new context that enhanced the experience. It was a metaphor for what we are discussing in this book.

The point emerged for me again. Different media have different strengths and capabilities. They yield distinct results. Some things media can replicate, such as the passing on of information, and others go missing, such as the face-to-face ability to sense a close connection. Yet in certain circumstances, technology becomes an alternative way to accomplish what needs to be done. As I donned the VR headset, it dawned on me that one could use VR to display God's glory in creation while speaking about His presence and power. In this way, simply through the use of a 360-degree photo, one could produce a different kind of appreciation for the general revelation of creation. I also sensed that VR could create an opportunity for audiences to stand closer to speakers than is possible in traditional auditoriums. VR can compellingly facilitate interactivity, but living side by side in an incarnated manner is not the same. Strengths and limitations coexist.

This book is about exploring the possibilities and limits of the virtual church. We aim to take a big step into the technological spectrum while engaging in careful reflection about it. It is a new world, and we are still learning what this new environment can and cannot do. Some circumstances make it an advantageous place to meet. Many potential examples leap to mind, such as: people who (1) live in the 10/40 Window and may not have many believers close by; (2) live in countries where meeting together in a church is illegal and where the church is persecuted, a situation not unlike the one created by the coronavirus crisis where people were prevented from gathering together; (3) seek to explore the church and theology in a digital world in order to reflect on God, the world, and life itself in a new way. We seek to explore that digital world, to assess what is possible and what is not, to help people appreciate what can be expected and what may need supplementing if this is how they choose or are forced to gather together with the saints. We invite you to explore this area with us, to ponder anew what the Almighty can do as God is in this new and highly intriguing space.

Chapter 1

NEW MEDIA AND THE GOOD NEWS

"I HAVE BECOME ALL THINGS TO ALL PEOPLE,
THAT BY ALL POSSIBLE MEANS I MIGHT SAVE SOME."

✦ The Apostle Paul (1 Cor. 9:22)

"I LOOK ON ALL THE WORLD AS MY PARISH."[1]

✦ John Wesley

O ver the six decades of his unprecedented career as an evangelist, "Hollywood-handsome" Billy Graham (1918–2018) stood up, Bible in hand, and preached crusade after crusade to a staggering 215 million souls. Endowed with the charisma of a movie star and possessing the spiritual vision of an apostle, Billy Graham made it his life's ambition to employ every means possible to reach as many people as possible for the sake of the gospel. Operating within the conventions of the twentieth century, Graham's priority to reach the world with the good news of Jesus Christ meant that he maintained a travel schedule that is simply unimaginable today. Graham missed the birth of his first daughter because he was away on a preaching tour, and even when he was home with his family, he could be elsewhere mentally.[2] Initial planning for the 1954 London Crusade so engrossed him that he entertained visitors in the hospital room where his wife was about to give birth to their fourth child. When Graham continued to conduct meetings in the hospital room after Ruth's labor pains started in earnest, a nurse transferred her to another room. Graham recounts in his autobiography that the nurse returned a few hours later to announce that Ruth had given birth to a son, and Graham confesses that he had been completely unaware.[3]

In addition to a superabundance of personal passion, a confluence of factors that Graham could not have orchestrated also fueled the phenomenal success of his preaching. In 1949 at the Los Angeles crusade, publishing magnate William Randolph Hearst famously directed his staff to "puff Graham"—that is, to feature positive stories of the crusade throughout his media empire, which was then the nation's largest. The spiritual hunger that permeated western societies and, in fact, the entire globe, in the wake of World War II opened doors not only into hearts but also into nations.[4] Billy Graham is celebrated for having spoken in person to more people in his lifetime than any other figure in human history.

There will never be another Billy Graham. When Billy Graham was asked in 1974 at the Lausanne Congress who the "next Billy Graham" would be, he responded "they will," pointing to the crowd of evangelists who had assembled for the congress. Graham followed in a train of American evangelists who translated the revivalist tradition—which had provided the framework for Billy's own conversion experience in 1934, when itinerant evangelist Mordecai Ham led a series of tent meetings not far from the Graham family dairy farm in Charlotte, North Carolina—into a worldwide movement. *Newsweek* declared 1976 "the year of the evangelical," and in this same year Jimmy Carter, who was vocal about his "born-again" faith, campaigned for and won the presidency. Billy Graham met with each of the US presidents since World War II, sharing vital spiritual conversations with all of them and fostering warm personal friendships with several of them.

"Graham was less a preacher than a Protestant Saint," historian Grant Wacker comments, noting that Billy Graham was listed on Gallup's "Ten Most Admired Men" sixty-one times between 1955 and 2017.[5] When one counts listeners and viewers who witnessed Graham's preaching via radio, television, and internet broadcast, the number touched by Graham's ministry surges to over two billion people—approximately one-third of the population of planet Earth at the time of Graham's retirement from public ministry in 2005. Unquestionably, Graham was used mightily by God. To this day, evangelicalism has been profoundly influenced by his ministry. Our understanding of the way church and ministry work have been shaped by his use of mass media, his broad-brush approach to denominational differences, and his gospel-centered theology.

But many sense a change in the winds. We are entering a new era that raises new questions and calls for new approaches. New technologies are now emerging that make possible social and religious movements of an unprecedented scale and complexity. At the beginning of the twenty-first century, the world was astonished that one man could preach to a third of the world's population over the course of his lifetime, but by the end of the twenty-first century—if not well before—the technological infrastructure will be in place for one person to speak to the entire world in a single instant. What does this mean for the church? What do these new possibilities in global telecommunication mean for the community on earth to whom God has entrusted the message of eternal salvation?

A small network of ministry leaders have seen these changes coming. These leaders have been watching the shifts in the technological landscape and have been able to pivot their ministries to take advantage of new opportunities. One of the most forward-thinking ministry strategists of his generation is Walt Wilson. "Everything is now shifting from the world of atoms to the world of bits," Wilson could write already in 2000 in his book, *The Internet Church*.[6] Wilson worked for Steve Jobs as one of Apple's first project managers before joining Computer Sciences Corporation (CSC), one of the dominant tech companies at the close of the millennium. While at a consultation sponsored by MIT about how to monetize the internet, Wilson sensed a calling from God to use the burgeoning technology of the internet to spread the gospel.[7] In 2004, as Mel Gibson was preparing to release *The Passion of the Christ*, Wilson approached Gibson and asked whether he could run a series of internet ads based on the film in order to solicit those who wanted to know more about Jesus to contact an online group of specially trained spiritual counselors. This was long before many of us began to think of the internet as a mission field.

Wilson received the necessary permissions and ran the ads, resulting in unexpected numbers of decisions for Christ. Global Media Outreach (GMO), as the ministry is known today, continues to connect searching souls on the internet with spiritual counselors online through a portfolio of ads and gospel-promoting websites. And the numbers of those making decisions for Christ worldwide continue to soar.

When I (Jonathan) interviewed Jeff Gowler, the CEO at GMO, the ministry was preparing to celebrate the milestone of having made its two billionth gospel presentation online. We conducted the interview under lockdown, as this was early in the coronavirus quarantine, and I asked Gowler how the pandemic had affected the ministry of GMO. Prior to the coronavirus crisis, GMO had been reaching about 350,000 people each day with a presentation of the gospel. Speaking in late April 2020, Gowler confirmed: "This last week our numbers have averaged 550,000 gospel presentations per day."

And Global Media Outreach is not alone in having discovered the massive opportunities of online ministry. As of October 2020, YouVersion could boast that its flagship *Bible App* has been downloaded on over 445 million unique devices.[8] One-Hope, in partnership with YouVersion, has developed a popular children's Bible storybook called *The Bible App for Kids*, which has now been downloaded over 50 million times.[9] With its colorful animations and theologically straightforward telling of the most memorable Bible stories, this app has become the stained-glass windows of the digital church, sharing the timeless stories of the Bible with a new generation of children. While experiencing our Christian life online or through computer tools still feels new for many of us, the reality is that for hundreds of millions of people, computer technology and the internet facilitate part of their daily religious experience.

Sean Dunn, a pioneer in innovative youth ministry, was doing crusade-style evangelism when he felt God calling him to reorient his ministry paradigm. "I started to realize that I was only influencing people who were willing to give me an hour to come to my camp, my conference, my church."[10] But the question to which Dunn really wanted to know the answer was: "How do you influence a generation that runs away?" In 2017, Dunn made the leap to digital evangelism, recognizing that "the younger generations consume media differently than we do, and so we jumped into the digital thing, and that's when our growth really began to accelerate." By the close of 2019, Dunn's ministry had witnessed 83,970 people come to faith over the course of the past twelve months. "Today, we're on track to have our first day in the US where we'll see one thousand people come to faith," Dunn said in late April of 2020. "We've grown 300 percent in the last four weeks since the pandemic started." He continued: "People are huddling in their corner, but they're taking their phones."

Ken Cochrum converted to Christianity while a mechanical engineering student at the University of Texas through the ministry of Cru (formerly Campus Crusade for Christ). After graduating from college, he joined Cru as a staff member and served in various positions, including one assignment overseas. In 2012, while in prayer in his office, Ken felt God calling him to do something new and bold—to form a team at Cru focused exclusively on digital ministry. And so the Global Digital Strategies team at Cru came into being.

Ken framed the problem that the Global Digital Strategies team is trying to solve this way in our interview: "What can we do to present Jesus Christ in a relevant way within fifteen seconds on a four-inch piece of glass, anywhere in the world, 24/7/365?"[11] Ken oversees a team of about five hundred people from around the world who together witness a remarkable response to their online missionary endeavors: "The fruitfulness that we see is about 205 million unique users in the last 365 days from over 200 countries." Ken reminded me: "Even though we see a lot of numbers and analytics in the Global Digital Strategies team, the heart behind it is really that behind every screen is a person, and every person has a story, and every single story matters to God."

What is going on as we push another decade deeper into the third millennium of the history of Christianity? What is the picture that emerges from the swirling torrents of change around us? For Walt Wilson, the story is clear: the internet is the new Roman Road. The Roman roads were built to ensure that the Roman military could move soldiers and supplies quickly from anywhere to anywhere within the empire. But this network of roads, crisscrossing the Roman Empire during the days of Jesus and the apostle Paul, was used not only by the Roman military; it also became the communication network through which the early church brought the gospel to every corner of the empire, finally leading to the conversion of Rome under Constantine the Great in the fourth century.

Like the Roman roads, Wilson notes, the internet was also built as a military tool, one designed to serve as a communication infrastructure so resilient that not even atomic warfare could neutralize it.[12] The roads that the Romans built to move their legions were traveled by the Christian missionaries of the first century. Now the network built by the US Department of Defense can be traveled by the Christian missionaries of the twenty-first century at virtually no cost. "It is hard for me not to be startled by the parallel nature of these events," Wilson writes.[13] For Wilson, the appearance of the internet represents a divinely orchestrated opportunity to access every person on planet Earth with the gospel and thereby to complete the Great Commission.

The purpose of this book is to explore the way that VR—one specific technology reflecting the wave of new technologies in development in our era—can be applied for the purposes of Christian ministry. We would not have chosen to write a book about VR if we did not believe that VR possesses potential to reshape our culture in profound ways in the coming years. But we also hope that, by showcasing biblical and theological reflection on one specific emerging technology, this study can serve as a guide for Christian leaders as they seek to adapt any number of telecommunication technologies for ministry purposes.

Technology has been progressing at such a rapid pace that some assume there is no rhyme or reason to what may show up next in the marketplace or in our homes. The speed of change is now so lightning fast that many of us have simply quit trying to understand what is going on around us. But stewardship of the gospel demands that we make an attempt to decode this revolution.

The Internet Revolution

I (Jonathan) was speaking to a small group of church leaders in Washington State about VR and the changes that I anticipate this new technology will bring for churches and educational institutions. After the presentation, a retired missionary approached me with a question. This saint had spent four decades on the mission field in Papua New Guinea, translating the

Scriptures into one of the country's more than eight hundred languages. Picking up one of the dry erase markers, the retired missionary began writing on the white board.

"So, let me get this right," he said, drawing out a timeline of the twenty centuries of Christian history. "You're saying that the Roman roads in the first century created a way for the gospel to reach the whole Roman Empire." He scribbled a cross to represent the beginning of the Christian era. "And after Rome fell in the fifth century, Western Europe remained a center for Christian learning and tradition," he continued. "And somewhere about here," he said, marking the middle of the fifteenth century, "Johannes Gutenberg invented the printing press in the 1450s, and this started the print age, eventually leading to the full flowering of the Reformation. Then we have the rise of the railroad and the telegraph, about here," he said, doodling his way through the nineteenth century, "which coincides with the apex of the British Empire and the Protestant missions movement. Then comes mass media—radio and television," he said, moving over into the twentieth century. "And what you're saying is that the rise of the internet and virtual reality is going to be the next chapter in that story?" This missionary, who had lived the majority of his life in one of the least developed countries on earth, had seen the picture more clearly than any of us.

The world is both bigger and smaller than it used to be. The world's population is larger, and everyone maintains more complex social networks than we used to, but at the same time, everyone's reach extends further, and so we feel like everyone is closer to us than they used to be. Tom Goodwin could write in 2015: "Uber, the world's largest taxi company, owns no vehicles. Facebook, the world's most popular media owner, creates no content. Alibaba, the most valuable retailer, has no inventory. And AirBnB, the world's largest accommodation provider, owns no real estate. Something interesting is happening."[14]

Can we map out this revolution? Since the first appearance of the internet, sociologists of religion began comparing the epic changes brought about by the printing press to an anticipated set of changes in Christianity that the internet would produce.[15] How can we get a handle on all of the technological changes taking place under our feet?

To many commentators, it is clear that the internet revolution is the fastest expanding and broadest technological revolution in human history.[16] In a mere three decades, the internet has developed from a single webpage created by the British computer scientist, Tim Berners-Lee, in 1991 at CERN in Switzerland into the world's primary communication channel for almost everything. The internet was initially developed in a nuclear physics laboratory in order to serve as a specialized research tool for scientists, yet it has become the way that most people on planet Earth shop, bank, experience entertainment, read news and product reviews, and countless other activities. Following the commercialization of the internet in 1995, the number of internet users worldwide skyrocketed. In 1995, there were about 16 million internet users worldwide; by 2001, this number had climbed to over 500 million. The number of internet users worldwide crossed the 1 billion mark in 2005, at which time this represented 15 percent of the world's population.

By 2010, the number of internet users worldwide crossed the 2 billion mark (representing 29 percent of the world's population), and then 3 billion by 2014 (representing 42 percent of the world's population). As of June of 2020, there were over 4.8

billion internet users worldwide (representing over 62 percent of the world's population).[17] It would be hard to exaggerate the breadth, depth, and suddenness of the internet revolution. At the very least, we could say that the advent of the internet has more profoundly affected the daily life of more people on planet Earth than any other invention in human history. What would its closest rival be? The invention of writing? We are clearly living in a unique juncture in history.

The extent of the revolution may be measured by counting the global numbers of internet users, but the depth of the revolution—that is, the myriad ways that technology shapes our daily lives—is not easy to assess. We do know that technology is gaining an ever-deepening influence in society. Not only are the lives of more people affected by the internet than ever, but their lives are affected in more areas than ever. As computers become faster and more capable of mimicking human interaction, their presence is becoming ubiquitous in every area of our lives.

Presently, driverless cars are at once a symbol of the revolution and one of its major frontiers, illustrating the depth of the social, economic, and cultural impact of this revolution. Around 2010, the scientific community was convinced that autonomous cars would remain impossible until deep into the future; now we can't imagine a future that does not include driverless cars.[18] As computer processing power has become ever faster and cheaper, the list of tasks that can be automated and entrusted to our digital personal assistants continues to grow. IBM's "Deep Blue" chess-playing computer lost in 1996 to Garry Kasparov, the world's then-reigning champion. But one year later in 1997, Deep Blue prevailed. A computer program, developed by a team of dedicated scientists, had defeated the world's leading chess champion at one of humanity's classic strategy games. Could computer programs begin to best people at other intellectual challenges?

In 2011, IBM's supercomputer "Watson" challenged the undefeated Brad Rutter and Ken Jennings at *Jeopardy!* Playing *Jeopardy!* required the computer to listen to and respond to questions in natural language, winning the highly publicized tournament with the answer "Who is Bram Stoker?" in the category "19th Century Novelists" to the question: "William Wilkinson's 'An Account of the Principalities of Wallachia and Moldovia' inspired this author's most famous novel." Watson could process five hundred gigabytes of information per second, or about the equivalent of one million books. In an interview following the tournament, Brad Rutter commented: "I would have thought that technology like this was years away, but it's here now. I have the bruised ego to prove it." Ken Jennings said: "My past *Jeopardy!* experiences have been great, but they weren't really weighty with this kind of technological-philosophical importance. I think we saw something important today."[19] Since Watson's gameshow triumph in 2011, IBM has been focusing its attention on applying the computer program to improving medical care.

The latest supercomputing feat in this litany came in 2017, when Google's AlphaGo toppled the world's leading Go player.[20] Go is a strategy game of mind-boggling mathematical complexity that was invented in ancient China. IMB's Deep Blue, which became the world's chess champion twenty years earlier in 1997, was capable of evaluating two hundred million moves per second, but this level of computing is magnitudes of order too little to play the game of Go effectively. Go has an unspeakable number of possible moves—to be precise, there are ten to the three-hundred-and-sixtieth-power possible moves in the game of Go. This means that Go has more possible moves than there are atoms in the visible universe! The game is so complex that it defies the "if this, then that" type of programing that Deep Blue had been able to harness in order to excel at the game of chess.[21] For AlphaGo to best the world's champion, the computer had to learn how to learn. Basically, the computer had to learn how to program itself, and the success of this project demonstrated that computers may be able to program themselves to accomplish other tasks that are too complicated for human programmers to reduce to a set of rules. At least for now, there is no end in sight to the limits of where this revolution is leading us.

MIT professors Erik Brynjolfsson and Andrew McAfee call this revolution "The Second Machine Age." If the Industrial Revolution in the eighteenth century began to replace the work of our hands with the work of machines, then the revolution that is now taking place all around us is replacing the work of our intellectual faculties with the work of digital computing.[22] The analogy has limitations, but it points us in the right direction. When I begin to prepare a sermon, I open Logos Bible Software and begin studying Scripture on my computer. Logos saves me hours of research time by performing a variety of search functions through the thousands of books in my digital library, tasks that had me combing the stacks of my seminary library for days at a time.

Other lucid writers speak of the same basic transitions at play in our cultural moment by other names. What Brynjolfsson and McAfee call "The Second Machine Age," Klaus Schwab, the founder and executive chairman of the World Economic

Forum, calls "the fourth industrial revolution."[23] According to this analysis, the first industrial revolution came with the rise of steam power (beginning in the 1760s), and the second came with the transition from steam power to electricity (in the decades around 1900). The third industrial revolution marks the transition from mechanical and analogue electronic processes to digital computing (beginning in the 1950s), and the fourth industrial revolution represents the internet revolution and its continual unfolding with artificial intelligence (from the 1990s onward).

In 2007, when Apple unveiled its first iPhone, it was about the only device consumers owned that they referred to as "smart." Increasingly, everything around us is becoming "smart"—that is, these devices automatically transmit data to the internet and modify their functions based on data that they receive back from the internet.[24] We are crossing a threshold whereby the majority of the data pulsing through the internet is no longer person-to-person communication (such as an SMS text or an email) but sensor-to-cloud (for example, the data generated by the smart components in airplanes, home security systems, and even our refrigerators). We are quickly moving to an era where the bulk of the information transmitted on the internet is data written by machines to be read by other machines.[25] It used to be that we watched our movies and read our books; now our movies watch us, and our books read us! Our smart assistants listen to our conversations, ready to do our bidding at any time. This silent and invisible transmission of data at an inconceivable pace and scale all around us is at the core of what the internet revolution is about. And VR is emerging as a new and compelling way for people to visualize and interface with these data streams.

Since the rise of digital computers in the second half of the twentieth century, we've watched as supercomputers that formerly only governments could afford have become consumer products in the span of a few decades. Thus, computers that once required the space of several tennis courts, the electricity supply of whole villages, and cost hundreds of millions of dollars have become affordable to average consumers within a generation. For example, the Cray-2 became the fastest supercomputer in the world when it was released in 1985, and Apple's iPad 2, which released in 2011, has an equivalent computing power.[26] The Frontier supercomputer, scheduled to be operational by 2021, is projected to be the world's most advanced supercomputer with the computational output of 1.5 exaflops—that is, the equivalent of the computing power of the 160 next most powerful supercomputers in the world combined.[27] If current trends continue, we could anticipate that, in the year 2050, our child or grandchild might unwrap as a Christmas present a device with technical specifications equivalent to the Frontier supercomputer. December 25, 2050, falls on a Sunday. After the festivities of opening gifts on Christmas morning, will our loved ones get in their cars and drive to a church service with this new device in their pocket? What will church services even look like then? How will the experience of worship and faith on Christmas Day of 2050 continue the tradition of the Christianity that we know?

What Is VR and Why Is It Important?

In August 2012, news outlets and technology forums were buzzing with reports of consumer VR. A new company called

"Oculus" had launched its Kickstarter campaign for a new virtual reality headset, which Oculus's founder, Palmer Luckey, called the "Rift." This Kickstarter campaign sparked hope that the dream of VR could become a consumer product in the near future. VR had been a popular theme in science fiction for some time, at least since Neal Stephenson's 1992 novel *Snow Crash*—which coined the term "Metaverse"—and the 1999 blockbuster film, *The Matrix*. In fact, VR was not merely science fiction but had been a working technology for some time, yet it was vastly too expensive and unwieldy to be made into something that people could actually buy and use at home. In 1968, while teaching at Harvard and MIT, Ivan Sutherland invented the first VR display system. The contraption was so large and menacing that they called it the "Sword of Damocles," named after the fabled sword that dangled over the head of the king in Greek mythology.

In 1984, Jaron Lanier founded VPL Research, which is generally regarded as the first company to develop and market VR products, such as VR headsets and haptic gloves. A quick review of the collection of products that Lanier developed way back in the 1980s will reveal why he is sometimes called the father of virtual reality. Not only did he coin the term "virtual reality" in 1978,[28] but the products that VPL Research created forty years ago are by and large the same as those on the market today, at least in terms of outer appearance and purpose. In the intervening years, computer processing power has accelerated significantly, so the level of detail in today's VR simulations is vastly greater and the cost of the equipment has plunged downward. VPL Research's VR systems cost millions of dollars in the 1980s, and by 2003, when Jeremy Bailenson founded the

Virtual Human Interaction Lab at Stanford University, a quality VR system cost notably less at about $100,000 per unit. Still, the basic concept of VR—that the user straps on a set of goggles in order to see stereoscopic imagery of a digitally created environment—has not changed over the past half century since Ivan Sutherland created the first VR system in a university laboratory.

Then, something rocked the tech world, something that convinced not only gamers and geeks but also investors that VR could soon become the next computing platform. In March 2014, Facebook bought Oculus for over two billion dollars. On August 17, 2015, *Time* magazine ran the cover story "The Surprising Joy of Virtual Reality: And Why It's about to Change the World."[29] In October 2017, at Facebook's developer conference, Mark Zuckerberg stood in front of a giant screen and announced his company's bold new goal: "1 billion people in VR." All of this generated a tremendous stir among creatives and those interested in emerging media. Facebook released the Oculus Quest 1 in May 2019 and the Oculus Quest 2 in October 2020. Although not the first VR headsets released by Facebook, the Oculus Quest 1 and 2 were in many ways the first headsets to deliver what enthusiasts had been hoping for all along since the initial Kickstarter campaign in 2012. The Oculus Quest 1 and 2 were stand-alone VR headsets (meaning that they did not require a desktop computer to operate, and they had no wires tethering them to any additional equipment); they were completely portable and could be configured to any room almost instantly (whereas previous systems required several hours to install and calibrate); and at the base price of $399 and $299 respectively, they were praised as affordable. In an interview in 2015, Jeremy Bailenson revealed that the VR lab at Stanford University had switched from its proprietary VR headsets costing tens of thousands of dollars to the $350 prototype released by Oculus. "My lab is very quickly becoming, from a hardware standpoint, not as special as it was," Bailenson confessed.[30] VR was becoming, for the first time, available to everyone.

How do we define virtual reality? It's not easy to do. Jaron Lanier, who knows VR about as well as anyone, compiles no fewer than fifty-two definitions of virtual reality in his book.[31] We are not technical specialists but biblical scholars, and so, for the most part, we are content to let the industry define for us what VR is. Nevertheless, it will be helpful to identify some key features of VR at this point. VR is a computer interface (analogous to the computer screen, which has served as the primary computer interface for the past several decades) that is capable of receiving input and delivering output in three dimensions. Some call VR "spatial computing," and this is an apt name, since VR allows the user to see and respond to data in a 3D environment. Basically, VR maps data over the top of a physical space and allows users to be actors in a digitally created world by their motions and manipulations in the real world. For many people, the experience of VR is like stepping into the computer world, and one can suddenly see all around the artifacts that used to be visible only through the computer screen.

Someday in the not-too-distant future, young people will be shocked to learn that our experience of computers was once limited to rectangular windows about twelve-inches wide. While we will reserve the terminology of "virtual reality" or VR for head-mounted display systems, we will use the term "virtual" somewhat more loosely. In keeping with the way that hospitals and schools now offer "virtual" appointments, we will speak of "virtual" technology as any internet-based platform for group communication and interaction.

At the present moment, tech companies tend to distinguish rigidly between VR and AR (augmented reality). In our view, these differences, which companies use to distinguish product lines from one another, will likely fade in the future as people begin to locate the real usefulness of the underlying technology. Some explain AR by calling it "headphones for the eyes," and this may point to a realistic vision of the future. When you walk through an airport terminal or down a busy city sidewalk today, you'll see that many people are wearing a pair of headphones or have in their ears a set of earbuds. Everyone is moving to and fro on the same walkways and in and out of the same stores and coffee shops, but everyone is engaged in their individual audio programing. In the near future, it may be that everyone will walk around wearing AR glasses, seeing and interacting with their own visual realities. Like the other technologies discussed in this book, AR has been around for some time. Augmented Reality entered public consciousness in 2012, when Google released its "Google Glass Explorer Edition" for $1,500, but the project was premature and cancelled by 2015. Nevertheless, almost all the tech giants have invested significantly in the research and development of AR and seem poised to release a panoply of AR devices in the years immediately ahead.

While we may think of AR as perhaps even more futuristic than VR, the reality is that many of us already use a primitive form of AR every day when we access the navigator app on our smartphones. When you enter an address into your smartphone and then follow the real-time driving directions that it provides to your destination, you may not think of this as "augmented reality," but it is. Your smartphone maps data over physical spaces, and you then interpret the real world based on the instructions that you receive. What would happen if, instead of receiving these real-time driving directions on the screen of your smartphone, this information was beamed straight onto the lenses of your glasses? This is the premise of AR. The distinction between virtual reality and augmented reality is currently emphasized by tech companies as they jockey for greater market share of this emerging industry. But for the purposes of this book, we see VR and AR as essentially the same technology. VR is emerging first, as the technical challenges in creating VR are fewer and more achievable than for compelling AR. In this book we will explore how the church can apply VR technology for the purposes of Christian ministry, knowing that AR is not far away and will bring many of the same opportunities and challenges.

What Is New about "New Media"?

At this point, your head may be spinning. But we are now ready to talk about what these changes mean for communication theory in general and for the communication of the gospel specifically.

"New media" is a term that began appearing in the early 2000s to describe the potential of the internet for communication. In some ways, the internet is not a new media type at all but simply a new way of reproducing old media types. Kevin Kelly—founding editor of *Wired* magazine and "Geek Theologian," in the words of *Christianity Today*[32]—conceptualizes the internet as the "world's largest copy machine."[33] You input digital information into the internet from one physical location, and the internet replicates this information instantaneously and at nearly no cost, outputting a digital copy at another physical location. In this analogy, the internet isn't really a new media type at all but a new mechanism to copy and distribute pre-existing media types. Most of the content on the internet can be represented as text, photographs, or video files, but the printing press has been around for about five centuries, photographs for about two centuries, and movies and film for about one century. So what exactly is new about "new media"?

We begin to uncover the novel communicative possibilities of the internet when we imagine converting the internet into an analog format. First of all, what would happen if we converted the text of the internet back into book form? Around the turn of the millennium, one could still find printed catalogues of the best sites on the internet. Based on the use of phonebooks at the time, people in the mid-1990s still turned to printed books in order to look up websites on the internet. Can you imagine a print directory of the contents of the internet today? In 2015, a *Washington Post* reporter attempted to calculate how many pages of paper it would require to print out the entire internet. The estimate came to just over three hundred billion pages.[34] If we were to say that an average book is three hundred pages long, then it would require one billion books to contain the internet in print form. By way of comparison, the Library of Congress in Washington, DC, which is the largest library in the United States, holds about thirty-nine million books. Quite obviously, it would be a physical impossibility to print out the entire internet.

But it is not only the sheer size of the internet that makes printing it physically impossible. Even if you could somehow find yourself in a library that contained a paper edition of all of the webpages on the internet, it would be almost entirely useless. Have you ever printed out selections from your social media accounts? Probably not, even though it would be easy to do and you may be an avid social media user. The way that we use many kinds of text on the internet is fundamentally different from the way we used to use text in book form.

Heidi Campbell identifies several key characteristics of "new media."[35] First, "new media" is bidirectional rather than unidirectional. This means that new media content is—more often than not—generated by the users of the platform rather than the creators of the website. Think of some of the most popular websites today, such as Wikipedia (founded in 2001), Facebook (2004), or YouTube (2005). These websites are analogous to an encyclopedia, a newspaper, or the television, but with one crucial difference—the content is all created by the users. Rather than paying a professional staff to create the content, these new media companies provide a platform for exchange between users. The line between content creator and user is blurred. Second, "new media" is nonlinear, meaning that users can continue to revise content after it has been posted. New media is therefore constantly being updated and corrected, and so "new media" feels unofficial and impermanent when compared to traditional media types like encyclopedias and newspapers. Third, new media can combine traditional media types in new ways. Because the internet is the single point of access for new media, creators are not limited by traditional distribution channels. We used to go to the movie theater to see a film, to the drugstore to purchase a newspaper, and to the bookstore to purchase books and music. Now we go online to buy almost everything, which in turn means that creators of new media have an opportunity to produce content of a dazzling, new variety.

New media is not merely a new way to access old information. By changing the way we access information, new media is changing the way we communicate and so is transforming what we communicate about and even what we believe the possibilities of communication to be. We used to hold up our phones to our ears and smilingly speak into them; now we hold our phones at arm's length and tap at them with our thumbs. The shift from telephone calling to texting illustrates how we communicate differently when we use different modes of communication.

Positive and Problematic Change

Every new technology brings positive and problematic change for the communities who adopt them. When we look to the future, it is clear that VR brings many strengths that could be applied to communicating the gospel across geographical, cultural, and linguistic borders. But how will the use of VR as a technology change the way we think about ourselves and our churches? How will VR and related technologies reshape the way that we think about God and speak about Him to the world around us?

"The medium is the message" is the mantra for which we remember Marshall McLuhan (1911–1980), the Canadian philosopher who for many years served as professor of literature and communication theory at the University of Toronto. In 1962, McLuhan published his breakout book, *The Gutenberg Galaxy: The Making of Typographic Man*, arguing that the printing press gave rise to a new mindset and a new way of seeing the world.[36] The proliferation of the printed page resulted not merely in an increase in books but produced a new way of reading. McLuhan, always a brilliant observer of twentieth-century Western culture, began to note the pervasive influence of television and other forms of non-print media on society. In a televised interview with McLuhan in 1965, literary critic, Sir John Frank Kermode, summarized: "You argue that for a long time, without actually understanding it, we've been living in a culture in which our whole way of looking at the world has been determined by typography."[37]

McLuhan was not only a penetrating analyst but also a persuasive presenter, and he disseminated his views in an array of radio and television interviews. His stately, elegant figure and polished voice made him a winsome communicator for his ideas about media. In his interviews, McLuhan plunges forward breathlessly, his words conveying explosive intellectual energy, and his willingness to respond to questions enigmatically led many to view him as something of a prophet. McLuhan embraced this role, consulting for some of America's leading corporations. Some credit McLuhan as having predicted the internet, and while McLuhan did not foresee the technical mechanisms that make the internet possible, he did anticipate the way that electronic communication reshapes our understanding concerning the very nature of information.[38] McLuhan coined the phrase "global village" and explained that a new paradigm of society was coming, not only because people would someday be able to travel faster and farther but because information would travel instantaneously to everybody.[39] Marshall McLuhan converted to Christianity while reading the apologetic writings of G. K. Chesterton during doctoral studies at Cambridge, and he remained a devout Roman Catholic his entire life.

McLuhan's thesis that the printing press had birthed a new way of thinking and that this way of thinking was then being superseded as typography was replaced by electronic modes of communication had echoes in the writings of other thinkers of his time. The French Jesuit philosopher and theologian, Pierre Teilhard de Chardin (1881–1955), had speculated about the "noosphere" (from the Greek word for "mind"), a term that he invented in order to speak of a collective consciousness encircling the earth that communicated the totality of human codes. Had de Chardin foreseen the faintest glimmer of the internet? Jacques Ellul (1912–1994), the Christian philosopher and sociologist whose *Technological Society* appeared in French in 1954, sounded many of the same notes as McLuhan. Walter J. Ong (1912–2003) studied under McLuhan and became perhaps his truest successor, dedicating his scholarly research as a professor of literature to the effect that the shift from orality to literacy has on culture.

Melding together many of the insights from the above-mentioned scholars, Neil Postman (1931–2003) became the best-known representative of these ideas through his popular books and academic work in founding the department of "Media Ecology" at New York University in 1971. In his most systematic book, *Technopoly: The Surrender of Culture to Technology*, Postman explains:

> Technological change is neither additive nor subtractive. It is ecological. I mean "ecological" in the same sense as the word is used by environmental scientists. One significant change generates total change. If you remove caterpillars from a given habitat, you are not

left with the same environment minus caterpillars: you have a new environment, and you have reconstituted the conditions of survival; the same is true if you add caterpillars to an environment that has had none. This is how the ecology of media works as well. A new technology does not add or subtract something. It changes everything. In the year 1500, fifty years after the printing press was invented, we did not have old Europe plus the printing press. We had a different Europe.[40]

This model of media as an ecology is, in our view, still one of the best ways to map out what is happening today with the rise of the internet and virtual reality. VR becomes not merely a new way of visualizing the internet but, in fact, produces a new world. And so the worlds that we experience inside the goggles also transform the way that we see and know the world outside the goggles.

In 1993, Postman, who was known for his warnings concerning the dangers that computers pose to education, delivered a lecture to the employees of Apple. In his address, Postman stated: "Anyone who has studied the history of technology knows that technological change is always a Faustian bargain. Technology giveth, and technology taketh away—and not always in equal measure."[41] Postman cites the invention of the mechanical clock, noting that it was invented by Benedictine monks who wished to orchestrate more precisely their times of community prayer, but in fact the mechanical clock served not principally to promote the interests of religious life but capitalism. Johannes Gutenberg was a pious Roman Catholic, and his intention in developing the printing press was to serve the church. The earliest dated printed document that we have from Gutenberg's printing press is a papal indulgence, and the printing press at first fueled the sale of indulgences, since it made indulgences extremely inexpensive and therefore also extremely profitable for the church.[42] But the printing press also empowered the Protestant Reformation, which was sparked when Martin Luther challenged the sale of indulgences.

The Greek philosopher, Plato, recounted that his teacher, Socrates, had been suspicious of the invention of writing. Proponents of writing claimed that it would allow people to remember forever. Socrates, who left nothing in writing and dedicated himself to teaching his pupils by dialogue, on the contrary argued that writing would undo the art of memory: "For this invention will produce forgetfulness in the minds of those who learn to use it, because they will not practice their memory. . . . You have invented an elixir not of memory, but of reminding; and you offer your pupils the appearance of wisdom, not true wisdom."[43]

We can be sure that the advent of VR will create a tidal wave of unintended consequences, as the invention of every media type throughout history has also done. But simply because all media carry certain inclinations and limitations does not mean that any media type is to be rejected outright. Storytelling is the grounds of communalism; literature inspires individualism. Music speaks to the transcendent; images envelop rituals. If the mode of communication transforms the meaning of the messages thereby conveyed, as McLuhan correctly observed, then what does the advent of the internet revolution and the rise of VR mean for the church, whose commission it is to proclaim the gospel to the ends of the earth?

Racing toward Every Person on the Planet

The VR of antiquity—the *viae Romanae*, or Roman roads—brought the gospel to every corner of the empire. VR presents colossal opportunities for the proclamation of the gospel and the witness of the church in the public square in our world today. Karl Barth, the famous Swiss theologian from the twentieth century, advised throughout his life: "Take your Bible and take your newspaper, and read both. But interpret newspapers from your Bible."[44] This book is an attempt to do precisely this for our own time. This is not a simple assignment, because many of the realities that we encounter today were never mentioned in Scripture. Of course, virtual reality, the internet, teleconferencing, avatars, and going to church in your pajamas are all phenomena that the Bible does not directly address. And yet, the principles that Scripture provides represent the wisdom that we need to face even the most surprising and complex questions of the present and the future.

God alone knows the future, and what God expects from us is not foreknowledge about coming events but responsible stewardship in the present. In the parable of the talents (Matt. 25:14–30), Jesus instructs us that we are to be faithful stewards of the resources that He has entrusted to us until His return. And technology is certainly one of these resources.[45] But to deal with technology is to deal with uncertainty. There are questions to which we cannot now know the answers but which will certainly shape the realities discussed in this book. One such question is whether internet access will reach the great majority of the world's population in the future. If billions of people still do not have internet access decades from now, then VR's deployment for the purposes of Christian ministry in general and for world evangelization in particular will be significantly curtailed. In 2020, there were over three billion people—or about four people in ten—who have no access to the internet, and by and large these are the same people who as of then have never heard the gospel.[46]

If the number of new internet users continues to climb at the same rate that it has for the past two decades, then nearly everyone in the world will have internet access by around the year 2035. However, it is currently not clear whether the number of new internet users will continue to expand worldwide at the same rate in the future as it has in the past. Several companies are in the process of devising ways to bring internet access to everyone on the planet. Facebook's method for accomplishing this is to launch a fleet of high-altitude, super-efficient, solar-powered aircraft that would return to earth only for scheduled maintenance and would relay internet communication to terrestrial transmission stations by laser beam. Google's solution to the problem is to send a flotilla of giant balloons up into the stratosphere, far above commercial airline traffic, which would then navigate to strategic locations by sailing on winds at different altitudes. Elon Musk, the South African entrepreneur behind Tesla, may have the best shot at creating internet access for everyone on the planet with his "Starlink" program from Space X. This $10 billion program, now partially underway, aims to launch 42,000 tiny satellites into space with the express purpose of providing internet access to all. From our perspective, it is probable that more or less the entire world's population will have internet access somewhere around the year 2035, but this is something that cannot be known at this point in time.

Another question which cannot be answered at this time is whether VR technology will become sufficiently inexpensive to serve the world's low-income and impoverished communities. The three billion people who currently live without internet access are, as a general rule, the world's poorest people—in the majority of instances, living on only a few dollars per day. Computing power has skyrocketed astronomically over the past seven decades, while the cost to consumers per computational unit has plunged drastically during this same period. This means that computers have become vastly more powerful while at the same time costing vastly less per measurable unit of performance. But the advances in digital computer technology do not translate to mean that personal computers are cheap.

In fact, the computers that run the programs we use every day to communicate at work and with our friends remain expensive. Nonetheless, certain technologies have demonstrated an ability to achieve adoption on a truly global scale. Mobile phones, for example, have become ubiquitous today, with the number of mobile phones on the planet surpassing the number of people sometime around 2015.[47] This would have been unthinkable even a couple of decades ago, when mobile phones were perceived as luxury goods affordable only to the world's elite. If VR becomes the primary interface for the internet of the future, then we can expect that VR will achieve an unprecedented depth in its global penetration.

Our predictions of the future virtually never turn out the way we imagine. In 1993, AT&T ran a series of television commercials ("You Will") about future technologies that the company aspired to create. These commercials are celebrated for their stunning accuracy in describing some of today's most iconic technologies, including video calling, GPS navigation systems for automobiles, media streaming, phones that are worn as wristwatches, and home security systems that can be monitored remotely. Still, the list of things that these commercials got wrong about the future is at least as long as the list of things they got right.[48] Visions of the future quickly wear thin once the future actually arrives. If the future were predictable, we all would be flying around in jetpacks by now. Remember the Jetsons, anyone? Even in cases where cultural expectations about future technologies are basically correct in outline, we are invariably incorrect about when and how these technologies will arrive. It was not too many years ago that everyone was talking about someday owning a car phone. But when the technology that made car phones possible materialized, we discovered that we were not really interested in car phones because it was so much more convenient simply to carry our phones in our purses and pockets.

The commission of the church has been and remains: "Go therefore and make disciples of all nations, baptizing them in the name of the Father and of the Son and of the Holy Spirit, teaching them to observe all that I have commanded you" (Matt. 28:19–20 ESV). This mandate requires us to evaluate carefully the missional potential of VR and related technologies. In 2000, Walt Wilson could already see where the internet was going, and he could not contain his excitement over the possibility that the internet could be a vehicle to reach the four million people in China who were then online.[49] There are now over nine hundred million people online in China. There is no less reason today to be ecstatic over the opportunities for ministry at present and in the immediate future. The virtual world may prove to be the most fruitful mission field in the twenty-first century.

Chapter 2

THE ONLY CONSTANT IS CHANGE

"NEW MEASURES ARE NO NEW THING IN THE CHURCH."[1]

✦ Charles G. Finney

"OUR TECHNOLOGY MAY BE NEW, BUT DEALING WITH THE EFFECTS OF THE CHANGE IT CREATES IS FAMILIAR."[2]

✦ Tom Wheeler

E vangelicalism has existed at the crossroads of tradition and innovation from its inception. On the one hand, evangelicalism is a form of Christianity that emphasizes the tradition of the authority of Scripture. When in the early twentieth century mainline churches were ready to conclude that the Bible had become irrelevant, evangelicals rallied to establish a network of Bible colleges and seminaries that would train up pastors with a firm conviction of the trustworthiness of Scripture. It is this tradition of *sola Scriptura* that perhaps represents evangelicalism's most resilient connection to Reformation theological priorities. It is no secondary concern for evangelicals that their churches adhere to historic Christian orthodoxy. On a Sunday morning at an evangelical church, it would not be surprising to find a class on the doctrine of the Trinity or even to witness the occasional recitation of the creed.

But on the other hand, evangelicalism is a movement that is intensely focused on the gospel. The word "evangelical" comes from the Greek word for "gospel" (*evangelion*). This relentlessness for gospel-first preaching and practice has translated into a history of religious innovation. From radio and television to missionary aviation, evangelical ministries have tended to be pragmatic and quick to apply new technology to the task of expanding access to the gospel. In this chapter, we will delve into the history of evangelicalism and see how Christian leaders in the evangelical tradition have always applied emerging technology in order to promote revivalism. The mass media of radio, television, and film came to prominence in the twentieth century, and evangelical leaders were ready in each instance to apply the emerging technology to the standing agenda of communicating the gospel to as many people as possible. Evangelicalism provided a framework for rapid innovation and entrepreneurial ministry, solidifying enormous gains for world evangelization. But the rise of mass media introduced new pitfalls as well as new possibilities. The idea of a "virtual reality church" may at first sound unprecedented, but Christian churches have been applying electronic media to extend their reach for at least a century. The story of the advent of the "church of the air" of the radio preachers and the "electric church" of the televangelists contains many lessons for us as we enter the age of the "virtual reality church."

Revivals and New Measures

The tradition of innovation within evangelicalism traces back to the very foundations of the movement, and we could cite examples of innovation already in the First Great Awakening. George Whitefield (1714–1770) used newspapers, the principle media of his day, to fuel expectation of revival during his preaching tours, and it is no coincidence that Whitefield could count one of the shrewdest publishers of the eighteenth century—Benjamin Franklin—among his close associates. John Wesley (1703–1791) refined and expanded the convention of circuit riding until the network of Methodist itinerant clergy resembled a preaching empire. Even Jonathan Edwards (1703–1758), who was more a theologian than a practitioner, had a profound interest in finding new ways to evangelize the Native American peoples. When Edwards lost his position as a pastor in the prominent town of Northampton, he relocated with his wife and eleven children to the outpost settlement of Stockbridge so that he could invest his time in learning the Mohican language and culture. Even the First Great Awakening witnessed significant religious innovation, but it was not until the Second Great Awakening in the early nineteenth century that this pattern of innovation came to light as a point of controversy.

Charles Grandison Finney (1792–1875) became the preeminent revivalist of the Second Great Awakening during the tabernacle meetings he conducted in upstate New York and Manhattan from 1825 to 1835. Although he had never attended university, Finney became professor of theology at Oberlin College in 1835 and then the institution's second president in 1851. He had practiced law for a few years before his dramatic conversion and baptism in the Holy Spirit, which he recounted vividly in his revival preaching and recorded in his autobiography. Aspects of Finney's legacy continue to elicit unanimous praise, such as his labors to abolish slavery and to create equal educational opportunities for African Americans and for women. However, his enthusiasm for pioneering new methods in promoting revivals and his results-oriented philosophy in conducting tabernacle meetings kept him ensconced in controversies until the end of his life. Finney called these innovations "new measures."

What were these "new measures" that so divided the church of his day? Finney preached in a business suit rather than donning clerical vestments. He preached extemporaneously rather than reading his sermon from a meticulously prepared manuscript. He asked women to preside at prayer services in conjunction with his revival meetings. But perhaps nothing drew more fire from Finney's critics than the introduction of the so-called "anxious seat," a special pew at the front of the auditorium where those who were particularly concerned about the condition of their souls could sit through the revival meetings. For proponents, the anxious seat served to remind the audience to pray for the souls of those who had yet to do business with God. From the perspective of the critics, the anxious seat made a spectacle of spiritual anguish and inclined people to come forward during the altar call not as a result of the Holy Spirit's conviction but as a response to social pressure.

Finney's outright rejection of the Calvinism of the Protestant establishment of his day did nothing to abate the controversy surrounding his revival preaching. In 1835, in *Lectures on Revival of Religion*, Finney posed a viewpoint that has remained contested when he stated concerning the success of revivals: "It is not a miracle, or dependent on a miracle, in any sense. It is a purely philosophical result of the right use of the constituted means—as much so as any other effect produced by the application of means."[3] In a devastating critique, the Princeton theologian, B. B. Warfield, claimed: "It is quite clear that Finney gives us less a theology than a system of morals. God might be eliminated from it entirely without essentially changing its character. All virtue, all holiness, is made to consist in an ethical determination of will."[4] Finney's position that revival does not represent a miracle continues to spark debate among evangelicals who wrestle with the same questions as they apply the techniques and technologies of the twenty-first century to the task of winning souls for Christ.

Finney and his critics symbolize the conflict within evangelicalism over the proper relationship between tradition and innovation. In a series of sermons titled "Measures to Promote Revivals," which he preached as pastor of New York's Second Free Presbyterian Church in 1834, Finney provides one of the clearest defenses of his tactics to promote revivalism. In a tour de force, Finney recounts a panoply of innovations that Christians have brought into the church for the purpose of effective gospel witness.

He commences by noting an innovation that was at that time likely to incite only minor controversy—clerical dress. Some of the ministers of Finney's day had set aside knee-breeches, cocked hats, and wigs, dressing rather in business suits. For the previous generation, who grieved the loss of distinctive clerical dress and who believed that this change in fashion signaled that the ministers were abandoning the authority of the church and selling out to secularism, this had been a point of genuine concern. Finney recalls a former day when "good people would have been shocked if a minister had gone into the pulpit with pantaloons on. They would have thought he was certainly going to ruin the church by his innovations."[5] Finney went on to cite the example of an elderly minister in New England who ferociously guarded against any man preaching from his pulpit in pants. The story concluded with an embarrassing confrontation in which a young visiting minister once had to change hastily into one of the elderly minister's pair of knee-breeches before ascending the pulpit. But all of this had been to prepare his audience to see the ridiculousness of the situation, for Finney concluded with a line that was sure to produce a roar of laughter from his audience: "I remember one minister, who, though quite a young man, used to wear an enormous white wig. And the people talked as if there was a divine right about it, and it was as hard to give it up, almost, as to give up the Bible itself."[6]

From Finney's perspective, in applying "new measures" in the pursuit of revival, he was simply following in a train of saintly innovators of incontrovertible standing:

> If we examine the history of the church we shall find that there never has been an extensive reformation, except by new measures. Whenever the churches get settled down into a form of doing things, they soon get to rely upon the outward doing of it, and so retain the form of religion while they lose the substance. And then it has always been found impossible to arouse them so as to bring about a reformation of the evils, and produce a revival of religion, by simply pursuing that established form.[7]

Even at a distance of almost two centuries, Finney still has a point to make. Are churches today so focused on maintaining the method by which we congregate that we have lost touch with the real spiritual business of the church?

Radio and the Church of the Air

Finney acted as a lightning rod in the controversy over the new techniques of revivalism in the nineteenth century, but not in his wildest imaginations could he have envisioned what would arise less than one century later. The scope and scale of innovations that would soon present themselves to the evangelical movement increased at an astounding pace with the advent of electronic communication. On May 24, 1844, Samuel Morse demonstrated the telegraph before an audience including members of Congress, sending the message "What hath God wrought" (a line from Numbers 23:23 KJV) in an instant over forty miles of cable running from Washington, DC, to Baltimore. In retrospect, no more fitting words could have been selected for the inaugural message of the age of instantaneous electronic communication. Commercially successful radio, television, and film would radically reshape the religious landscape in the United States, and this saga of profound transition begins in the decade between 1920 and 1930—the period when the majority of Americans gained access to electricity.[8]

Radio was not only the first available form of mass media to emerge during the electronic age but also, arguably, the most successful for evangelistic purposes. Radio had several traits that seemed to align it naturally to the purposes of Christian mission. First of all, radio is oriented toward the spoken word, in clear consonance with the theological priorities that evangelicalism had inherited from the Reformation. Martin Luther's principle of *sola Scriptura*, as well as the iconoclasm of Ulrich Zwingli and John Calvin, had oriented evangelicalism to the priority of preaching. Evangelicalism's insistence on the Bible as the very words of God and the vision of the church as a gospel-preaching community of believers translated clearly and powerfully to the medium of radio broadcast. The apostle Paul's dictum, "faith comes from hearing" (Rom. 10:17), might as well have been written with radio in mind.

But there is a second reason why radio became such a re-markably effective instrument for the purposes of Christian mission, and that is that radio is relatively inexpensive to pro-duce and extremely inexpensive to receive. Because radio was an affordable medium, religious broadcasts could be financially backed by churches and missionary societies, and the audiences radio reached did not require expensive equipment to tune into the programs. The so-called "crystal radio" could be constructed by hand and did not even require electricity to operate, as the radio signal itself could be amplified by an antenna and ren-dered audible in an earphone. The fact that crystal radios could be operated without electricity greatly sped the adoption of the technology in the early 1920s, when significant numbers of the population still did not have access to electricity.

In 1922, the US Bureau of Standards published a pamphlet titled "Construction and Operation of a Very Simple Radio Re-ceiving Equipment." The pamphlet was written for use by boys and girls radio clubs, and the pamphlet outlined how a basic radio kit could be assembled for under $10. Almost anyone with access to minimal tools and materials could build a functioning radio. When I was a child, I (Darrell) built one of these radios from a kit available in the '50s and '60s in order to listen to baseball games. The radio I constructed with my own hands did not function as well as the models available from Radio Shack, but it worked well enough for me to enjoy listening to my game! Radio had served as a decisive military technology during World War I, and in the wake of the war it became the world's first electronic mass medium. The first commercial radio broadcast in the US was conducted on November 2, 1920, by KDKA of Pittsburgh and covered the presidential election of Warren G. Harding.[9] The first religious radio broadcast in the US followed only several weeks later on January 2, 1921, when the Reverend Edwin J. Van Etten of Calvary Episcopal Church in Pittsburgh preached on the airwaves.[10] One of the listeners among the several hundred who tuned in that evening was a woman who lived some four hundred miles away and who preserved the following account in a letter she sent to Van Etten:

> Last night for the first time in twenty years, I heard a full church service. My son recently became interested in wireless, with the result that he installed a radio receiving set. I had no idea of ever using the apparatus, but when he told me that Westinghouse Electric and Manufacturing Company had a test station at East Liberty and that they were going to transmit services of Calvary Church, I was anxious to hear them. Everything in the house had been prepared to await the start of the service that night. My son had placed on my head the 'phones through which he said I would hear the service. I could scarcely believe my ears when the

organ music and choir sounded distinctly. Then afterwards the voice of the pastor thrilled me as few things have in the long suffering years. I kept the 'phones on all through the service and at the end felt at peace with the world, "the peace that passeth all understanding."[11]

By January 1, 1922, there were only 30 licensed radio stations in the US. By March 1, 1923, this number had exploded to 556 stations. One hundred thousand radio receivers were sold in 1922; 500,000 were produced in 1923.[12] Religious radio broadcasting was booming, too. In 1923, churches and Christian institutions owned at least 12 radio stations, but this number climbed to 29 in 1924 and to 71 in 1925.[13] The widespread adoption of radio in a very short span of time parallels in some ways the global adoption of the smartphone following the release of Apple's first iPhone on June 29, 2007. It was immediately clear to all that these new inventions would radically reshape culture and religious life.

On June 17, 1922, the mayor of Chicago, William Hale Thompson, invited Paul Rader to preach from the radio station that had been newly erected on the top floor of the city hall. Paul Rader had at that time recently stepped down from his position as pastor of the Moody Church in Chicago, which he had held from 1915–1922. This was to become the first gospel broadcast in Chicago's history. Rader brought with him a brass quartet to play on the air before he preached, and the trombonist was Clarence Jones, who had worked with Rader as a staff member at the Chicago Gospel Tabernacle.[14] Jones later graduated from Moody Bible Institute and served as the producer for Rader's weekly radio programs on WJBT ("Where Jesus Blesses Thousands"). In 1931, patterning his ministry after that of Paul

Rader in Chicago, Clarence Jones founded a missionary radio station in Ecuador that would expand into the massive worldwide radio network HCJB ("Heralding Christ Jesus' Blessings"). Jones could say, "Our whole creed of service is 'Use everything we can that God has given us in this twentieth century to speed the taking of the first-century message.' Thus we restate Paul's challenge: 'By all means save some.'"[15]

Radio not only renewed traditional streams of Christianity but also empowered the creative emergence of new forms. Perhaps nowhere do we see this more clearly than in the life story of Aimee Semple McPherson (1890–1944), who, as a woman, Pentecostal preacher with a bewildering personal life, became one of the most famous representatives of Christianity of her day. Following her meteoric rise to fame as a faith healer immediately following World War I, she became the most popular evangelist in America, surpassing even the aging Billy Sunday (1862–1935), who was the last of the tabernacle evangelists to resist mass media. Aimee had a love for novelty and adventure.

In 1918, Aimee drove her "Gospel Car" (a seven-passenger Oldsmobile emblazed with the words "Jesus Is Coming Soon— Get Ready") from the East Coast to Los Angeles, conducting crusades along the 4,000-mile itinerary. In April 1922, Aimee became the first woman to preach on the radio, broadcasting from the Rockridge radio station in Oakland, California. The year following, in 1923, Aimee opened the Angelus Temple in Los Angeles, considered by some to be the first megachurch. The church had a seating capacity of 5,300 people, and crowds filled the auditorium twenty-one times each week to hear her preach. Her "illustrated sermons," which she delivered as theatrical pieces, complete with sets and musical accompaniment, achieved acclaim in the city that was quickly becoming the international symbol of the film industry.

Aimee's life story also resonated with the people of Los Angeles, almost all of whom had come from elsewhere in order to seek employment. The population of Los Angeles had swelled from approximately 100,000 in 1900 to over 1,200,000 by 1930, making Los Angeles the fifth-largest city in the nation and perhaps the most volatile and dynamic. Aimee's powerful revival preaching, compassion for the downtrodden, and genius for showmanship drew gigantic crowds. In 1924, Aimee became the second woman to receive a broadcast license from the Federal Radio Commission when she opened KSFG, which then was the third radio station to open in Los Angeles. Two colossal radio spires were erected on the massive concrete dome of the Angelus Temple when the radio station opened, creating a visual symbol of the merging of the church and her radio ministry. Aimee had a deep sense of the power of radio as a communication medium for the gospel, and she referred to radio ministry as the "Cathedral of the Air."[16]

Aimee led a dramatic, even reckless, personal life. Her first husband, Robert James Semple, whom she married in 1908, died shortly after the couple's arrival in China as missionaries in 1910. Aimee became a widow at only nineteen, and at this time she was eight months pregnant with her first child, Roberta Star Semple. After returning to the US, she married her second husband in 1912, Harold Stewart McPherson. When a voice that she could not silence continued calling her to preach, she suffered a nervous breakdown, left her husband one night in June 1915, and embarked on an itinerant ministry of faith healing and crusade evangelism. In his biography of Aimee, Daniel

Epstein remarks: "Whether this was an auditory hallucination or the voice of God is known only to Aimee and to God, and God has remained silent upon the matter."[17] The impulsivity of her personality did not make life easy for Aimee, but it translated almost perfectly to the pioneering days of radio. Early on the morning of June 29, 1925, one of the Angelus Temple parishioners called to tell Aimee that there had been a devastating earthquake in Santa Barbara. Aimee rushed next door to the KSFG radio studios and, interrupting a live broadcast, announced the crisis to the world. She then called for donations of emergency supplies and for volunteers to drive the cargo to the people of Santa Barbara. Even before newspapers had reported the earthquake, a convoy of relief supplies from Angelus Temple was on its way to Santa Barbara.[18]

Aimee's penchant for the dramatic appeared boundless. On May 18, 1926, the course of her life and career was permanently altered when she disappeared from Ocean Park Beach in Santa Monica, California. At first it was believed that she had drowned, but five weeks later Aimee reappeared, reporting to the police that she had been kidnapped and held captive in a shack in the Mexican desert. She claimed that she had escaped and walked twenty miles through the desert before arriving in the Mexican border town of Agua Prieta.

However, when the shack in which she had allegedly been held captive could not be located, the district attorney accused Aimee of perpetrating a public fraud. Aimee was subpoenaed before a grand jury, and the coherency of Aimee's recounting of the story soon began to unravel, but the case was finally closed on January 10, 1927, since no real evidence could be presented. Aimee continued to preach until the end of her life, but her influence waned after this episode. Her third marriage, to David Hutton in 1931, lasted for only three years before ending in divorce in 1934. Aimee died on September 26, 1944, in Oakland, California, where she had traveled to conduct revival services. Her son found her dead in her hotel room after she had accidently overdosed on sleeping pills. Wildly popular but perpetually embroiled in controversy, Aimee personified the new opportunities that mass media opened for ministry as well as the perils of courting show business.

From the beginning, religious radio had its critics. Clarence Macartney (1879–1957)—the pastor of the First Presbyterian Church in Pittsburgh who, along with J. Gresham Machen, became one of the champions of Fundamentalism during the modernist controversy—was vocal in his disapproval. He was appalled that audio recordings of church services would be stripped of their context and blasted over the airwaves, arguing that church services "sent indiscriminately into all kinds of places" would be "grotesque and irreverent."[19] And yet, it was clear even early on that electronic mass media would radically reshape the church. Writing in 1935, one commentator could declare: "Radio religion is here to stay—a part of the matrix of our complex civilization. To those who are distressed at the decline of the power of the Church and religion in our day, it may very well be that out of this 'marriage of science and religion' a new quickening of the spiritual life of America will emerge."[20]

Television and the Electric Church

Television had been an experimental form of telecommunication up through the end of World War II. Franklin D. Roosevelt became the first American president to appear on television when he delivered an address for the opening ceremony of the 1939 New York World's Fair.[21] Roosevelt delivered his address to a live audience gathered at the fair because at that time almost no one owned a television set. By the end of the war in 1945, television sets were still extremely rare, but by 1955 half of all households in America owned at least one television set.

The application of television for the purposes of Christian ministry proved to be far more problematic than had been the case for radio. First, sermons translated naturally and effectively to radio, and many religious broadcasts over radio had not been studio productions at all but simply relays of live church services. But something changed with television. Watching television broadcasts of church services tended to strike viewers not as an opportunity to participate from afar in the religious life of a particular community but rather simply as poor entertainment. The medium of television carried with it the possibility of showcasing all kinds of imagery, but most of this potential was left unexplored in television broadcasts of religious services. Second, television proved to be vastly more expensive than radio to produce, and the financial burden of producing television overwhelmed all but a few of the preachers who ventured into this space.

For a generation of evangelists in the post–World War II era, early experiences with radio ministry acted as the training grounds for later work in television. Billy Graham learned production as the announcer for the radio program, "Songs in the Night," which aired for the first time in 1944. But already by 1951, Graham had made the leap into television and was starring in studio-produced evangelistic programs. By 1957, Graham was producing live broadcasts of his crusades on television networks. Oral Roberts (1918–2009) also began working in radio in 1947 before transitioning to television in 1954. The most successful television ministry among Roman Catholics in the US was that of Fulton Sheen (1895–1979), the Emmy Award-winning Archbishop from New York who hosted "Life is Worth Living" (1952–1957) and "The Fulton Sheen Program" (1961–1968). Sheen came to television after twenty years of anchoring the popular radio program, "The Catholic Hour," from 1930–1950. Fulton Sheen is credited as the clergyman to preside over the first televised Christian church service when he celebrated an Easter Mass over the airwaves on March 24, 1940, broadcast on NBC's W2XBS.[22]

Even in the early days, it was clear that producing television was a massively more costly proposition than producing radio. The expense of producing television required that the evangelists who entered this arena be capable of capturing the attention and dollars of astronomically large numbers of people. Some succeeded. In 1976, the television show, *Oral Roberts and You*, attracted a weekly viewing audience of 2.5 million households. By way of comparison, *The Merv Griffin Show*, which was then the top-ranking program on national television, attracted a weekly viewing audience of almost three million households. At the peak of his ministry, Oral Roberts, the Pentecostal evangelist and university founder, could claim to command a viewership of fifty million people for his one-hour television specials.[23] Finding the sums necessary to launch television ministries mandated some of the most aggressive fundraising appeals the evangelical world had ever seen.

In 1954, when Oral Roberts felt pressed to raise $42,000 in order to televise his first crusade, he landed on the idea of the "Blessing-Pact." In his 1961 autobiography, *My Story*, Oral Roberts explains the concept in his own words: "I will use your gift to win souls; and because of this, I will earnestly pray that the Lord will return your gift in its entirety from a totally unexpected source. And if at the end of one year this has not happened, you may write and tell me, and our Evangelistic Association will refund you the same amount immediately and no questions asked."[24] The crushing financial burden of producing television certainly played a part in redirecting many television ministries toward the prosperity gospel.

Televangelists handled a lot of money. In 1980, the television ministry of Oral Roberts received an estimated $60 million in annual donations, making it the leading television ministry in fiscal terms. Pat Robertson came in as a close second at $58 million, with Jim Bakker and Jerry Falwell trailing only slightly at $51 million and $50 million, respectively.[25] These numbers alone caused concern.[26] Then there was the criticism that the televangelists were not merely repeating the old-fashioned gospel, which so many of them had claimed in the titles of their programs. The contours of a distinct theology were beginning to emerge, and this theology was not in alignment on all points with traditional church doctrine, especially concerning wealth and prosperity.[27] Then there was the question of the public influence of television. When strictly religious programming failed to generate the interest necessary to finance nationwide television broadcasts, some turned to political issues in order to reach greater numbers of viewers. No one contested that television accrued social power to its stars and producers. What was not clear was how religious and political objectives ought to be kept distinct in organizations that produced religious television.

Jerry Falwell's move from *The Old-Time Gospel Hour*—the television ministry that he started in 1956, which propelled him to national influence—to found the Moral Majority in 1979 alerted some commentators to the need to examine these questions.[28] Pat Robertson's departure from *The 700 Club* in order to run as a Republican candidate in the presidential election in 1987 signaled to many that architectonic shifts were underway.

Finally, scandal erupted. In 1987, it was publicly disclosed that Jim Bakker, who hosted the *PTL Club* with his wife, Tammy Faye Bakker, had committed adultery and received an annual salary in excess of $1 million.[29] Bakker's affair was criticized sharply by Jimmy Swaggart, whose *The Jimmy Swaggart Telecast* ranked among the most popular religious broadcasts in America. One year earlier, Swaggart had exposed the infidelity of rival televangelist, Marvin Gorman, whose ordination was subsequently revoked by the Assemblies of God. Gorman then hired a private detective who secretly captured photographs of Swaggart standing outside of a highway motel with a prostitute. When confronted with the photographs, Swaggart delivered a tearful confession on live television. The confession, which was devoid of all details, communicated personal remorse and the bravado of show business in equal measure. The empires of the televangelists were falling like houses of cards.

It is difficult to assess how deeply the enormity of these scandals changed the public perception of televangelism and the attitudes of Christian leaders about engaging media for ministry purposes. The time for deep soul searching had come.[30] For many Christian evangelists, the initial impulse to turn to television had been to "increase the capacity of the tent to seal millions"—to bring revival preaching from the tabernacle directly into the homes of the American people.[31] But television proved itself to be a behemoth far more challenging to tame than anyone had anticipated. Television promotes the dangerous impression that visibility equals credibility. Those who listen to preaching in traditional churches can discern at some level the motivations of their pastors, but the medium of television masked almost completely the motivations of the televangelists.

The Jesus Film (1979)

The history of Christian cinematography could fill volumes, but for the purposes of this book we will restrict our comments to films that were created explicitly for evangelistic purposes. In 1951, the Billy Graham Evangelistic Film Ministry (BGEFM) was formed as a subsidiary of the Billy Graham Evangelistic Association (BGEA). On the heels of the astonishing success of the Los Angeles crusade in 1949, Graham commissioned Christian filmmaker, Dick Ross, to produce a film version of the crusade scheduled for the following year in Portland, Oregon. In setting up the film ministry, the BGEA purchased Ross's company and placed him as the president of the new subsidiary. The original charter for the BGEFM was closely tied to creating publicity for Billy Graham's live crusades and producing films of the crusades. One of the more innovative pieces created by the BGEFM was *Man in the Fifth Dimension*, a film that acted as a part of the Billy Graham pavilion at the 1964 New York World's Fair. This twenty-eight-minute film played twelve times per day, seven days per week, and in every showing the filmed likeness of Billy Graham made an impassioned appeal that viewers step forward to the front of the theater to commit their lives to Christ. "This tremendous change in your life could take place right here and now," Graham promised his viewers. Spiritual counselors who had been trained specifically for this interactive exhibit met those who proceeded to the front of the theater.

Films on the life of Christ abounded from the earliest days of the film industry.[32] Cecile DeMille's 1927 *King of Kings* is sometimes viewed as the greatest antecedent to *The Jesus Film* (1979), but Passion plays had been a staple of theater for centuries. This tradition of portraying the gospel in dramatic form continued on even as the film industry began to develop. When one counts films in which Christ is portrayed in a supporting role, there have been literally hundreds of films featuring Jesus. Even immediately before *The Jesus Film* would be produced, Robert Powell stared as Jesus in Franco Zaffirelli's internationally acclaimed TV mini-series, *Jesus of Nazareth* (1977).

While perhaps not extraordinary as a piece of cinematography, *The Jesus Film* (1979) is extraordinary in its legacy and impact. No film in the history of the medium can claim such a universal viewership as *The Jesus Film*, but its beginnings were not particularly auspicious. In an article anticipating the release of Mel Gibson's *The Passion of the Christ* in 2004, a journalist for the *New York Times* recounts the story: "Bill Bright, an Oklahoma-born confectioner who would go on to found the Campus Crusade for Christ, spent a good chunk of his early career in Los Angeles trying to convert Hollywood stars. He dreamed of creating a powerful film about the life of Christ, and tried unsuccessfully to persuade Cecil B. DeMille to direct a talkie remake of his 1927 silent film, 'The King of Kings.'"[33] The idea continued to fail to gain traction until Bill Bright was introduced to John Heyman (1933–2017).

Heyman was born to Jewish parents in Leipzig in Nazi

Germany and had been brought to England when he was seven months old. There, his father worked as a naturalized citizen for the Ministry of Information during the war and then as a financial correspondent for several newspapers. In 1959, John Heyman founded the International Artists Agency, which brought him into contact with a wide network of personalities and producers in the film industry. Heyman began producing films in 1963, experiencing critical success with *The Go-Between* (1971) and *The Hireling* (1971), which won the Grand Prix at the Cannes Film Festival. John Heyman would become the producer of *The Jesus Film*.

In 1973, Heyman founded *The Genesis Project*, the aim of which was to translate the Bible into film. *The New Media Bible: Book of Genesis* released in 1979, and *The Jesus Film* released later the same year, originally conceived as the gospel of Luke for this multidecade, Bible-to-film translation project. Eleanor Blau could report in 1976 in the *New York Times*: "They are making what they call a film translation of the Bible. . . . It is designed to be a high quality series of film segments for religious schools and libraries, and attempt to present virtually every bit of the Old Testament and New Testament, without interpretation. It is to be based on meticulous research and consultation with Bible scholars of many denominations, archeologists and other experts."[34]

"The aim is to transmit the faith and ideas of the Bible in an age of television in which people 'don't read anymore,'" Heyman explained.[35] The article provides an "optimistic estimate" that *The New Media Bible* would be complete in 33 years, or approximately by the close of the century. From the beginning, *The New Media Bible* was not conceived as a series of feature films but as a library of fifteen-to-twenty-minute film segments. The business plan for the project included selling *The New Media Bible* to churches and synagogues as part of an educational curriculum. In fact, only the Book of Genesis and the Gospel of Luke were ever created. When *The Jesus Film* was released in 1979, it premiered in 250 theaters in the US.[36] The film, which had been financed by Campus Crusade for Christ, cost $6 million to produce and earned $4 million at the box office. Even though the film had not been a financial success, Bill Bright immediately recognized the potential of the film to bring the gospel to nonliterate peoples around the world.

Several factors conspired to make *The Jesus Film* apt for global distribution on an unprecedented scale. First, because the film represented a performance of the words of the Bible, translations of the film could be produced quite rapidly. Second, because the film had been conceived as a translation of Scripture, it attracted a missionary enterprise dedicated to showing the film everywhere on Earth, including extremely remote areas where electricity and the alphabet were unknown. Bill Bright set up the Jesus Film Project in 1981, an evangelistic mission that exists to distribute *The Jesus Film*. In 2004, there were an estimated five thousand missionaries serving under the auspices of this project.

The Jesus Film had reached an estimated 5.4 billion viewings by 2005 and then 7.4 billion viewings by 2015.[37] Not only is *The Jesus Film* the most viewed film of all time, but it has also been translated into the most languages of any film. *The Jesus Film* reached 500 translations by 1999, 1,000 translations by 2007, and 1,500 translations by 2017. And it is currently available in over 1,800 languages.[38] By any measurement except financial profit, *The Jesus Film* would surpass its nearest competitors by a vast margin.

Irv Klaschus came into contact with Campus Crusade for Christ as a computer science student at California State University in Sacramento. When Klaschus went on a mission trip to Kenya in 1984 with about ninety other students, showing *The Jesus Film* in remote areas of the country, he discovered his life calling and has remained with The Jesus Film Project ever since. Renowned today as a leader in innovation, the Jesus Film Project started unassumingly. "The studio was two guys in a room with some tape machines," Klaschus recalls, but "I knew this is where I was supposed to be."[39]

Initially, translation teams traveled with up to five hundred pounds of equipment when dubbing a new translation, but each year the equipment became smaller and lighter. When I (Jonathan) asked Klaschus about what made this cinematic portrayal of Jesus unique, he responded: "*The Jesus Film* was a pretty humble endeavor. . . . [The film's success is] more attributable to God and His power, prayer, and partners across missions agencies all over the world." Klaschus continued: "It's just a testimony to the body of Christ and the work of the Holy Spirit. There is no other way really to explain it." With its message focused exclusively on the story of Jesus, its distribution aimed for those who have never heard the gospel, and with no expectation of financial return, *The Jesus Film* is one of the best examples of the application of media for the purposes of the gospel in the past century.

The Gospel and Global Communication

Instantaneous global telecommunication has been around for almost as long as Charles Finney's defense of the use of "new measures" in revival preaching. The first transatlantic telegraph was sent on August 16, 1858, which was a letter from Queen Victoria to US President James Buchanan. The royal telegraph was the inaugural communication of an undersea cable stretching from Newfoundland to Ireland. Messages that formerly required weeks to transmit via ship could now be exchanged in a matter of minutes. Telegraph technology at this time was not fundamentally unlike the texting of today, except for the fact that only tiny numbers of people were privileged to send messages via this medium. In 1914, Wilhelm II of Germany and Nicholas II of Russia famously exchanged a flurry of telegrams as they witnessed the onset of World War I. The telegrams were sent back and forth so quickly that sometimes outgoing messages had already been sent before incoming messages could be read, not unlike the texting of today.

From the earliest days of the movement, evangelicalism has fostered the adoption of emerging technology for the purposes of gospel proclamation. Predictably, this inclination toward innovation has produced stunning successes as well as spectacular failures. But the criterion for success was always clear—whether the application of new technology resulted in more people knowing the story of Jesus. With its roots extending back into the Reformation, evangelicalism has tended to express suspicion toward traditions that could not be derived from the Scriptures or clearly tied to gospel priorities. Whether devising new pathways for missionary service abroad or engineering responses to social crises, evangelicalism's proudest moments have been ones of innovation and overcoming obstacles in order to advance the gospel. As we look to the future, it should come as no surprise to find that evangelical churches would be among the first to explore the application of VR to devotional life, education, and missionary service.

Not without struggle and scandal, Christian churches began applying electronic forms of mass media in order to extend their ministries somewhere around one century ago. As early as 1925, Aimee Semple McPherson perceived that mass media could cross divides that had become impassible in conventional society. The "Cathedral of the Air"—as Aimee described the airwaves of her day—could bring the good news and spiritual encouragement where traditional churches could not. Although her language concerning race and color reflects the terminology of her time, her spirit was in exactly the right place. She wrote:

> The Cathedral of the Air am I, the church with no boundary line. And under my broad, canopied expanse I house the sons of men—the black, the white, the yellow; the brown and red man, too. Brothers all sit side by side in the church with no color line. The rich and the poor, the old and the young, The sad and the gay of heart, the strong and the weak, the sick and the well, all worship at my shrine.[40]

Over the past century, countless people have converted to Christianity through radio and television ministries. Not every sermon that reached the airwaves could be likened to gold, silver, or precious stones. Some were more like the wood, hay, and straw that the apostle Paul warns us will be burned away at the last judgement (see 1 Cor. 3:14). Far too many listeners and viewers uncritically accepted the success that preachers experienced with mass media as an indication of spiritual success. But for the untold millions of Christians in the twentieth century whose spiritual lives were shaped and deepened by preaching transmitted through radio and television ministries, the "church of the air" in the era of radio or the "electric church" in the era of television required no particular theological justification. It was simply how they heard God's Word preached.

The best of traditions are never really static but give fresh life even in the most surprising places, and the best of innovations are always anchored in tradition. In the axiom attributed to Jaroslav Pelikan: "Tradition is the living faith of the dead, not the dead faith of the living."[41] One of D. L. Moody's most striking innovations was the "Gospel Wagon"—a pulpit mounted on a horse-drawn buggy that allowed preachers to travel to any street corner and address the crowds who were pouring into Chicago for the World's Fair of 1893. If Jonathan Edwards were alive today, would he advocate the use of VR for preaching and doctrinal instruction? The question is not entirely ridiculous. Jonathan Edwards—the man who served as the third president of Princeton for only thirty-four days because he died of an experimental vaccine against small pox—was a lifelong believer that discovery in any realm reveals the glory of God. He might have had to remove his wig when strapping on the VR googles, but we think he would be interested in giving it a try. He was, after all, particularly fascinated by optics.[42]

Chapter 3

THE CHURCH STEPS INTO VIRTUAL REALITY

"ONLINE CHURCHES ARE ALWAYS AND ETERNALLY NEW."[1]

✦ Tim Hutchings

"HISTORY NEVER LOOKS LIKE HISTORY WHEN YOU ARE
LIVING THROUGH IT."[2]

✦ John W. Gardener

W e who have been churchgoers for any period of time can recall moments when we have prematurely judged cultural shifts. Amy Grant's crossover album, *Heart in Motion* came out in 1991, and Hillsong's *The Power of Your Love* began making its way up from Sydney through churches around the world in 1992. Should the hymns that have been sung in churches for generations be set aside for the new genre of contemporary Christian music? For some pastors and churchgoers at the time, this was a question of real interest. It had not been many years prior when rock and roll had been summarily condemned as "the devil's music."[3] But today the issue has been settled, and on any given Sunday morning rock-and-roll-style worship wafts its way up to heaven from evangelical churches from across the entire planet. This is not to say that there was nothing really at stake in the debate, but the "worship wars" of the late 1980s and early 1990s illustrate how even the best-intentioned of Christian leaders can misinterpret cultural change. In moments of controversy, we can jump to conclusions and render opinions that later seem not a little naïve.

And yet, for every time that we churchgoers can point to an embarrassing moment when we were slow to accept cultural changes that everyone eventually agreed were inevitable, we can probably also point to moments when we enthusiastically embraced something that turned out to be a fad. Drive-in churches may be a case in point. Until the coronavirus crisis brought about a sudden return of drive-in church services, the phenomenon had been relegated to the archives of church history for all practical purposes.[4] Drive-in churches never achieved mainstream status in the twentieth century, even though some commentators believed their success to be assured.

In 1955, Robert Schuller opened the first drive-in church in Southern California. Disneyland had opened just a few miles away earlier that same year, and Schuller's drive-in church became popular with vacationers. In 1961, Schuller opened a new, hybrid church that featured pews to accommodate a traditional congregation as well as a parking-lot-sanctuary with a drive-in capacity for five hundred cars. Modeled after Schuller's highly publicized success, other churches around the country began offering drive-in services. However, the success was short-lived, and when Schuller opened the Crystal Cathedral in 1981, there was no provision for drive-in attendance.

As churches around the world navigate the pitfalls and possibilities of VR, how will we reflect back on this period from the vantage point of another several decades? Will VR become a seamless part of the everyday operations of churches, like email or word processing today, miracles of technology which have become more ordinary in churches than steeples? Or, like robot butlers from the dreams of yesteryears, will VR become a relic of the future that never was? In an attempt to give us the best possible perspective on how VR will most probably be applied for the purposes of Christian ministry in the decades ahead, we will offer an overview of the history of virtual churches and VR churches in this chapter.

Digital Christianity at the Dawn of the Internet: 1991–2004

The absence of a consensus concerning the definition of a "virtual church" makes it problematic to pinpoint the exact date of the founding of the very first virtual church. However, when online chatrooms first became popular in the early 1990s, they quickly became places for experimental social communication, including experimental dialogue about the Christian faith.[5] Once logged on, chatroom users could send text messages in real time to other users who were also logged on to the chatroom. Except for military personnel, most people had never experienced this type of communication before. This was the era of dial-up internet and the unforgettable sound of a modem establishing a connection to the internet via copper telephone wires. Being online meant blocking the use of the landline telephone for everyone else in the house, and many users paid for the internet by the hour or even by the minute. Being online was inconvenient, expensive, and required a fair amount of "geekiness," that is, technical expertise. Although the internet was initially released on August 6, 1991, web browsing tools simple enough for the average person to use did not appear for several years. Netscape and Yahoo were both initially released in 1994. It wasn't until 1998, when Google came on the scene, that the mystery was taken out of even the most elementary internet searches.

Nevertheless, by the early 1990s, some Christians had ventured online and were frequenting chatrooms, practicing their faith in this new venue. Stephen D. O'Leary, one of the first sociologists to study the influence of new media on religion, documented his own explorations and discovery of Christian communities online: "What intrigued me about this type of connection to the network was that it allowed for group interaction of a sort not possible through basic email, people were not merely exchanging letters with each other but actually engaged in collective devotion, much as they would at church or in a Bible study group."[6] Churches and Christian networks began practicing their faith online in various ways, such as by sharing prayer requests in chatrooms, writing out prayers and Scripture verses, and posting links to recordings of sermons and sacred music. An abundance of forums sprung up and hosted detailed discussion threads on a wide variety of topics within Christian theology. Some Christian networks turned to email as a primary means of interaction, arranging for occasional "list-meets," where members could meet in person at specific times and places.[7]

When Facebook arrived on the scene in 2004, the company strove to ensure that people's online personas matched their real-world identities, thus reversing the trend among early chatrooms for users to assume false names and false identities as part of a practice of social experimentation. Flushed with a sense of anonymity, some chatroom users engaged in sexually explicit or gleefully eccentric conversations, resulting in a tarnished reputation for chatrooms in mainstream society. As a general rule, groups that had been unsuccessful in securing space in the public square for one reason or another were the first to experiment with cyberspace as a medium for facilitating their networks and practices.

Neopagans turned to the internet in such numbers that *Wired* coined the term "Technopagan" in 1995.[8] But as the internet began seeping into the culture at large, commentators began asking how the internet might influence religious faith as practiced by the mainstream. In 1996, *Time* ran a cover story titled: "Finding God on the Web: Across the Internet, Believers Are Re-Examining Their Ideas of Faith, Religion and Spirituality."[9] The article exclaims: "Almost overnight, the electronic community of the Internet has come to resemble a high-speed spiritual bazaar, where thousands of the faithful—and equal numbers of the faithless—meet and debate and swap ideas about things many of us had long since stopped discussing in public, like our faith and religious beliefs. It's an astonishing act of technological and intellectual mainstreaming that is changing the character of the internet, and could even change our ideas about God."

Prior to the turn of the millennium, only about a third of Christians had email addresses, and only about a third of churches in the US had websites.[10] The Vatican opened its website in 1995, principally in order to make its vast store of official documentation available to its priests worldwide, and in this the

Roman Catholic Church was strikingly progressive when compared to other Christian churches. At this time, the Catholic Church did its own web serving on three impressive computers that were named after the archangels, Michael, Gabriel, and Raphael. The "email the pope" feature proved too popular to sustain, as the flood of email kept overwhelming even the archangels. The opening of the Vatican website received significant media coverage, but it was clear from the outset that the Vatican website was simply a church website, not an online church.

The first claim to the status of a virtual church seems to have come from the Reverend Charles Henderson, a graduate of Princeton University and Union Theological Seminary. After retiring from thirty years of ministry in the Presbyterian Church USA, Henderson founded "The First Church of Cyberspace" (www.godweb.org) in 1994. Henderson had witnessed firsthand the decline of church attendance in his denomination, and he determined to do something about it. In explaining his reasons for founding the online church to a journalist, Henderson noted that about only one in ten members of his denomination attended church services on any given Sunday, and he intended "The First Church of Cyberspace" to be an outreach to the nine in ten. Reverend Henderson's online church was therefore designed as a mission to those who were officially church members but no longer attended services in brick-and-mortar churches.

The website showcased breakthrough creativity in appealing to the internet as a platform for facilitating religious experience. One journalist commented that visiting the online church created "the sense of a real walk-in church."[11] She continued: "Packed with images and reading material you'd expect to find in a church atmosphere, the site includes inspirational music, sermons and fellowship in the chat room." The virtual sanctuary was represented by a webpage with a perfectly black backdrop. On either side of this dark canvas appeared a pair of icons at an angle, creating the illusion that the icons lined the walls of a darkly lit room. At the center of the webpage lay a graphic tile representing a flame, which "flickered" every time visitors reloaded the webpage by rotating to the next graphic tile on an animation loop. Many commented on the impression that spending time in the virtual sanctuary had made on them. The Presbyterian Church USA never recognized "The First Church of Cyberspace" as an official church in the denomination, although representatives of the denomination expressed their appreciation for Reverend Henderson's ministry on the internet.

Douglas Estes began his journey into the study of the relationship of faith and technology while a graduate student in the mid-1990s. "Like many Christians, I have a deep desire to see the gospel go out around the world," Estes explained.[12] "When the internet first came on the scene, I was one of those people who spent some time sharing the gospel in chatrooms and online. It was a brave new world, so to speak, of opportunities for mission in that way." Through these experiences, Estes landed on the idea of publishing a book on internet evangelism. After completing doctoral studies in theology and serving as a pastor for several years, Estes published his reflections in 2009 in one of the first books from an evangelical perspective on virtual churches: *SimChurch: Being the Church in the Virtual World*.

For many readers, this book was their first exposure to the phenomenon of virtual churches, that is, online communities that identified themselves as Christian churches. Estes argues that virtual churches should not be regarded simply as online evangelistic tools to bring the unchurched into brick-and-mortar churches. Those who see virtual churches from this perspective, Estes claims, "misunderstand the capacity of the virtual world for discipleship. They think of the virtual world as equivalent to broadcast television, when it is a completely different medium."[13] Estes concludes that virtual churches are not merely online extensions of physical churches but rather open unique opportunities for experiencing community life as Christian churches: "The best way to reach and disciple people in virtual worlds is with virtual churches."[14]

Concepts of online churches began to coalesce in the years leading up to the new millennium. In 1997, London-based futurist and business consultant, Patrick Dixon, published *Cyberchurch: Christianity and the Internet.*[15] Dixon was truly a man ahead of his time, documenting some prescient insights concerning what would unfold over the next quarter century. When he published his book, there were about forty million internet users in the world (or about 0.68 percent of the world's population at the time), but Dixon correctly comprehended that this number would skyrocket in the immediate future. In 1997, Dixon could document the number of times that certain theological words occurred online (the word *Jesus*, for example, occurred 515,747 times), and Dixon could tabulate the number of webpages that pertained to specific theological topics (for example, there were one hundred thousand websites that in some way dealt with the Bible).[16] As a graduate of Cambridge University, he visualized the internet as the equivalent of one hundred thousand books, which he remarked was "miniscule" compared to the Cambridge library he had known during his student days.[17] The internet that Dixon describes seems impossibly small in comparison to the internet of today, and yet Dixon correctly perceived that a revolution was underway. He writes with an excitement that approaches ecstasy over the possibilities that he believed the internet would present to Christian churches.

Based on his experiences with global telecommunication as a frequent traveler and business consultant, Dixon predicted that churches would someday livestream their services over the internet: "I predict that it will not be long before a number of the larger churches worldwide begin to go live with cameras and sound, allowing people to drop in on live services."[18] Dixon owned a Nokia 9000 Communicator, which was released in August of 1996 and which has since been called the first smartphone-like device, though the word "smartphone" had not been coined at the time. After listing out the many impressive functions of the device, Dixon comments: "It's really a perfect example of the next generation of computer devices. Is it a phone? Is it a computer?"[19] Dixon also conceptualized teleconferencing with near perfect accuracy: "In the future it might be possible to see a composite image of an electronic congregation of fifty or a hundred faces on your screen, refreshed every minute or two. Each participant's camera image could be sent live to a central computer on the Net, which builds up the total view of the congregation before transmitting it to every participant."[20] What Dixon theorized in 1997 became reality for countless Christian congregations in the wake of the coronavirus crisis in 2020.

Dixon's overarching message was that the internet would grow explosively, and he urged churches everywhere to begin learning to use the internet wisely. He explored several practices that continue to have relevance for virtual church and VR churches today. For example, he notes that the practice of prayer translates well to telecommunication media, and he extrapolates from his experience on prayer conference calls that the internet could someday facilitate large-scale prayer assemblies.[21] Dixon's most enduring contribution may be his advocacy that, in applying the internet as a medium for ministry, the church is simply doing what the church has always done: "Paul was the first cyberapostle. His overwhelming desire was always to be present personally with a local church, but when in prison he used all the communication technology at his disposal to make himself virtually present throughout the known world."[22]

About the time that George Barna released the 1998 report, "The Cyberchurch Is Coming: National Survey of Teenagers Shows Expectation of Substituting Internet for Corner Church," many evangelical leaders in the US started to think seriously about virtual churches for the first time. The report opens with the sensational line: "Fifteen years from now you may tell your grandchildren that back in the old days, when people wanted a religious experience they attended a church for that purpose. Chances are good that your grandchildren will be shocked by such a revelation."[23] The bold report continues:

> Our research indicates that by 2010 we will probably have 10% to 20% of the population relying primarily or exclusively upon the Internet for its religious input. Those people will never set foot on a church campus because their religious and spiritual needs will be met through other means—including the Internet. Whether or not the cyberchurch is a "true" church may not be [as] pressing an issue as what current church leaders will do about the inevitable gravitation of tens of millions of

people away from the existing church and how they can help to shape this emerging church form.[24]

The document reminds the reader that, when Willow Creek Community Church popularized the "seeker church" in the 1970s and 80s, many Christian ministers refused to recognize such communities as legitimate churches, arguing that these communities were far less intimate and far more focused on stage performance than the neighborhood churches of the 1940s and 50s. As 2013 came and went—the year that the report supposed that young people would have all but forgotten traditional churchgoing—"The Cyber Church is Coming" began to be criticized as inexcusably inaccurate.[25]

The Beta Phase of the VR Church: 2004–2016

In 2004, Mark Zuckerberg founded Facebook, Google released Gmail, and *Wired* announced that they would no longer capitalize the "Internet," since the internet had become a mundane part of everyone's life.[26] This same year also witnessed a burst of creative energy in the development of online churches. With the disruption of Y2K and the catastrophe of 9/11 receding into the past, churches now started anew to develop strategies for Christian mission in the third millennium. The Anglican Church published the report, *Mission-Shaped Church: Church Planting and Fresh Expressions of Church in a Changing Context.* As Tim Hutchings explains, this document called on the Anglican Church "to rethink how they did church in the modern world, to start looking for ways of doing church that went outside the parish and into networks."[27] This document served as the charter for the "Fresh Expressions" movement, a church-planting initiative started within the Anglican Church that seeks to bring the lived reality of church out of the cathedral and into people's everyday lives. The foundation of ministry in the Anglican Church is the parish system, observed the authors of *Mission-Shaped Church*, but people today connect "through the networks in which they live, rather than through the place where they live."[28] In his foreword to the report, Rowan Williams—who served as archbishop of Canterbury from 2002 to 2012—said that the church was living in a "watershed" moment and explained: "The essence of this is in the fact that we have begun to recognize that there are many ways in which the reality of 'church' can exist."[29]

In 2004, i-church became the first online church to be an official congregation of a major denomination.[30] The Anglican Diocese of Oxford established i-church in order to facilitate the assembling of its first online congregation. The project was the brainchild of Richard Thomas, the director of communications for the Diocese of Oxford.[31] When i-church opened, its leadership presumed that it would attract visitors from the Diocese of Oxford, but they quickly discovered that people from everywhere on earth—both those who ascribed to traditional Christian doctrine and those who espoused no faith—were attending services regularly. Set up as an innovative church plant, i-church has persisted now for nearly two decades as an official, online congregation of the Anglican Church. The BBC announced the story with the headline, "First Web-Pastor Appointed," explaining: "The Church of England has appointed its first web pastor to oversee a new parish that will exist only on the net."[32] i-church was designed as a forum-based online community, and the congregation has continued to assemble in this format ever since.

i-church was launched on a budget of £15,000 per year (approximately equivalent to a half-time salary). The first minister at i-church stayed for about one year, followed by a second minister who remained in office for about three years. The Reverend Pam Smith assumed office in 2008 and continues to serve as the third minister of the congregation. Smith connected to Christian faith via the internet early in her own spiritual journey before becoming a pioneer in online ministry. When caring for a relative's health concern required her to change her lifestyle and stay at home for periods of time, Smith became an early adopter of the internet. She describes her first encounters with the internet: "The noise of the dialing tones gave the impression of travelling a long distance to reach the mysterious place called 'cyber space' where I could read what other people had posted on the world wide web."[33] She explains that she "had only been a Christian for a few years" at that time, and the exchange with Christians online helped her come to a deeper understanding of the faith.[34]

She found that the forums on the Ship of Fools website made for especially profitable reading and became an avid member of this online community. Smith remembers the feeling of freedom that accompanied online communication, allowing her to readily express questions that she feared would have been perceived as elementary had she asked them in traditional churches.[35] "It was this experience of encountering so many different points of view, and engaging directly with people who held them, which convinced me that Christians should be online, not just explaining their faith but exploring it in the company of others."[36] Smith now ministers to church members who have joined a virtual church for many of the same reasons that first attracted Smith herself to the Christian community online.

In 2014, at the ten-year anniversary of i-church, Smith could write: "Our members are a mixture of those who can't get to a physical church, members of small churches who enjoy the opportunity for fellowship with the wider Christian community online, and people who are exploring or returning to the Christian faith."[37] Reverend Smith articulates the philosophy of ministry of i-church:

> The aim of i-church is both evangelical—to connect people online who are looking to find out about Christianity—and pastoral—to help people to develop in their spiritual journeys. I'm licensed as the priest in charge, but in practice other i-church members are quick to respond to questions and prayer requests. We don't just want people to find out information about Christianity, but to experience Christian community as well, since as Christians we believe that Jesus is present among us when we gather.[38]

Only weeks after the launch of i-church, the world's first VR church—the Church of Fools—opened its portals. This inauspiciously named project pioneered an interactive, three-dimensional interface for the purposes of conducting church services. The project was sponsored by the Methodist Church of Great Britain as well as the Anglican Church, although neither church recognized the experiment as an official congregation.

The stated purpose of the experiment was to "create holy ground on the net."[39] The Anglican Bishop of London, Richard Chartres, delivered the opening sermon on Tuesday, May 11, 2004. The project received substantial amounts of press through media outlets all around the world.

An article that appeared in the *New York Times* described the experience: "Visitors who log on to a vaguely Romanesque church control the speech and movement of on-screen figures known as avatars. Acting through the avatars, visitors can kneel in prayer, talk or whisper in text messages, extend a hand in blessing or raise both arms in ecstatic praise. They can also sit in pews or gather for conversation in a crypt equipped not only with chairs but with a 'holy water' water cooler and vending machines as well."[40] Those attending services at the Church of Fools joined via their desktop and laptop computers, not by stereoscopic head-mounted display systems. However, it seems reasonable to consider the Church of Fools the first VR church, since visitors interacted via a platform that simulated spatial position.

The Church of Fools experiment developed from a magazine titled *The Ship of Fools*, which Simon Jenkins and his associates had founded in the 1970s.[41] While a student at London Bible College (now London School of Theology), Simon Jenkins served as the editor of the school's newspaper. Jenkins launched *The Ship of Fools* during his final semester before graduation in 1977. From Jenkins's perspective, the spin of Christian publications at that time was almost exclusively toward the positive and inspirational, and he felt that some of the most pressing issues in the church could not be addressed effectively by this genre of publication. "How can we get better at being church?" Jenkins began to ask.[42] "It struck us that the only way to get better at living in our culture was to be more critically aware of ourselves and how we came across and the things we did wrong." The aim of the magazine was not to celebrate failure but to learn through critical engagement, Jenkins explained, and so the magazine launched with the tagline, "The Magazine of Christian Unrest." On April 1, 1998, *The Ship of Fools* was relaunched as an internet website, and its online readership quickly outnumbered what the readership had been for the print edition.[43]

The leadership and community of *The Ship of Fools* launched the Church of Fools in 2004. Jenkins delineated the principles of the experiment. First, he said, "we wanted to try translating church into the medium of the net."[44] The second aim of the project was to facilitate authentic spiritual experiences for visitors, and the third aim was to share the message of Christianity with people who would not normally come to a church building. "Just as the Methodist church leader John Wesley took his preaching out of churches and into the fields and streets in the 18th century, we wanted to take church to where people are in the 21st century—on the Net,"[45] Jenkins stated. In terms of the numbers of visitors, the experiment proved overwhelmingly successful. There were an average of 7,337 visitors per day for the first 52 days of the project, with a record attendance of over 41,000 on May 25, 2004.[46] Jenkins reflects: "In other words, we were drawing cathedral-sized congregations to our little church."[47] This unique experiment ran from May 11 to September 26, 2004.

By other measures, the experiment demonstrated itself to be untenable. The most pressing concern faced by the community was the wretched manners of many of the visitors. The church was soon overrun by "trolls"—visitors who, charged with a sense of anonymity and power, rushed in and seized the opportunity to shout (that is, to text) the obscene or profane during services. Mark Howe, one of the leaders involved in both the computer programming and the spiritual direction of the project, commented: "All churches need to hold mission and pastoral care in creative tension, but few congregations experience this tension as dramatically as Church of Fools, which attracted massive interest from both the unchurched and those with a grudge against churches in general. An unfortunate and unforeseen clash of cultures meant that what for the Church's creators was a sacred space looked to many newcomers like a computer game."[48]

Howe went on to lament: "Within a few weeks, the leadership team was spending almost all its time dealing with sustained attacks rather than engaging in the mission and pastoral support that they had signed up for."[49] These security issues had not been anticipated by the leadership of *The Ship of Fools*. The interactive platform by which the church met was a proprietary software created by a London-based studio specifically for the experiment, and redesigning the platform with additional security features contributed to the financial strain that ultimately brought the experiment to a close. The Church of Fools held its final service on September 26, 2004, at which time the experiment had already outlived the three months that the creators had originally intended for the project.

Through a flood of newspaper articles and other international media releases, the Church of Fools brought the concept of VR churches into public awareness.[50] There were many aspects of the church services that were overtly experimental—and a few that were perhaps flippant, like the holy water vending

97

machine in the church crypt. The spiritual purpose of the project was to discover through experience how best to practice faith as an online community. Jenkins reflected on the outcomes of the experiment: "Does prayer work in a virtual environment? Does preaching work? Does worship work? How does this feel? We proved it quite quickly—well, to our satisfaction, on a kind of felt basis—that, yes, this really was prayer. And that when you gathered in a circle, and people started praying, you—imaginatively—you were there—you were in a prayer meeting. You were creating sacred space."[51] Jenkins describes his discovery of the real spiritual power of prayer, albeit in a virtual space: "The experience of praying the Lord's Prayer together focused attention on our togetherness in prayer and worship, despite our distance in terms of geography, culture, language and faith expression. . . . Theologically speaking, it was like the coming together of the church on the Day of Pentecost, showing the unity of the church regardless of time and space."[52]

After the Church of Fools officially closed, the congregation reconfigured itself as "Saint Pixels" and continued to meet via a standard chatroom platform until migrating to Facebook in 2012. Second Life, the online interactive social platform founded in 2003, became a popular gathering place for Christian groups. The "Anglican Cathedral of Second Life" is probably the best remembered of the churches that assembled in Second Life. While not recognized as an official congregation by the Anglican Church or by any other denomination, services were conducted regularly from 2007 to 2009 by the Reverend Mark Brown, who continued on to become the CEO of the Bible Society of New Zealand.[53] By this time, internet speeds had climbed to sufficient levels to incorporate bidirectional audio streams, allowing visitors in the Anglican Cathedral of Second Life to speak to one another in real time. The Reverend Brown delivered his sermons as speech instead of the text format which had been the only possible form of communication in previous VR churches. Second Life also sported advanced computer graphics, and many found the visual experience of visiting the cathedral to be stunning. Other virtual social platforms emerged following the success of Second Life. In 2011, Daniel Herron, then a middle-schooler, founded a Christian community on "Roblox," a platform released in 2006 that features Lego-like avatars and sets. Herron called the group "The Robloxian Christians," and the church website explains: "We are a youth-led online church that has served on the Roblox gaming platform since 2011."[54]

While the above projects raised questions and sparked curiosity, another transition was quietly underway that probably has done more than anything else to cause mainstream church-goers to ponder the possibilities of virtual churches. Founded in 2005 and acquired by Google in 2006, YouTube introduced video streaming to the majority of internet users. Prior to YouTube, sharing a video on a website usually required the user to download the entire file before beginning to watch the video, and because software had not been standardized, additional downloads were sometimes necessary to playback the video file in the correct format. YouTube quickly became one of the most popular websites on the internet, and by 2010, there were thirty-five hours of new video material uploaded to YouTube each and every minute.[55] In 2013, Google introduced "Hangouts," which allowed users to broadcast live video for free. By 2014, there were over three hundred hours of new video material uploaded to YouTube every minute. Countless churches started posting video recordings of their services to their webpages. Some churches began broadcasting services live, so that church members who could not be physically present for one reason or another could still join the congregation in viewing the services in real time. A small number of churches, usually those with sophisticated media teams, even began producing special editions of their weekly services specifically designed for online congregations. In August of 2012, Rick Warren's Saddleback Church appointed Jay Kranda as the church's first full-time Online Campus Pastor. Livestreaming was becoming mainstream.

To Be Virtual, Or Not to Be, That Is the Question: 2016 and Beyond

The Oculus Rift, arguably the first successful attempt to bring virtual reality to the consumer market, launched on March 28, 2016. This system was followed by the HTC Vive (a competitor to the Oculus Rift with slightly superior technical specifications) released on June 7, 2016. These systems sold for $599 and $799 respectively, and these prices did not include the souped-up PCs necessary to power the VR goggles. Sony also released a consumer VR headset for its PlayStation 4 gaming console on October 13, 2016. While the graphical performance of Sony's VR headset was somewhat inferior, its price point of $399 and the fact that it did not require the purchase of a PC translated into increased sales. By the close of the Christmas season of 2019, Sony had sold five million VR headsets, dwarfing the sales of the Oculus Rift and the HTC Vive combined.

In early 2016, D. J. Soto stepped down from his position on the staff of a megachurch in Reading, Pennsylvania, intending to take up a new mission of church planting. In his own words, Soto recalls "this turmoil within us to go from our comfortable environment, which was at the megachurch—we had a salary and benefits—and to leave that to start something new. We didn't know what 'new' meant. We thought that meant starting new churches across America. And at the same time, VR started to come out. And I remember reading about the Oculus Rift, and I was thinking to myself, 'Oh, man, I got to try it out.'"[56] Within a year after leaving his position at the megachurch, Soto's new vision of planting VR churches had coalesced. As a former filmmaker, Soto was an experienced producer of digital media.

By late 2016, Soto had sold his home and, along with his wife and five children, moved into a thirty-foot trailer and started trekking across the country. *Wired* reports: "Soto imagined bringing religion directly to the people by offering sermons or Bible study in unusual places, like backwater towns, CrossFit gyms, campgrounds, and bars. . . . Their plan was to head to California, by way of backroads, launching a series of pop-up churches along the way."[57] Soto started hosting meetings for Bible study and prayer on a VR social platform called AltSpaceVR in June of 2016, and throughout the next months of travel Soto continued to host these meetings on an occasional basis. By May of 2017, a leadership team had formed and determined to host these meetings on a weekly basis.[58] Soto explains that from this point on the aim of planting a VR church seemed straightforward: "That mental shift set the church plant in motion. And then I suppose it was a gradual evolution of thought to come to the realization that we were a 'legitimate' church that existed entirely in VR."[59] D. J. Soto's VR Church started as an experiment. The initial purpose was purely exploratory: "What can we do in this space? Is church viable?" Soto asked himself. "And then it just evolved into a church plant."[60]

VR Church is surprisingly similar to a traditional, evangelical church, D. J. Soto explains: "People ask, 'What's VR church like?' And I say, 'It's probably what your church is like, just in VR.' We have church services, we have prayers, we have sermons, and we have small groups during the week. We also do sacraments in VR. The life of the church has been for us an immersive experience translated into the virtual reality."[61] Services at VR Church are church as normal, Soto urges, "just in a 'Ready Player One/Matrix/Inception' kind of virtual world."[62] While the form of services at VR Church is strikingly familiar for many evangelical churchgoers, certain elements at Soto's VR Church are unquestionably different from traditional churches.

Soto notes that VR Church attracts many who profess to be neither evangelical nor Christian. "We haven't done surveys, but probably over fifty percent of our attendees would not identify as an evangelical or a Christian *per se*," Soto explained.[63] *Wired* notes: "To find an atheist in a church is not so strange. Plenty of people visit with their families to keep the peace. But to find an atheist who seeks out religious services, one who talks about his atheism in church, and intends to return for more—that is unusual."[64] Soto has consistently expressed awareness of the experimental nature of VR Church: "We're trying to figure this out," he said. "It's uncharted territory. It's a different thing, and our team is just trying to navigate through those waters."

In the spring of 2020, I (Jonathan) drove past a sign outside a church that read: "Can we uninstall 2020 and install it again? This version seems to have a virus!" While many were aware of the phenomenon of virtual reality churches in early 2020, probably only an infinitesimal percentage of Christians worldwide would have answered in the affirmative if they had been asked whether they had ever attended a virtual reality church service. With the onset of the coronavirus crisis, the question of whether churches could assemble via virtual technology became a serious question for Christians of all traditions. Only weeks into the crisis, Gallup Senior Scientist, Frank Newport, could state: "The abrupt cessation of in-person worship in churches, synagogues and mosques around the country is one of the most significant sudden disruptions in the practice of religion in U.S. history."[65]

During the weeks leading up to Easter of 2020, many ministers were scrambling simply trying to cope with congregational life under lockdown measures, drawing up plans for only the next couple of weeks. Few imagined at that time that the crisis would permanently impact the practice of Christianity worldwide. But one by one, and then as a flood, churches began announcing that their Easter services would be canceled or conducted online. As the hope of assembling in person on Easter morning drifted further away and then was altogether abandoned, Christians from across the spectrum of traditions began to ask whether attending church services virtually was to attend church services for real. On Easter Sunday, April 12, 2020, almost every church building on planet Earth stood empty, for the first time in nearly two millennia of Christian history.

VR churches may still seem like novelties today. Tim Hutchings reflects: "Somehow this is a medium that is always strange to the church. It is always being rediscovered for the first time."[66] From the historical survey in this chapter, we can see that the migration of activities that were traditionally conducted in designated church buildings to an array of internet-based telecommunication platforms has been ongoing since the earliest days of the internet. We can also see from this review that, because different Christian traditions adhere to different definitions of what properly constitutes a church, certain Christian communities are more or less willing to label their online ministries "churches" and to develop them as such.

For some Christians, the words of Jesus constitute the definition of the church when He said: "For where two or three are gathered in my name, there am I among them" (Matt. 18:20 ESV). For those of this persuasion, it is obvious that Christians have gathered as the church via the internet for as long as chatrooms have facilitated community prayer. For Christians for whom official status within a denominational structure is part and parcel of what it means to be a church, 2004 probably marks the year of the appearance of the first virtual church with the founding of i-church under the Anglican Diocese of Oxford. But even for the most ardent skeptic of the concept of VR churches, the response of Christian communities worldwide to the coronavirus crisis demonstrated that real people can assemble as the real church in virtual reality in order to receive real spiritual nourishment.

Chapter 4

THE NATURE OF VIRTUALITY

"WHERE IS THE WISDOM WE HAVE LOST IN
KNOWLEDGE? WHERE IS THE KNOWLEDGE
WE HAVE LOST IN INFORMATION?"[1]

✦ T. S. Elliot

"TECHNOLOGY IS A GIFT OF GOD. AFTER THE GIFT OF LIFE
IT IS PERHAPS THE GREATEST OF GOD'S GIFTS. IT IS THE
MOTHER OF CIVILIZATIONS, OF ARTS AND OF SCIENCES."[2]

✦ Freeman Dyson

I f we are to be skilled ministers of the gospel in the virtual age, then we need to have a thoroughgoing grasp of the nature of virtual reality. What is *virtuality*? The dictionary defines *virtuality* as the state of being virtual or being one way in power, force, or effect but another way in actuality. Attempting to ferret out the exact nature of virtual reality therefore would seem to be a nearly impossible task. But everything in God's universe has a nature. Every new technology operates by a set of principles, and we will deploy this technology best when we understand these principles and reflect on their relation to the types of problems that we intend to solve by applying them.

We have heard a lot about the "limitless possibilities" of VR in recent years. Ernest Cline, author of the 2011 novel, *Ready Player One* (the film adaptation produced by Steven Spielberg appeared in 2018), explains that he wrote the book because he wanted to explore the technology's "limitless application."[3] In the hype that has poured out from the VR industry over the past couple of years, there has been no shortage of claims that essentially everything is within the reach of VR. But every new technology has its limitations, and VR is no exception. When a new technology first lands in the awareness of the public, it may seem that the technology has no bounds. But sustained experience with the new technology and reflection on this experience will reveal its limits, and understanding these limits will allow us to begin setting the technology to its best use. When we as church leaders and Christian educators are first introduced to VR, we may falsely assume that the technology is capable of absolutely everything, including replicating a church service or a seminary-level theology class down to the minutest detail. But this is not the case. VR may be the most powerful communication medium yet invented by humankind, but it will nonetheless require great creativity, patience, wisdom, and expertise to develop effective forms of Christian ministry in VR.

In a way, the applications of new technology are indeed limitless, but this does not mean that the technologies themselves do not have limits. Let me explain. If any invention ever stirred the imagination of humanity to dream about limitless possibilities, it would be the book. The book superseded the scroll as the medium of choice for written materials not long after the close of the first century AD. Books beat out the competition for several reasons. First, books are more convenient for retrieving information (transitioning from one passage to another in a scroll takes far more time). Second, books can be revised with relative ease (individual pages can be excised or inserted with minimum repair work necessary, whereas patching a scroll is laborious and never looks quite right). Third, books are less troublesome to store and transport (small and large books stack neatly on shelves, but scrolls become unwieldy when they are too small or too large). Today, hundreds of thousands of new book titles are published each year, and yet we come no closer to exhausting the value of books. If any invention ever offered "limitless possibilities," surely it would be the book.

But seen from another angle, books are not limitless but bound, and it is precisely this boundedness that creates the value for which we use books. Even after many centuries, the basic "look and feel" of books has remained remarkably static, from the time of Julius Caesar to our own day. Even after centuries of improvements and technological advances, books continue to be burdensome to carry except a few at a time, are susceptible to water and fire damage, and still consume significant amounts of paper—a resource that we today understand to be more precious than ever. The invention of the book has opened up limitless possibilities, but these possibilities are directed and shaped by a very specific set of limitations.

This principle is true not only for the book. The nineteenth century witnessed one of history's profound technological revolutions with the invention of the steam locomotive and the rise of the commercially successful railroad. To the nineteenth-century citizen, the railroad certainly seemed to open up endless possibilities, and in a way the railroad did change everything. Intellectual historian Jacques Barzun explains that the rise of the railway marks "the completest change in human experience since the nomadic tribes became rooted in one spot to grow grain and raise cattle; it was in effect a reversal of that settling down. Locomotion by the force of steam, the railroad, uprooted mankind and made of it individual nomads again."[4] In the US, the history of the railroad is intertwined with the history of the settlement of the western territories, the assimilation of the "wild west" into the forty-eight contiguous states. On June 4, 1876, the Transcontinental Express arrived in San Francisco after having left New York City a mere eighty-three hours and thirty-nine minutes prior. Newspapers across the nation exploded with the tidings. The famed Oregon Trail, which had been the principle route to the west previous to the rise of the railroad, required a six-month journey on foot, people trudging alongside the oxen who pulled the covered wagons filled with supplies. It seemed that anything would be possible in the wake of the revolution that the railroad promised.

The railroad certainly reshaped America, as well as almost every other nation on earth, and yet trains today still carry some of the same basic limitations that they did when they first appeared two centuries ago. Because trains run steel wheels on steel rails, they roll forward and backward with astoundingly low levels of friction. This means that trains can transport cargo in a vastly more efficient manner than traditional wheeled vehicles, such as horse-drawn wagons or modern automobiles with rubber tires on asphalt roads. The incredibly low levels of friction between steel wheels and steel rails means that locomotives need to be extremely heavy in order to have pulling power. The extreme heaviness of locomotives and their cargos further means that trains require great distances to start and stop.

This cascading sequence of causes and effects translates to the fact that trains today still operate similarly to the trains of the past in several ways: trains travel on rails (and therefore cannot roam in any direction the engineer may desire), trains are long (the expense of maintaining a railway dictates that the payloads of trains are, on average, far greater than that of cars or trucks), and trains abide by tightly governed schedules (if you were ever the passenger who imagined that the train would wait for you, you will know what I'm talking about). In one sense, the railroads did change everything. But, seen from another angle, railroads continue to be limited by many of the same factors that have always defined railroads. Does VR carry limitations equivalent to the bounded pages of the book or the unmovable tracks of the railroad? We suspect the answer is yes, and in this chapter, we will present ten principles that articulate what we believe these limitations to be. We will deploy VR technology for the purposes of Christian ministry best if we have a clear sense of what VR can and cannot do.

Before we dive into the principles below, two quick caveats are in order. First, while we believe that VR technology does carry basic limitations, we admit that distilling precisely what these limitations are is a process that is far more simply done in hindsight than with foresight. When VR technology is understood better in the future, experts will no doubt be able to state VR's fundamental capacities in a fewer number of principles than we can now. Second, for each of the ten principles below, the reader can silently append the phrase, "for the foreseeable future." It should be stated explicitly that all of our conclusions are extrapolations from the constellation of technologies that we know currently as virtual reality.

1. VR Is, After All, Virtual

Users will remain aware that VR experiences are simulations of actual reality. Therefore, the value of VR technology will be that it allows users to engage in simulations of experiences that in actual reality could be unsafe, expensive, or impossible.

In its present incarnation, VR is a series of wearable apparatuses that simulate sense perception. The VR headsets of today deal with the senses of sight and sound, but there are consumer products available that simulate the sense of touch. These so-called "haptic devices" can take on a variety of forms, for example, gloves that one can wear in order to "touch" virtual building blocks or vests that one can wear in order to "feel" simulations of physical objects (such as rain) or abstract phenomena (such as music). Haptic devices are currently not as common as VR headsets, but the technology is showing promise, and experts anticipate that select haptic devices will become widely accessible in the years ahead. The technology to simulate the senses of smell and taste is in development in laboratories, but it is not clear at present whether consumer VR will deal with smell and taste within the decade. However, it is clear that VR systems in the future will provide simulations of sense perception of an increasing realism and across a broadening spectrum of senses. The experiences that VR systems will become capable of delivering will become progressively more immersive.

One of the controversial questions in the VR industry today is whether the technology will ever become so compelling that the simulations will be indistinguishable from actual reality. Will the sense of "presence" that VR delivers ever be so powerful that it renders users incapable of detecting whether they are in a simulation? From our perspective, the answer to this question is clearly "no." The plotline of many dystopian science fiction films and novels hinges on the idea that VR simulations become so good that they are indistinguishable from the real world. This lost ability to differentiate between virtual reality and actual reality is then exploited by the villains of the movie or book. Not all experts agree, and some enthusiasts seem to think that VR's value cannot be realized unless the technology reaches this point, but we are quite convinced that it is extremely improbable that VR will ever be able to replicate reality so compellingly that users are incapable of distinguishing the simulations from actual reality. This is not to say that people will not use VR for escapism or to block out their experience of actual reality, which to them seems too painful or too banal to face. But the basic fact that users will remain psychologically capable of perceiving that their experiences in VR are simulations means that most VR users will be content to engage in VR for a specific set of uses. These use cases include simulations of experiences that in actual reality would be unsafe, expensive, or impossible.[5]

Why do we conclude that VR will never really fool people into thinking that the simulations are actual reality? As the founder of Moody Bible Institute's VR Lab, I (Jonathan) have had the privilege of proctoring first VR experiences for hundreds of people. While I have witnessed many responses of amazement and even awe when people don the VR headset for the very first time, no one at any point has ever mistaken VR for reality—not even for a second. One of my favorite initial responses came from Jon Guerra, the artist who wrote the popular worship song, "I Will Follow." After Jon put on the goggles, and I started to showcase our latest VR learning environments, he exclaimed: "I want to vacation here!" But in all the hours of VR experiences that our lab has cumulatively clocked, no one once forgot that they were in a simulation. I can attest that small children, too, do not confuse virtual reality for actual reality. I personally own VR equipment and, as a prelude to family game night, I occasionally allow our children a quick experience in VR. One of our children's favorite VR experiences features a pet dragon (modeled in visual appearance and personality after a puppy) that one can give treats to, play fetch with, or stroke lovingly on the top of the head. After my third-born daughter took one of her first forays into VR, I asked her whether the pet dragon were real. I might as well have asked her whether "Todd the Frog" were real, whom I impersonate when I place her on my back and hop up the stairs to tuck her into bed for the night. Even my three-year-old daughter thought the question was silly and could not for a moment imagine that her VR experience had not been a simulation.

But what will happen as VR technology becomes more advanced? We conclude that people will still be able to distinguish the difference between VR and actual reality. Consider for a moment how tremendously the technology of photography has advanced over the course of the past two centuries. We have moved from black-and-white images, which were barely focused and required days to develop, to images of brilliant color and astounding resolution that can be communicated anywhere in the world in an instant. But despite these massive technical advances, how many times in your life have you looked at a photograph and mistaken it for actual reality? In 1886, when the Lumière Brothers premiered in Paris their fifty-second film, "Arrival of a Train at La Ciotat," it was reported that people screamed and jumped out of their seats, terrified that the approaching train would crash into them. But it turns out that this story is an urban legend, and so virtually no one in the whole history of cinema has ever mistaken film for real life. From our experience with current VR technology, we see no clues pointing to the conclusion that VR will someday be indistinguishable from actual reality.

VR theoretically allows us to experience simulations of anything, but because we will remain aware of the fact that our VR experiences are simulations of reality, we will choose to access VR to facilitate basically only three kinds of experiences: those that in actual reality are potentially unsafe, expensive, or impossible. Many of our everyday experiences in real life would feel like agonizing wastes of time in VR (for example, emptying out the recycling bin). However, we might expect a lot of people to queue up if we were offering VR experiences that in real life were potentially unsafe (for example, driving a sports car down the winding streets of Monaco), expensive (for example, hosting an evening with friends on your own private superyacht), or impossible (for example, walking alongside a brontosaurus in a prehistoric habitat). VR experiences that contain value to users will present elements from at least one of these three categories, and sometimes elements from all three. Scuba diving with blue whales or learning to perform open-heart surgery could qualify for all three criteria.

How then might we apply VR technology for ministry purposes? Let's work through these three categories one at a time. Are there activities that the church and institutions of Christian education engage in on an ongoing basis that are potentially unsafe? Training for missionary aviators comes immediately to mind for us.[6] Learning to land an airplane on an airstrip in the jungle is a process that can be improved by VR simulations. What about first-aid training or intruder response training for church staff and volunteers? Medical schools are among the earliest educational institutions to adopt VR broadly, and VR simulations offer benefits over traditional techniques when teaching many medical procedures. Those training for missionary service in the medical field may be the first Christian workers for whom VR is a normal part of their educational experience.

VR experiences create value when simulating experiences that are perceived to be potentially unsafe in real life, but what is perceived as "potentially unsafe" will vary for different people and need not pose an objective threat of bodily harm. VR experiences can create value in simulating experiences that are perceived as psychologically unsafe or merely notably uncomfortable. Studies are emerging that demonstrate that VR can be used as an effective tool in overcoming anxiety in an array of situations. JoAnn Difede, professor of psychology at the medical school of Cornell University, became internationally famous for her work in applying VR to the treatment of patients suffering from PTSD following the terrorist attacks of September 11, 2001. There are many possible ways in which VR simulations could be applied to reinforce the effectiveness of Christian counseling.

Are there expensive activities that the church and institutions of Christian education have traditionally pursued? The list of use cases for VR technology here could be extremely long. Christian communities have historically invested significant resources in travel, either for the purposes of missionary service (whether this be a missionary team or an individual), communication within a network (for example, conferences or synodal assemblies), or for educational and spiritual enrichment (for example, study tours and pilgrimages). As VR technology advances, it is probable that the need for travel will decrease significantly. International travel is incredibly expensive, and the costs are measured in environmental impact and personal health as well as dollars.

Leaders of denominations and mission agencies know what it is like literally to fly to the other side of the world in order to attend only a few days of meetings. Not infrequently, more hours are spent in the airplane than in the conference room, and the road warrior can live perpetually in the wrong time zone. These have been the trials faced by the leaders who have maintained solidarity among our international Christian networks for the past decades. This is not to say that the relationships that people form in VR are equivalent to the relationships formed when people assemble in person. Nonetheless, churches and Christian networks stand to gain a great deal by learning to identify what components of their community life can be effectively conducted in VR and by migrating these specific components to VR platforms.

Sometimes we board an airplane and fly across the ocean not to see other people but to see extraordinary places. The tradition of pilgrimage—whether to sail on the Sea of Galilee in Israel or to visit C. S. Lewis's home in Oxford—has a long and deep history within Christianity. Who among serious Bible students would not be interested in a VR tour of the Temple Mount in Jerusalem? It fires the imagination to think of seeing the paintings on the walls of the Vatican Museum right from one's living room. VR pilgrimages are unlikely to forge the same depth of spiritual transformation traditionally associated with this kind of journey, and yet VR pilgrimages also come with real advantages, perhaps the first being that they will cost far less money and therefore will be available to a far broader audience. Even for those who are privileged to travel in person to the sites of the Holy Land, the ability to return to these sites in VR and relive their memories will prove attractive.

Tourists at famous historical sites almost never receive the pristine and solemn experiences promised in guidebooks. Rushed through the exhibit alongside hordes of other tourists, with feet aching for the next cappuccino break, sometimes facing dehydration and practically at the point of heatstroke, we discover that real-world pilgrimage is not only expensive but extremely tiring. Whether it is the number of miles we can walk on our feet in a day or the number of hours we can ride on a bus, our physical limitations frequently interfere with our ability to experience sacred sites. VR pilgrimages will not supersede actual pilgrimage, but the fact that VR pilgrimages can be accessed conveniently and repeatedly will have real value for Christian education and spiritual formation. We should also point out that there are no crowds and no security guards in VR museums, which means that visitors may come as close to the paintings or artifacts as they please.

Lastly, are there experiences that are impossible in actual reality but could be simulated in VR for the purposes of deepening spiritual life? We suspect that there are, and we suspect that this is where VR will ultimately produce its most significant contributions. First, as an abstract example of such an impossible experience, VR could provide a new liturgical language for the global church. The experience of worshiping with Christians from other places in the world is often a powerful source of spiritual renewal in our own lives. Perhaps you have experienced the invigoration of dancing in praise with African Christians in a remote village. Perhaps you have knelt on the floor of a house church in Shanghai and prayed fervently in a circle with Chinese believers from the underground church. Perhaps you have awakened in Europe on a Sunday morning and followed the sound of church bells into a cathedral, discovering God amid the majestic organ music and serene order of service in a way that you did not expect. In these moments we discover echoes of God's cosmic plan to draw every tongue, tribe, and nation to His eternal throne in never-ceasing worship and adoration (see Rev. 7:9).

Many streams of Christian worship find their source in the quest to recreate this heavenly scene, as our liturgical practices seek to resonate with the worship of the saints in God's presence. Could VR provide the new alphabet and musical notation by which we sing praise to God, the new cathedral in which we worship as the global church? What could this impossible experience possibly look like when performed in reality? Maybe for the immediate future all that we should hope for is the opportunity to visit churches from around the world in VR. If given the opportunity to do so, I would gladly don my VR headset during the Christmas season and join an Anglican carol service or sign up to learn to paint icons in the Russian Orthodox style in the weeks leading up to Resurrection Sunday. This might be a first step in allowing Christians from around the world to share the riches of their traditions with one another.

Second, let us consider a concrete example of how VR might facilitate an impossible experience for the purposes of Christian ministry. There is a long history of Christian artists and authors placing their viewers or readers into the stories of the Bible. Ludolph of Saxony (ca. 1295–1378), for example, whose *Vita Christi* inspired Thomas à Kempis's *Imitation of Christ*, developed the technique of imagining oneself as an active participant in the Gospel stories as a spiritual exercise. VR could be applied to facilitate such experiences in sermons. Imagine a sermon from the story of Noah about judgement and grace (Gen. 6–9). Now imagine hearing that sermon from inside Noah's ark, the closing of the colossal, wooden door and the sound of the rain beginning to pound on the exterior of the vessel punctuating the preacher's points.

Imagine a sermon about the faith of the four friends who brought the paralytic to Jesus at Peter's house (Mark 2:1–12). Now imagine listening to this sermon while you watch as the roof is opened, tile by tile, and the sick man is lowered down in front of your eyes before Jesus. Sermons on passages from Paul's Prison Epistles sometimes start with an explanation of why Paul had been imprisoned. Imagine your pastor delivering this explanation as an avatar of Paul, while you and the other members of the congregation listen from across iron bars. One would appreciate the gospel in a new way if one experienced the sacrifice that the apostle Paul made in order to share this good news. There is a great deal to be done in developing a new kind of Bible storytelling through the medium of VR.

If VR technology is never able to compete with the intimacy, vividness, and memorability of real life, then the value of VR experiences will remain confined to activities that in the real world would be potentially unsafe, expensive, or impossible. VR will be an amazing place to explore but a poor place to live.

People will want to visit a reconstruction of first-century Jerusalem in VR, but they will also want to be able to take off the goggles and share their excitement and learning with family and friends over a real plate of falafel.

2. In VR, the User Is Not a Spectator but a Participant

Unlike traditional theater and film, which position the user as a spectator of an external performance, VR places the user within the scene. The user of a VR experience therefore assumes himself or herself not to be a passive viewer but an active participant. This shift in perspective and role renders VR a remarkably powerful medium for shaping attitudes and creating empathy.

Theater and film critics sometimes speak of the "fourth wall." This phrase refers to the convention that, although spectators can see into the world portrayed by the actors, the actors pretend that the spectators are not there. The traditional theater stage can be conceived as a box with three closed walls and one open wall, through which the audience peers. This has been the basic setup of theater stages even as far back in the Western tradition as the sixth century BC, when ancient Greek actors performed at the Theater of Dionysius on the slopes of the Acropolis in Athens. But in VR, the convention of the fourth wall feels unnatural and constrictive. When you strap on a VR headset, you expect not to be an observer of a performance from the other side of the room but to be an active participant in what is going on all around you. Audiences in traditional stage and film theaters are spectators who are not asked to do anything but not to interrupt the performance. Users of VR experiences will instinctively expect to be able to shape the outcome of the experience.

Chris Milk, a pioneer in VR cinematography, addressed how the absence of the "fourth wall" renders VR productions different from traditional theater and film. In a 2015 TED Talk titled "How Virtual Reality Can Create the Ultimate Empathy Machine," Milk noted: "Film is an incredible medium, but it's essentially the same now as it was then."[7] Milk explained that film has remained for the past century a window through which viewers looked into another world, but VR allows users to step through that window. The act of stepping through the window—passing through the "fourth wall" that has kept the audience divided from the story of which they are spectators—creates an emotional connection to the story that is not possible in traditional theater or film. Milk tested his theory in his critically acclaimed short film, "Clouds over Sidra." This film of eight minutes and thirty-five seconds was shot at the Za'atari Refugee Camp in Jordan, which is occupied primarily by refugees from Syria. The film is narrated by a twelve-year-old girl, Sidra, who guides you on a tour of her life in the refugee camp. For a few minutes, the fact that Syrian refugees face dire circumstances and extreme deprivation is not a distant fact but your own reality. The stories we experience in VR become our own stories, because, in a way, we embody them and actually live them.

The fact that the user of a VR experience can turn his or her head in any direction at any time creates endless problems for producers of cinematic VR content. In film, the director can control with incredible precision the focus of the camera and the exact timeline of events. In this way the director can control where and when the audience looks. For example, in a detective film, the director might flash a clue on-screen, raising just the right level of suspense and suspicion. But in a rendition of the story in VR, the director cannot control where the audience may be looking at any point in time, and therefore the director's intention that the audience discover the pistol on the piano may be thwarted because the audience is more interested in the curious-looking Chinese vase on the opposite end of the room. The difference between film and VR on this point may seem slight, but it has profound ramifications.

I (Darrell) once counted the number of seconds of each clip in an MTV-style music video. I discovered that no image stayed on the screen for more than four seconds. Processing information this way is very different from contemplating an argument in words. The genius of film is that it can present scenes one after another in perfectly timed sequences of events. This makes film a remarkable medium for fast-paced action sequences. This same set of qualities also makes film a generally poor medium for philosophical discourse, which requires the opportunity to stop and reflect. The genius of VR is interaction—that the experience is reshaped by participation.

VR is a new medium with exciting new possibilities, but learning to use any new medium effectively requires a process of trial and error. Jeremy Bailenson reminds us: "People using a new medium have a difficult time breaking out of the thinking involved with the previous ones. We see this in the history of Hollywood filmmaking. Many of the early storytellers in Hollywood came from the world of the stage. Consequently, early directors essentially filmed stage shows—one camera angle in front of a proscenium arch, with few to no cuts."[8] The pivot from spectator to participant represents one of the greatest challenges posed to producers of VR content, including producers who seek to create VR for the purposes of Christian ministry.

Just as Hollywood filmmakers initially reproduced stage shows in the new medium of film, so our first inclination may be to reproduce the form of church services as we now know them in VR, but this will probably prove to be a misstep. Each element from our church services today will require careful translation into the medium of VR in order to express the spiritual purpose of each element properly.

3. VR Simulates Sense Experience but Cannot Directly Present Abstract Concepts

VR excels at articulating spatial relationships and physical movement. VR is an extraordinarily effective platform for visualizing data that can be sequenced by spatial relationships, such as models of complex structures or intricate maneuvers. VR simulates sense experience but cannot directly present abstract concepts or spiritual realities.

If you were attempting to teach me about something complicated but concrete—let's say how the components of a Boeing 747 airplane are assembled—a well-constructed VR experience could be a tremendous aid. It is relatively straightforward to imagine how VR could significantly improve the process of learning about this complicated but concrete process. You could set out in VR a series of jumbo jets in various stages of completion, and reviewing these models would provide me with a clear sense of each step involved in the process. Setting up this visual aid in VR rather than in real life would also come with the advantage of not requiring hundreds of millions of dollars of inventory and showroom space. For some learning experiences, VR offers incredible resources. But VR does not improve our capacity to learn and communicate about everything.

While VR is a powerful tool to help us imagine spatial relationships and the manipulation of physical objects, the medium is uncannily concrete. If you were teaching a Bible lesson on the story of David and Goliath, for example, you could use VR to pinpoint on the map where the confrontation took place. You could use VR to allow your audience to see from all directions a digital replica of an ancient Israelite sling, and VR modeling could help participants understand how such an innocent-looking weapon could propel lethal force. You could create an interactive exhibit that would allow audience members to see exactly how tall Goliath would appear to them if they were standing next to him. VR would excel at communicating all of these concrete realities.

But VR could do very little to help you explain the source of David's faith and how the audience can find this faith for themselves. If you wished to note in your Bible lesson that David's motivation for slaying the giant was not for personal glory but to defend the name of the Lord, it would not be obvious how VR could improve on a simple verbal statement of this point. VR can reproduce digitally realities that we can see with our eyes and hear with our ears, but what about realities that we feel, intuit, and perceive spiritually?

This is not to say that standard tool kits will not be developed for VR that facilitate the communication of abstract concepts. Emoticons are an interesting case study in the way that elements that are not native to one form of communication can be transposed into another. Text messaging does not natively communicate information about the emotional state of the author, except when the author explicitly states such information. If you receive a text from a family member that reads, "I'll be there in an hour," you may not have all of the information you need in order to interpret her message. Is the sender expressing excitement that she will see you soon or disappointment that her train is running late? The smiley face—one of humankind's noblest inventions—has been devised in order to help us in precisely this predicament. The sender of a text can communicate her approximate emotional state by appending an emoticon (that is, a symbol of a specific feeling, represented by a face that is at once recognizable but not personal) to the words of her message. In spoken language, emotional information is communicated by vocal tone, but because text messages do not reproduce vocal tone, this information is missing unless it is translated into an emoji or expressly stated.

It may be that standard tool kits are devised in order to allow ministers and Christian educators to communicate about the abstract concepts of theology and the interior realities of Christian spiritual life. In fact, the Christian tradition already possesses a rich library of symbols and allegories in order to articulate the spiritual truths of the faith. As Christians, we receive the stories of the Old Testament as lessons of faith for us today (see Rom. 15:4; 1 Cor. 10:11). These stories all point to deep, spiritual realities through concrete, historical events. Jesus' parables are a treasure trove of specific spiritual symbols that can be applied in teaching Christian doctrine. Even more than this, Jesus becomes for us the master teacher from whom we learn to teach theology through the mundane. The farmer sows the seed, which is the word of God (see Matt. 13:3); a man discovers in a field a pearl of immeasurable value, which is the kingdom of God (see Matt. 13:44); the wise virgins await the entrance of the bridegroom, who is the Son of God (see Matt. 25:1); the sign of Jonah, who was swallowed by a great fish and remained in its belly for three days and three nights, points to the death and resurrection of the Messiah (see Matt. 12:39). Jesus is the vine, and we are the branches (see John 15:5).

This abundant library of symbols, embedded into the Christian tradition at its very foundation, has been an inexhaustible fount of inspiration for Christian artists of all ages. It is waiting to be exposited compellingly, beautifully, and faithfully in virtual reality. VR by itself cannot overcome the spiritual blindness about which Jesus warned when He said to the audience of His own parables: "You will indeed hear but never understand, and you will indeed see but never perceive" (Matt. 13:14b ESV). The telephone has turned out to be a useful tool for the purposes of Christian ministry; most pastors use them everyday. But despite frequent jokes to the contrary, there are no direct phone lines to heaven to allow us to hear the voice of God through our telephones. The same will prove true with virtual reality. VR will be a useful tool for Christian ministry, but bringing spiritual sight has always been and will remain the work of the Spirit. As we labor as Christian teachers to bring into visible form the spiritual realities of the faith, we trust that God will illumine our minds and increase our love for Himself.

4. VR Can Facilitate Cross-Cultural Communication

VR opens many doors of opportunity to improve cross-cultural communication. VR is a composite media type that allows creators to set side-by-side, text-based communication and other forms of media (such as, audio files, images, and video content).

Let's imagine that we set up an experiment to study how cross-cultural communication works. For this experiment, we form two teams. Team A is composed of five people whose primary language is French, but each of whom have varying degrees of ability to communicate in English. Team B is composed of five people whose primary language is English, but each of whom studied French in school for a couple of years. We then task these teams to play the following game. Team A will hide a red flag somewhere in the Willis Tower in Chicago. After hiding the flag, Team A will have the next six hours to prepare a five-minute briefing session for Team B. Team B will then be immediately dispatched in search of the red flag, and we will measure the time Team B requires to retrieve the red flag as an indication of the effectiveness of the cross-cultural communication of these teams. If we ran this experiment over and over again, and we allowed some teams to use VR to facilitate their cross-cultural communication and required other teams to rely solely on verbal forms of communication, we would discover that VR can dramatically increase the effectiveness of certain forms of cross-cultural communication.

What is going on here? Pictures aid cross-cultural communication. Language teachers have known this for a long time. This is why, when your teacher wanted you to learn that the French word for "apple" is "pomme," she brought to class a picture of an apple. VR can be conceived as an interactive picture, and as such it will open many avenues for cross-cultural communication. You may have noticed that the instruction manuals of today are far richer in visual content than the instruction manuals of the past. If you assembled toy models decades ago, you will probably remember that the instruction manuals consisted of verbally precise step-by-step instructions. It required a lot of mental energy to figure out exactly what one was supposed to do.

Compare this experience to what it is like to assemble a piece of IKEA furniture today. The instruction manuals that accompany IKEA products generally have very few words whatsoever and are instead composed of a series of sketches and diagrams. By publishing their instruction manuals as pictorial booklets, IKEA can ship the same instruction manual to any region of the world, regardless of the language of the purchaser. In the same way, VR will be capable of facilitating communication between people who do not share a common language or who have limited ability in a common language.

Computer translation is still far from perfect, but it is making strides in the right direction. Skype introduced an automated translation service in 2015, which theoretically allowed speakers of different languages to hear one another in their own language in real time. As of 2020, Skype offers automated voice-to-voice translation in ten languages and text-to-text translation in sixty languages. Communicating through automated translation about anything more complicated than the weather and time of day can quickly become convoluted, but it is not difficult to imagine that this technology will improve in the years ahead. It may be, therefore, that VR technology and automated translation technology can be coupled in the future in order to facilitate quality communication between individuals and teams who do not speak the same language. Presumably human translators will always be needed to run interference for automated translation services, but computer tools will almost certainly speed the process of translation and extend the possibility of translation to new communities.

How might such technology be applied for the purposes of Christian ministry in the future? Imagine that a team of American medical professionals is preparing to travel to Bolivia in order set up a free clinic for one week in partnership with a local hospital. Everyone from the American team is able to meet everyone else from the Bolivian team during a preparatory meeting in VR, and while automated translations are not perfect, all team members are able to speak freely to one another during periods of socialization. When the American team arrives in Bolivia, the logistics have already been mapped out and communicated clearly, allowing the teams to work together to set up the clinic as efficiently as possible, freeing up valuable time for personal exchange. At key moments throughout the week, members from one team are willing to ask for help from members of the other team because they have already had the experience of speaking through automated translation, sometimes continuing their relationship through automated translation and sometime resorting to old-school Spanglish.

5. VR Renders Users
Unaware of Their Real-Life Surroundings

VR is an immersive media experience, which means that the attention of users is so focused on the sights and sounds of the VR content that they frequently become unaware of the people and activities around them. In order to ensure the physical safety of the user, VR experiences will need to be proctored in controlled environments.

VR's power is presence. But to be present in VR is to be functionally absent in one's physical location.[9] At least concerning the current generation of VR headsets, when one is present in VR, one cannot see one's actual physical surroundings. Augmented Reality (AR) aspires to merge our experience of the physical with the digital, and it is probable that commercially successful AR products will become available in the next several years. But, at least concerning VR experiences as we know them today, you are going to want to check yourself in before stepping into virtual reality. Museum visitors know the routine of checking in their coats and handbags at the cloakroom. For VR experiences, people will basically need to check in their bodies at the door when they enter.

I (Jonathan) access VR experiences from only one of two physical locations: the VR Lab at Moody Bible Institute and my living room at home. I can control the environment in both places in order to have a safe and positive VR experience. When I access VR from my living room, I first check in with any family members who might be around to see whether anyone needs me for the next while. This check-in procedure is the equivalent of what I do when I am about to leave the house for a quick run to the grocery store. Glancing at a text on your mobile device requires only a few seconds and is acceptable in most social contexts. Donning VR goggles, on the other hand, is an entirely different proposition. When you place the headset over your face, your expressions become masked, and your interactions with the invisible personalities and artifacts all around you can feel absurd or even disturbing to those nearby. In its current state, VR is best experienced in carefully controlled spaces where you are free to disregard your physical environment for a few moments. It is not a media experience that people will want to step in and out of quickly.

In the world we know today, there are certain activities which people are willing to check themselves in for—in order to see a film at a movie theater, for example. We check ourselves in at the airport in order to fly across the ocean, or at a restaurant for an elegant dinner. For these activities, we are willing to commit our physical presence for a set period of time. It is worth noting that people also check themselves into church—sometimes literally, as is the case with many nursery programs. Churchgoers are familiar with the embarrassment of having to get up in the middle of a service and leave for one unexpected reason or another. The commitment of time and effort that we invest in preparing to attend church services is not entirely unlike the steps prerequisite to attending appointments in VR. Churchgoers know the Sunday morning routine of dressing in church clothes, eating breakfast more or less punctually, and then driving across town to attend church services. Appointments in VR require a different setup routine, but nonetheless some preparation is in order to ensure that the experience is as successful as possible.

6. Users in VR Are Disidentified

It is almost equally simple for users in VR to represent themselves according to their physical appearance as it is according to an alternate set of preferences. People can choose to enter a VR social platform as an avatar that reflects the way they look in real life or as a purple lobster. Because we present ourselves and encounter others in VR as disidentified personae, establishing trust in relationships will be a perpetual problem.

Users in VR are disidentified. By "disidentified" we do not mean unidentified (that is, that users simply do not receive information concerning the identity of other users). When someone or something is "unidentified," we are conscious of the fact that we do not know the identity of the person or object. And by stating that users in VR are "disidentified," we also do not mean "misidentified" (that is, that one user could be mistaken for another user). When on a nature walk, I might misidentify an ash tree as a beech tree, or I might misidentify a basalt rock as a piece of granite. Here my mistake would be to confuse one category for another. But imagine living in a world where it was possible to mistake your pastor for a pink elephant.

During the Cold War, both Eastern Bloc and Western Bloc countries staffed "disinformation" bureaus, which were assigned the ignominious charge of generating large quantities of false information with the intent of confusing and misleading public opinion in enemy territory. It is in this sense that users in VR are "disidentified." In VR, everyone has access to disguises more sophisticated than even the KGB could devise at the peak of the Cold War. In 1993, Peter Steiner published in *The New Yorker* a cartoon that showed a picture of a dog at an office chair with one paw on the keyboard of a computer. Looking down from his desk at another dog sitting on the floor, the first dog exclaims: "On the internet, nobody knows you're a dog." Today we worry about our email accounts getting hacked; tomorrow we'll worry about people stealing our avatars.

One of the early debates about VR churches surfaced in 2009 in the context of the Anglican Cathedral of Second Life. The question concerned whether one could lead church services while represented by a dragon avatar.[10] The church had opened its portals to allow volunteers to lead the liturgy, but could a volunteer dressed as a dragon perform this service? Is coming to a church in VR as a dragon avatar simply a personal decision—like what kind of necktie to wear—or are church members and visitors bound to abide by some kind of dress code? Worse still, does coming to church as a dragon hint at subversive intent?

Let's face it—Christians have argued a lot through the centuries about what constitutes proper attire for church attendance. Tertullian, the notoriously cantankerous bishop of Carthage in the early church, argued that Christian women should not wear any unnecessary adornment, such as makeup, jewelry, or fancy clothes.[11] Countless others have felt it their duty to add their opinion to the discussion ever since. Should ministers wear vestments with clerical collars that identify them as members of the clergy or business suits, or jeans with holes in the knees? Even the most welcoming and progressive churches have unspoken dress codes about what would be too relaxed or too ostentatious for church services. Conducting church services in VR will not sidestep the question of proper dress in church.

Some may mistakenly conclude that, because an avatar is "not really real," its appearance should be unimportant, but this is clearly not the case. Painted and photographed portraits are also not real in the same way that an avatar is not real, and yet there is a long tradition of people spending fortunes to ensure that portraits are exactly according to their tastes. Fortnite Battle Royale set a new record in video game history when it earned $1.8 billion in 2019.[12] What is particularly remarkable about this is that Fortnite Battle Royale is a free-to-play video game. How then did it generate such astronomical earnings? By selling cosmetics and accessories for players' avatars. These optional purchases do not improve the players' performance in the game and are strictly fashion items. As in the real world so in VR, fashion is big business because people care a great deal about the way they present themselves to other people.

The clothes we wear help reinforce the role we intend to play, whether we are dressing to join a parent-teacher conference, a board meeting, a family vacation, or going to church. But avatars possess capacities for communication that extend beyond those associated with traditional fashion. The Reverend Pam Smith speaks of the problem of "sock puppetting" in the context of providing pastoral care in online environments.[13] "Sock puppetting" is when one person controls several online profiles and impersonates multiple people in order to manipulate a conversation or social situation. For example, one person might pose as an offended student as well as the student's irate parent in order to gain increased leverage. The question of appropriate dress in the context of worship has always required discernment and Christian charity. But because users have such complete control over the way they "dress" or appear to be in VR, even to the point that distinguishing between one person's identity and another's can become genuinely problematic, special consideration is required.

If churches aspire to be places of spiritual transformation, then they must also be places where people can trust each other. And here VR presents serious but not insurmountable problems. In traditional churches, there is a menu of rituals to help people build trust and establish rapport. When you enter through the doors of traditional church, you are welcomed with a smile and hearty handshake by a member of the greeter team. The smile is perhaps the first and most universal of all human behaviors for building trust, and smiles are infinitely easier to fake in VR than in real life. The Facebook profile picture proves this point.

Eating and drinking as a community is one of the oldest and best rituals for establishing trust, and traditional churches can create the opportunity to enjoy community meals on occasion. But none of these conventional methods of establishing trust are available to VR churches.

These serious concerns lead us to a couple of preliminary conclusions. First, it is not possible to replace in VR the trust that can be established through building relationships in person. This does not mean that every member of the congregation needs to meet with every other member of the congregation every week in order to have a healthy church, but it does mean that in-person communication will continue to play a unique role in establishing trust between members of Christian churches and ministry partners. Perhaps leadership teams meet face-to-face over coffee once per week, or prayer services that are usually conducted one per week in VR assemble in the church building once per month or once per quarter. Once relationships have been formed and some level of trust has been established, telecommunication in general, and VR specifically, can be used to sustain these relationships with some success. Even churches that intend to maximize the use of VR for ministry purposes should still retain mechanisms to facilitate in-person communication and interaction.

Our second preliminary conclusion is that VR churches should pay special attention to creating opportunities for church leaders and members to build trust with one another. There are innumerable ways to do this, even when speaking about communities who meet in VR and who do not come with any prior relationships. Sharing testimonies is an especially effective way for members of a community to give one another a clear picture of where they stand in their spiritual journeys. The consistent practice of prayer over a sustained period of time frequently leads groups to discover a surprising depth to their relationships. As technology advances and the audio quality of VR telecommunication improves, we suspect that the ancient practice of singing together will become a mainstay of VR congregational life. Educational experiences can provide opportunities for exchange and dialogue that can provide a foundation for strong relationships of mutual trust.

And so we come to the question: "What about going to church in your pajamas?" Paul could not have delivered for us a more perfect principle by which to respond to this quandary than when he said: "All things are lawful, but not all things are helpful" (1 Cor. 10:23a ESV). Paul then goes on to say that he does not seek his own advantage but the edification of the community (1 Cor. 10:33). The principle is that, while individual Christians are free in many ethical decisions, Christians are also called to do what is best for the good of the community.

With this principle in mind, the answer to the question above will depend on what is meant by "going to church in your pajamas." If we are speaking about attending church services in VR while still dressed in sleepwear in real life, then the question is really a nonissue. Not only will no one else in the VR church see your sleepwear, but you also will probably pay little attention to whatever you may be wearing in your house. If we mean selecting pajamas for your avatar to wear while attending church services in VR, then we would recommend asking a representative of the church about the dress code first. All cultures exhibit different sensitivities, and one of the sensitivities of internet and VR culture is the perpetual problem of establishing trust. Unless you are sure that the VR church welcomes such attire, coming to church with your avatar decked out in sleepwear could easily send the message that you find the sermons soporific.

7. VR Cannot Simulate Anonymity

As is the case with other modes of telecommunication, VR creates data trails or the electronic records of the transactions of the users. However, VR is unique among other modes of telecommunication concerning the volume of data that it generates. VR use generates such a vast quantity of data that it is impossible to use VR anonymously.

Literally and figuratively, the jury is still out on many questions concerning internet privacy. Ever since Edward Snowden's revelations to journalists of the National Security Administration's mass surveillance program of the American people in 2013, many have come to the conclusion that "internet privacy" is an oxymoron. The Cambridge Analytica scandal in 2017, in which the personal data of millions of Facebook users was leaked, as well as Mark Zuckerberg's congressional hearings in 2018 concerning Facebook's sale of ads to Russian propagandists during the 2016 election have done little to restore the confidence of the public.[14]

The data collection techniques used by the tech giants of the past several years have by and large been voluntary. Users consciously choose to upload photos to their Facebook profiles and to enter data into their Google spreadsheets. But VR processes unprecedented amounts of data on users, and necessarily so. It turns out that we all move our bodies in ways that are as unique as the human fingerprint. VR headsets track head and hand motion, and it is probable that soon most headsets will also track eye motion. The way I look about with my head and reach with my hands, the way I bob forward and backward on my feet, and the rhythm with which my eyes circle the VR environments creates a pattern of data that can be traced to me and uniquely to me. This data can be anonymized such that human editors are not aware of whose data they may be reviewing, but the data itself cannot but reveal who the user is. Internet security and data privacy is one of the pressing technological and legal questions of our time, and our concern here is neither to give false assurances nor to sound unnecessary alarm. However, at the very least, we can say that churches and Christian ministries that conduct activities in VR should do due diligence to ensure that their activities will not inadvertently affect Christians abroad who do not have the protections of religious liberty in their own countries.

To those of us in the West who have lived with the benefits of religious freedom, coping with the ambiguities and complexities inherent in online communication and VR can seem burdensome. But for believers in countries where religious freedom is limited, the new rules of the internet open up opportunity as well. In one such country where Christians live under threat of persecution, one mission agency devised a Bible software program that appeared as a functioning calculator app. When a certain equation was entered into the app, the "calculator" turned into a program for Bible study. In 2015, the Urbana Student Missions Conference held its first "hackathon," where students with coding skills teamed up for an intense period of attempting to broker technological solutions to the hardest problems in missions. One such challenge was to develop an app that would guide the user through the process of starting a new business in North Africa. Another challenge was to create a secure way for Christian missionaries to communicate in countries where religious liberty is limited. Tom Lin founded the event in order to respond to the question: "How can we stand alongside the persecuted church?"[15]

From a Christian point of view, it should come as no surprise that our words and every action are being recorded. In Matthew 12:36, Jesus tells us we will stand on trial for our every word: "On the day of judgment people will give account for every careless word they speak" (ESV). In this way, the Christian standard is already that God hears everything and that we are accountable for every word we say. The apostles set a precedent for Christians when they stated, "We must obey God rather than men" (Acts 5:29 ESV). Christians ought to speak and act in measured ways first in order to be accountable to God. The concern about whether our data is being recorded by tech giants and will be leaked at a later time is in this sense a secondary concern.

8. VR Places the User in Control

In VR, the user is at the center of the virtual universe. When compared to traditional media types, VR cedes almost total control to the individual user. VR therefore can support addictive behaviors and reinforce prejudices.

The internet creates a million and one ways for people to practice the art of self-deception. The internet can be an echo chamber where those who shout the loudest hear only their own voices coming back at themselves. As Sherry Turkle, professor of sociology and psychology at MIT, points out: "The web promises to make our world bigger. But as it works now, it also narrows our exposure to ideas. We can end up in a bubble in which we hear only the ideas we already know. Or already like."[16] As a media type based in internet technology, VR perpetuates this basic feature. Shane Hipps reminds us that, when technology fails us, the unintended consequence can be precisely the opposite of the effect for which we applied the specific technology in the first place.[17] The purpose of the automobile is to allow us to travel quickly and efficiently to our destinations, but the traffic jams that plague our cities today represent exactly the opposite effect. The purpose of the internet is to give us access to the instantaneous exchange of information, but we all know that the internet can become an enormous waste of time and even create greater confusion, either because of the overwhelming quantity of information available online or because of the inability to verify sources.

Technology is not bad, but it does fail. When our technology fails, we sometimes suffer from precisely the opposite effect of that which we had hoped to achieve. The purpose of VR is to allow the user to experience an alternate reality in order to increase our understanding of actual reality. When VR fails us as a technology, the failure will be that VR will cause users to see actual reality with less clarity and perception. When VR fails us, it will reinforce our prejudices and preconceptions rather than allowing us to discover new knowledge.

The advent of the automobile opened up a new era of "church shopping." Because people could drive to whatever congregation they wished to attend, rather than remaining faithful to their neighborhood churches, churches began catering to personal preferences in a new way. VR churches will continue to grapple with this same set of problems. When you go to VR looking for a church service, do you want a liturgical church service? It's there. Do you want a contemporary worship service with a slick worship band? It's there. One comedian's video "Virtual Reality Church" hilariously parodies the way that virtual churches can cater to the personal preferences and laziness of their parishioners.[18] But the point still stands: as an extension of the internet, VR provides for us what we search for. VR can proctor the experience for anyone to do anything anywhere, and at first glance, it seems that this possibility would wildly expand our imaginations. Yet, paradoxically, if we fail to look beyond the reality portrayed in VR simulations, VR can profoundly limit our imaginations. Precisely because VR caters entirely to our preferences and notions of reality, VR can prove to be a dull instrument to challenge our preconceptions about reality. And because the internet and VR are shared social spaces, these technologies can be used to reinforce societal prejudices and preconceptions.[19]

And what about the tragedy of pornography?[20] Christian communities are becoming increasingly aware of the pervasive and destructive influences of pornography. Pornography addiction is no doubt one of the most widespread expressions of addictive behavior on the internet. A recent study by the Barna Group has exposed the high percentage of Christians and church leaders who use pornography on an ongoing basis or have used pornography in the past.[21] We contest that one of the terrible consequences of pornography use in the Christian community, in addition to its deleterious influences on personal and professional relationships, is the way in which it cripples church leaders from responsible investigation and deployment of digital strategies for ministry. If we ourselves have experienced digital addiction in the past—whether pornography or other addictive online behaviors—we are likely to be reserved in our applications of digital media for ministry purposes in the future. It is true that the pornography industry will certainly fight hard for market share in the VR space. Some may need to opt out of VR ministry because of a past addictive behavior, and this is appropriate. But it would be tragic for the Christian community *en masse* to step away from the technology merely because it has a tainted reputation or because the technology is set to perverse uses elsewhere.

VR no more belongs to the devil than does the electric guitar. Mark Howe could write in 2008: "Much Christian reaction to the Internet is quite superficial, and, predictably, obsessed with sex. Yes, there's unsavoury content on the web, but a previous generation found their unsavoury content by mail order or in their corner shop, and Corinthian debauchery didn't seem to be hampered by a lack of peer-to-peer networking."[22] In this instance as in others, reflective observers will note that the internet can be an agent of good or of evil.[23]

While pornography may be the most destructive form of addictive behavior supported by the internet today, pornography is not the only insidious addiction that the internet perpetuates. Arguably more pervasive is the addiction of distraction. Far more difficult to recognize than many other sins, distraction is just as effective in removing our focus from God. Alan Noble comments: "For the vast majority of Americans who are above the poverty line, technology of distraction is an everyday experience."[24] And although we tend to view distraction as a social or a technological problem, it rapidly translates into a theological problem.

Distraction lulls us into indefinitely postponing questions about life's meaning and purpose, questions that historically have led people to uncover the conviction of God's existence, love, and presence. "If I feel like there are no real answers to life's big questions, I can stay entertained all day long, and I don't have to deal with that anxiety," Noble observes. "At the end of the day, when I'm falling asleep, how do I know that I've done right today? Well, that used to be a problem for people—the few minutes that you had between the time you turned off your light and the time you fell asleep. You used to have to sit and stare into the darkness and look at your own soul. But now, with a smartphone that has all this technology, all this access to infinite entertainment, you can really just stare at a screen until you collapse." In a similar vein, Craig Detweiler laments: "So many of Jesus' transformative moments occurred on the road, where he is walking with his disciples between spaces. And we have now filled up so many of those in-between spaces with these digital distractions."[25]

The fact that the internet can create echo chambers where we hear only the opinions that we want to hear, or that the internet can support pornography addictions, or that our smartphones can simply keep us in a state of perpetual distraction is not an argument against the reality that the internet can also be used responsibly. Good decisions are a matter of the heart, not the devices we use. VR, as an extension of internet technology, has these same pitfalls, and church communities will need to learn to guard against these by creating cultural boundaries of accountability and pastoral care.

9. VR Platforms Tend to Carry
Hidden Biases in Their Definitions of Success

Like the social media platforms of today, the VR platforms of the future will likely carry hidden biases in their definitions of success. Analyzing the biases of these platforms and differentiating between the objectives of the VR platform and the objectives of the VR church will be an integral part of responsible Christian stewardship and effective ministry in these environments.

Whether it is "the Metaverse" in *Snow Crash* (1992), "the Matrix" in the eponymous film (1999), or "the Oasis" in *Ready Player One* (2011), science fiction of late has assumed that VR will produce a single, monolithic alternate reality. Following the model of the tech giants and social media platforms of today, it may be that VR gives rise to just a few, super-popular platforms. Based on the business model of the tech giants and social media platforms of today, we can anticipate that VR platforms will operate in a way that is quietly as profitable as possible for their parent companies. It will be important for Christian users to analyze these pressures and ensure that their use of the medium aligns with their own mission and goals. When a team of Christians plants a church in a new city or in a new country, it is important for this team to analyze the local culture and to get a clear sense of how social expectations may conflict or align with the ministry model that the team is trying to foster. When conducting ministry on a digital platform, it is important to analyze first how this platform defines success and sets up expectations for use cases. The way these platforms define success is invariably tied to the business model of the company supporting the platform.

Google, Facebook, and the pantheon of social media platforms earn their income by selling advertising. This means that these companies give out their products for free (e.g., Google searches or Facebook profiles) but then collect as much data about their users as possible in order to sell advertising that is as profitable as possible. The Harvard Business School professor, Shoshana Zuboff, titles this precarious socioeconomic arrangement "surveillance capitalism."[26] When I write an email via a free email service, the company pays its bills by having its computers read my emails and selling this information to advertisers in a legally sanctioned packaging. As former Chairman of the Federal Communications Commission, Tom Wheeler, says: "If you are not paying for an online product, then you *are* the product as information about you is collected and monetized."[27]

Facebook's business model is also based on advertising. The more time you spend on Facebook, the more money Facebook earns from its advertising sales. This means that while Facebook is also a "free" product, you actually pay Facebook for the use of their product by the time you spend on their platform. After all, time is money. This may help to explain why social media platforms seem to perpetuate controversy. Social media platforms are incentivized to do anything—including foster fruitless and spiteful arguments—that lead users to extend their sessions longer or to check back again sooner. And if the isolation from broken relationships in the real world leads to further use of the social media platform, then this only fuels advertising sales and reinforces the company's business model. The business plans of the tech giants of today is to sell advertising, which means that these companies traffic in wasted time. If we intend to use these platforms for the purposes of Christian ministry, we will need to guard fiercely against distraction.

What this boils down to is that Christian ministries cannot rely on the metrics provided by the social media platforms themselves to define success. Success on YouTube is represented by the number of views for each video uploaded, because this drives advertising revenue back to Google. But the aim of a Christian ministry is not to enrich Google. Success on Facebook is defined as the number of Friends in one's network and the level of interaction between these Friends, again because this strengthens Facebook's brand, but churches exist for something more than to fill Facebook's coffers. When using VR platforms for ministry, we must first analyze the inherent biases in the medium and design our ministries to navigate and even mitigate these biases.

It's not easy to find exact data about the amount of time that the average user spends on social media, but a reasonable estimate appears to be that there are about four billion users of social media globally, and that the average user is on social media for about 2.5 hours per day.[28] What would happen if social media companies noted a clear correlation between profession of Christian faith and reduced social media use? What would happen if those who had been discipled in VR churches tended to use social media less, maybe for thirty minutes each day on average? Presumably this could lead social media companies to create policies that make it tougher for Christians to use their platforms for ministry purposes.

But we trust that Christian groups would have the courage to do the right thing, pursuing what is best for society even when this is at odds with the business models of powerful companies. When Paul had spent about three years preaching in Ephesus, his presentation of the gospel proved so successful that the silversmiths in the area detected a dip in revenue from the sales of their statues of the goddess Artemis (see Acts 19:21–41). This finally led to a riot that drove Paul and his missionary associates out of the city. We shouldn't expect that online platforms will always be welcoming places for Christian mission.

10. VR Is Based in Digital Computer Technology

For the foreseeable future, VR will inherit the limitations of digital computer products.

VR technology is a product of the digital computer industry, and as such VR products will remain relatively expensive, will require significant amounts of electricity, will have to be updated or replaced often, and will probably remain vulnerable to impacts, water damage, and extreme changes in temperatures. VR equipment will likely not soon overcome these basic limitations inherent in all digital computer products today. VR carries with it not only the limitations of electronic technology generally but also the specific challenges of a brand-new electronic technology. VR places tremendous pressure on even the most powerful computers and the fastest internet connections.

Will new kinds of computers become available in the future that will dramatically change the performance of our VR headsets and maybe even the fundamental way they work? The answer to this question is almost certainly "yes," but the next question of "when" is almost totally unknown. Many advocate quantum computing as the platform most likely to supersede digital computing, but will this revolution take place fifteen years from now or in a hundred and fifty years? Some theorists posit that biological computers may yet be developed next after quantum computing, but determining which new computer platforms may arrive in which order and when is entirely incalculable at this point. For the foreseeable future, while VR remains firmly planted within the industry of digital computer products, this means that part and parcel of doing ministry in VR will be ensuring that everyone has adequate access to the technology and skills to use the technology. Just as the construction and upkeep of church buildings of the past and present is no small undertaking, so the development and maintaining of technology networks for ministry purposes will require skill, wisdom, and hard work as we move forward.

What will the VR of tomorrow look like, and how will we use this emerging technology for ministry purposes? To return for a moment to our illustration from the world of the nineteenth-century railroad, if we could somehow go back in time to around the year 1876 and conduct a study about the future of trains, we probably would have correctly articulated some of the dynamics that continue to govern the use of trains today. But there would have been no way possible for us to anticipate that new kinds of trains would emerge, such as the New York City subway, or airport people movers, or the proposed Hyperloop. Although each of these inventions could be considered a new kind of train, these "trains" are substantially different from those that first conquered the western plains. From an intimate knowledge of the machinery of steam locomotives of the early nineteenth century, there would have been no way to anticipate that the trains of the future could operate underground, inside cavernous depots, or even be propelled by magnets at supersonic speeds through airless tubes, and this is because in each instance the technology was reimagined with significant advancements in its power supply and also with a significantly different purpose and context.

VR will continue to change and develop in the years ahead, and at each turn there will be an opportunity for ministers of the gospel to apply this technology to new ministry contexts. There is an immense opportunity on the horizon to apply the emerging medium of VR to communicate the gospel and to advance the mission of the church in the world. But acting as wise stewards of these technological possibilities will require us to understand the medium. Mark Howe makes this point with the ironic statement: "Email becomes a way to send a letter without having to lick a stamp, and websites are a way to publish huge screeds of Calvinesque text without the irritation of proof readers. Of course, it is perfectly possible to use the Internet this way, but doing so can create a false impression that nothing has really changed, and thus postpone the need for a radical response."[29] Only by carefully analyzing the particular strengths and weaknesses of VR as a distinct media type will we be able to take advantage of its unique communicative abilities to convey the gospel message to the world.

Chapter 5

GOD, CREATION, AND NEW CREATION

"GOD IS FAR TOO REAL TO BE MET
ANYWHERE OTHER THAN IN REALITY."[1]

✦ David G. Benner

"ALL TRUTH IS GOD'S TRUTH."[2]

✦ Arthur F. Holmes

At this point, you have probably come to your own conclusions about how and to what extent VR technology may affect Christian ministry in the future. Maybe you're excited about what VR ministry could look like in your own church, or maybe you're convinced that your church should postpone the adoption of the technology for now. Our next task is to sketch out an outline of Christian theology for the age of virtual reality. Whether or not the leadership team at your church decides to apply VR technology to any specific ministries in the immediate future, your church will be ministering to a generation that is increasingly influenced by VR and related technologies. What does it mean to explain the gospel to people whose reality is deeply shaped by video games or the constant stream of workplace teleconferences? How will VR technology reconfigure our own theological imaginations? Sherry Turkle has long observed in her books that our interactions with computers recast our self-identity and what we believe the world to be.[3] In 2018, Elon Musk sparked renewed conversation about whether what we perceive as reality is in fact a simulation when he opined in a podcast that this is the most probable scenario.[4] What does it mean to frame the gospel so that it can be received as good news in the world we live in today? In the remaining chapters, we will begin to analyze the theological issues at play in the application of VR for ministry purposes.

In the following chapters, we appeal to the outline that has served as the structure of systematic theology through the course of church history: God's trinitarian nature. The three persons of the Trinity—God as Father, Son, and Holy Spirit—has served as the outline of theology since the very beginning of the church, from the Apostles' Creed to John Calvin's *Institutes* to the statements of faith of contemporary churches. This telling of Christian theology is another way of stating the gospel. God the Father so loved the world that He sent His only Son, Jesus Christ, to save all who believe in Him, and He pours out the Holy Spirit richly on those who believe in order to sanctify and guide the church until His glorious return (see John 3:16; 16:13; Titus 3:4–7). This is the gospel in outline, and its structure is the three persons of the Trinity. Our purpose in the theological survey in the chapters that follow is not to uncover all the intricacies and beauty of the Scripture that will showcase the gospel in the age of virtual reality. Our purpose is rather to identify the questions about God, humanity, sin, salvation, and the church that are emerging as people see the world differently in light of virtual reality and to begin to outline responses to these questions from the Bible and the Christian tradition.

We begin where all the creeds begin: "We believe in one God, the Father, the Almighty, maker of heaven and earth, of all that is, visible and invisible."[5] Of course, this is not only where the creeds of the Christian church begin. It is where the Bible begins.

Does God Exist in Cyberspace?

One of the most basic aspects of the Christian faith is the belief in God as the Creator. According to Christian theology, it is as Creator that we first encounter God and learn to know Him. When the apostle Paul preached to the philosophers of Athens and proclaimed to them the "unknown god" whom they worshiped, he started at the very beginning of the story: "The God who made the world and everything in it, being Lord of heaven and earth, does not live in temples made by man" (Acts 17:24 ESV). When Paul spoke to those who were completely unversed in Jewish tradition and with whom he could assume no commonality in religious education, he opened his preaching with the unmissable fact that the God whom he proclaimed was the Creator of the world and the Creator of the human race.

The Bible does not shrink back from introducing to the reader God as the Creator, as though this were somehow a mundane or unenlightened perspective on God's identity. The Bible opens with the duly famous words: "In the beginning, God created the heavens and the earth" (Gen. 1:1). The Bible frames human existence, as well as the existence of the planet and the universe beyond, as an outcome of the creative and loving act of God. "It is he who made us, and we are his" (Ps. 100:3), the psalmist reminds us. From this frame of reference comes a fundamental posture of humility and deference toward God and His ways. The psalmist asks in wonder, "When I look at your heavens, the work of your fingers, the moon and the stars, which you have set in place, what is man that you are mindful of him, and the son of man that you that care for him?" (Ps. 8:3–4 ESV).

The prophet Isaiah tells us that God's position renders Him wholly above our conventions and convenience. His thoughts are truly not our thoughts (see Isa. 55:8–9). There is no avenue for humanity to comprehend God's being and nature other than to learn to recognize Him first as Creator. It is noteworthy that the Bible makes no attempt to construct a philosophical argument concerning the question of whether God exists. Why this is, the Bible does not explain. But we may conclude that the biblical authors would deny the question's presuppositions—namely, that our own existence and reasoning capacity could be possible apart from God's existence. In the worldview of the biblical authors, our existence is necessarily dependent on God's existence.

Throughout human history, people have shown interest in questions about who God may be and what His interactions with the world may be like, but in each era these questions are framed with different preconceptions. The Enlightenment still impresses many of its preconceptions into our musings today about whether God exists. The scientific revolution in the sixteenth and seventeenth centuries and the philosophical summations of these discoveries during the Enlightenment in the eighteenth century reframed almost completely our understanding of what the world is and who God may be. Christian apologists since that time have spilled a great deal of ink arguing for the existence of God from this frame of reference. What these arguments amount to is the contention that scientific inquiry, when reasonably exercised, leads back to the hypothesis of God's existence. Conceiving the world as a great machine, God is imagined as the designer of a great machine. In a world governed by the laws of nature, God becomes the author of these laws. During the Enlightenment, people postulated that the God of the Bible was a "watchmaker god," whose creation of the universe was analogous to the invention of an inexpressibly intricate mechanism. After assembling the universe and setting it in motion, the "watchmaker god" allegedly left the universe alone, a timepiece that would presumably tick on until the last star in the last galaxy burned out of existence.

As Charles Darwin's theory of evolution gained a hearing in our culture, beginning in the nineteenth century, and then achieved broad acceptance in the twentieth century, the assignment of Christian apologetics became to create space to imagine that there could be a God in a world controlled by biological evolution. This deity is sometimes referred to as the "god of the gaps," because he is perceivable only in spaces where current scientific theories are insufficient to account for natural phenomena. Today, few people espouse the concept of a "watchmaker god," and this is probably more due to the fact that our culture has lost touch with mechanical watches than because the philosophical argumentation that introduced the concept of a "watchmaker god" to us has been proven defective.

The pocket watch—once the marvel of the age, assigned with the noble task of orchestrating the opening and closing of businesses and the arrival and departure of trains—is no longer a known face in our culture. Our visions of who God may be change with our notions of what the world is. If the world is an unbelievably complicated mechanism, then God is a watchmaker. For many ancient peoples, the world was a tabletop display, and therefore God was a builder or a carpenter. Emerging in our own day is the notion that the universe is information, and from this worldview the God about whose existence we postulate is an omniscient network administrator, a superintelligence beyond that which we can imagine, whose universe is the ultimate VR simulation. Does this God exist?

Before we try to answer that question, it may be wise of us to step back and reflect on what we assume ultimate reality to be, lest we postulate the existence of a God who will soon seem as naïve as the "watchmaker god" or the "god of the gaps." If we are not careful, we will end up inventing a god who will quickly become as antiquated as punch cards.

God compares His relationship to humanity with many sets of relationships in Scripture. In His parables, Jesus often speaks of God as the master of a household (see Matt. 18:23–35; 20:1–16; 21:33–45; 24:45–51; 25:14–30). God is proclaimed as a king throughout Scripture (see, for example, Ps. 97). Kingship is a relationship of sovereign to people so ancient and so deeply embedded in our histories that it still carries currency almost everywhere, despite the fact that there are few countries in the world that are ruled by kings today. God meets us in explaining His identity to us in a variety of cultural forms.

It is apparently not God's concern that we cling to a particular image to make sense of His authority, but what is a concern to God is that humanity understands its state of rebellion. As differently as we may conceive of God in different ages, the temptation to place ourselves above God and thus usurp His position as God is astoundingly predictable. If God is a king, then our temptation is to rule the earth in His stead. If God is a watchmaker, then our temptation is to reengineer the universe so that the laws of physics subject everything to our designs. If God runs the universe like a computer program, then our temptation is to rewrite the code, to read morality and human nature as sociological constructions that we can reprogram according to our predilections.

From the Bible's point of view, humanity has been in a state of rebellion against God from the moment that Adam and Eve ate the forbidden fruit in the garden of Eden (see Gen. 3). Thousands of years after Babel, humankind is still striving to build a tower to heaven. We are still engaged in the project of erecting a means of our own salvation apart from obedience to God. The Bible frames our quest to find salvation—that is, ultimate meaning and purpose—apart from God as idolatry. Isaiah 44 is one of the most striking confrontations of the folly of idolatry anywhere in Scripture. The passage begins: "Thus says the LORD who made you, who formed you from the womb and will help you" (Isa. 44:2a ESV). God's prerogative is that He is the Creator; life comes from God and only from God. As medical science continues to progress—and we thank God for the many benefits of modern medical science—we come no closer at all to being able to create life. God is jealous of the fact that He is God. God sternly warns against the self-deception that takes place when we presume to occupy God's place or to have knowledge or power that is proper to God alone. The Lord declares, "I am the first and I am the last; besides me there is no god" (Isa. 44:6b ESV).

Isaiah then launches into a paragraph exposing the utter madness of idolatry. Idolatry is baseless at best and diabolical at worst, forgetting completely that God is the Creator and sustainer of all. Isaiah speaks of the ironsmith who wearies himself while forging an idol (Isa. 44:12). By lunchtime, the ironsmith's work on his "god" has left him with nothing but an empty stomach and a sore arm! Isaiah had no way of knowing that someday humanity would aspire to create a god of silicon dust—a digital superintelligence whose supposed destiny it is to possess and redeem the entire universe—but if he had, Isaiah's answer would probably run something like this: "If the machine that humanity is building is truly divine, then why after all these millions of cumulative years of human labor invested in digital computers is it that a bent back and blurry eyes are all that most of us have to show for it? If global warming teaches us one thing, it is that the only thing rising faster than the speed of computer processors is the speed at which humanity creates new problems with computer processors. Some rescuer this god turned out to be!"

Isaiah continues by speaking of the carpenter, who exercises great skill—one must admit—in fashioning a block of wood into an idol, but it was not the carpenter who created the wood. The tree grew without the aid of the carpenter, watered for years by faithful rainfall (Isa. 44:14). Living in an arid environment, the Israelites had an appreciation for the scarcity of water, and the fact that a tree reached maturity bespoke divine providence.

Psalm 115 echoes this strong note against idolatry. The psalmist warns the makers of idols: "Those who make them become like them; so do all who trust in them" (115:8; see also 135:18). If we could teleport ancient people into the modern world and ask them to comment on our technology, it may well be that some would suppose that humanity in the digital age had finally conquered the gods. But other, more reflective observers, would probably point out that the internet was not our slave but our master. Staring into our computers all day, bent over our desks, and punching away at the keys of our laptops, we have no more arrived upon apotheosis than humanity had with the discovery of fire or the invention of the steam engine. We have not created the gods! We have ourselves become subservient robots!

Computers are thus revealed not to be our saviors but the dust of the ground that God cursed after the fall. We will till this silicon dust for our daily bread until the day we die (Gen. 3:19). If an idol is anything from which we seek salvation and ultimate purpose that is not God, then our modern technological world is surely no less full of idols than was the ancient world. As we set our hearts on the release of technology products each new season, John Calvin's aphorism proves true again—our hearts are idol factories.[6]

We need to be clear at this point that the problem is not that humanity exercises creativity, a point that we will directly address in the next section in this chapter. God made humanity in His own image, and this means that people are designed by God to be creative. We are created to create. God delights in human ingenuity. After all, the plotline of the Scriptures is a thread tracing from a garden to a city, from the garden of Eden to the New Jerusalem (see Gen. 3; Rev. 21). God's intention for humanity is not that we remain in an uncultivated, unexplored, undeveloped world. The problem is not that we create but that we can forget God in the process. It is not the manufacturing plants of the tech giants but in fact our own hearts that are the idol factories.

The answer to our question of whether God exists in cyberspace is right there in Paul's words to the Athenian philosophers: "The God who made the world and everything in it, being Lord of heaven and earth, does not live in temples made by man" (Acts 17:24 ESV). God does not exist in cyberspace—cyberspace exists because God is Creator. That is to say, cyberspace no more constrains or delimits God's existence than did the temples of antiquity or do our modern church buildings. But God, who so desperately loves humanity that He would send His own Son to die for us, can be encountered in temples and church buildings, whether made of stone or made in virtual reality.

Solomon exclaimed as the opening words of his prayer at the dedication of the temple: "LORD, God of Israel, there is no God like you, in heaven above or on earth beneath. . . . Heaven and the highest heaven cannot contain you; how much less this house that I have built!" (1 Kings 8:23, 27 ESV). The author of Hebrews tells us that Christ's priesthood is fulfilled not in man-made holy places but in a heavenly tabernacle (Heb. 9:24). The Israelites learned again and again the awful lesson that God cannot be kept in a box (see 2 Sam. 6:7). God's existence is not contained in a physical location, but God can be encountered anywhere. This truth empowered the early Christians to spread throughout the entire Roman Empire, as they came to see that, even though the temple in Jerusalem had been destroyed in AD 70, God's presence was not limited to their former way of worship. God would go with them as they congregated in new places and in new ways.

Does God exist in cyberspace? The answer is "no," if we mean that cyberspace is a precondition of God's existence. The Bible introduces God as the one from whom are all things and for whom we exist (1 Cor. 8:5–6). But the answer to our question is surely "yes," if we mean that God allows Himself to be encountered in virtual reality. In this sense our question is analogous to asking whether God exists in a novel or in a film. Of course, God is not the creation of a novelist or a film director, but God can be encountered and transformatively so in the worlds created by novelists and film directors. As Tim Keller's innumerable references in his sermons to J. R. R. Tolkien's *The Lord of the Rings* demonstrates, God can be found in a man-made world.

When we don our VR headsets, God is still as present as ever, peering into our hearts and souls. God occupies all spaces and is to be related to in all spaces. God is not really floating above the candles in the front of the chapel, but one can kneel before God in adoration at the altar rail, whether in a church of stone or in a church in VR. In the unforgettable words of the psalmist: "Where shall I go from your Spirit? Or where shall I flee from your presence?" (Ps. 139:7 ESV). The clear implication of the verse is "nowhere!" Perhaps VR is the "nowhere" we have gone where God is still available to us and where we still have the opportunity to be in God's presence.

All Reality Is God's Reality

The early church fathers introduced the principle that all truth is God's truth. The second-century apologist, Justin Martyr concluded: "Therefore, whatever things were rightly said among all people are the property of us Christians."[7] Christian authors of antiquity articulated this principle as theologians began to address many of the questions raised by Greek philosophy. The principle does not mean that everything claimed to be true by the Greek philosophers should be received as true, but it does mean that Christians should be fearless in endorsing truth wherever it is stated, whether by Greek philosophers or by Christian authors. Saint Augustine continued this tradition when he formulated the maxim: "All good and true Christians should understand that truth, wherever they may find it, belongs to their Lord."[8] Perhaps if Augustine were alive today, he would formulate the principle as "All reality is God's reality." The principle does not mean that everything portrayed as reality in VR actually is reality, but it does mean that Christians should be bold in accepting the truth shown in artistic representations wherever they may appear, including in VR. Virtual reality, along with all other forms of creative expression, can showcase the glory of God.

God created humankind to be creative. The Bible says that God created humankind in His own image (see Gen. 1:26), and part of what it means to be made in the image of God is that we have a capacity and a calling to be creative. To the man and the woman, God says in the creation narrative: "Be fruitful and multiply and fill the earth and subdue it, and have dominion over the fish of the sea and over the birds of the heavens and over every living thing that moves on the earth" (Gen. 1:28 ESV). In this passage, God assigns humanity the noble task of cultivating God's own creation. We are to be good stewards of the creation. This is why so many of Jesus' parables discuss our stewardship and accountability before God. We are called to manage this creation well and to do so in community. We were created male and female in order to be able to complement each other in the task. We come to know and love God through cultivating the world and through participating in the fulfilment of the creation mandate. We honor and glorify God in so doing. Andy Crouch argues that, while only God could bring the world into being from absolute nothingness, as God's image bearers, we do have the capacity to create that which did not exist before. Our creative capacity, Crouch explains, is to "make something of the world," both in the sense that we fashion new artifacts from preexisting material as well as in the sense that we frame new perspectives and compose new knowledge about the world.[9] The responsibility that God has entrusted to us is truly breathtaking.

God created us to create. But evangelicals have tended to be unsettled in their attitudes about art, concerned that the making of images—paintings, photographs, films, and now VR worlds and avatars—might infringe on the second commandment. Francis Schaeffer's *Art and the Bible* (1973) helped a generation of evangelicals think through what Scripture means when it prohibited the making of images. Schaeffer traveled to Switzerland in 1948 and founded L'Abri in 1955, a community dedicated to Christian formation. Schaeffer rediscovered for evangelicalism the artistic and intellectual tradition of the West in postwar Europe. Through his lecturing and media productions, Schaeffer opened the eyes of many to the message that human culture—whether philosophy, art, music, literature, or film—all properly reflects God's truth.[10] Schaeffer contends with many of the perennial evangelical suspicions that would consign all artistic expression to the idolatrous.

The second commandment reads: "You shall not make for yourself a carved image, or any likeness of anything that is in heaven above, or that is in the earth beneath, or that is in the water under the earth. You shall not bow down to them or serve them, for I the LORD your God am a jealous God, visiting the iniquity of the fathers on the children to the third and the fourth generation of those who hate me, but showing steadfast love to thousands of those who love me and keep my commandments" (Ex. 20:4–6 ESV). In some strains of Protestantism, the second commandment is effectively read as a prohibition against image-making of all kinds. But this interpretation runs against the clear sense of Scripture.

In the Bible, God commanded the making of certain images, and we do not worship a God who contradicts Himself. God commanded a specific design for the fashioning of the cherubim, the two angelic figures that were to rest atop of either side of the arc of the covenant (Ex. 25:18–20). The Bible records that Bezalel—of whom the Lord says, "I have filled him with the Spirit of God" (Ex. 31:3; 35:31)—followed these instructions precisely in his work, designing and casting these golden images (Ex. 37:6–9). In executing this design, Bezalel was not setting up the image of an idol. Bezalel was reflecting the image of God by creating as God had created him to do.

Bezalel is commended repeatedly for his actions, and Exodus 38:22 explicitly states that Bezalel fulfilled the commandment that the Lord had given him. There can be no mistake that Bezalel's creations were not like the golden calf worshiped by the people of Israel while Moses ascended Mount Sinai (Ex. 32:4). But the difference between the cherubim made by Bezalel and the golden calf was not found in the materials that comprised the statues or in the tools that the artists used to craft their designs. The difference is that, while the images that Bezalel made pointed upward to God, the golden calf had been set up to absorb the glory that is proper to God alone. The golden calf did not reflect glory back to God but deceitfully laid claim to worship.

As God's image bearers, our divine assignment is to create culture that reflects glory back to God. The Bible clearly distinguishes between the making of idolatrous images and the making of God-glorifying images. Christians can enter any creative sphere confident that every medium can be used to represent reality for the glory of God.

Will the Computers of the Future Save Our Souls?

We use computers to save almost everything today. Our pictures, our emails, our calendars, our bank account information, and our medical records all are examples of things that we care about and that we entrust to the saving power of our computers. We rely on our computers so constantly to supply us with the information that we require that the line between where our computer's memory ends and where our brain's memory begins sometimes feels a little blurry. If we want to know whether we have sent a communication to a family member, for example, our first instinct may be to look at the screen of our smartphones rather than go through the mental exercise of trying to remember. And computers are saving more and more of our lives every day.

Have you ever wondered what happens to a person's Facebook account when they die? Our loved ones may die, but their data continues on in an unchanged state. In February of 2020, South Korea's MBC aired a documentary titled "Meeting You" that featured a woman and her daughter who had been brought back to life as a VR avatar. The daughter had died in 2016 from a rare blood disease at age seven. The encounter between the woman and her daughter's avatar was emotional and filled with tears, as the woman played hide-and-seek, received gifts of flowers, and even celebrated a birthday party for her daughter's avatar in a VR environment. The avatar had been reconstructed by a team of researchers from photographs and other digital artifacts. What will happen in the future when we have thousands or millions of times more data points about our loved ones than we do today? What would happen in the future if we had not merely millions of times more data points than we do today but a perfect digital record? Is a perfect digital record of a human life even possible? Will the computers of the future save our souls?

The movement known today as "transhumanism" is broad and on many points not clearly defined. But many who identify themselves as transhumanists would claim that a perfect digital record of human beings will be possible in the future, and that the indefinite perpetuation of this record will be as close to fulfilling humanity's universal hope for immortality as can be achieved in the physical universe.[11] The word "transhumanism" was coined by Julian Huxley in 1957 in an essay with this title.[12] In outline form, Julian's vision of tranhumanism has remained intact—humanity is on an evolutionary ascent, the destiny of which is to bring consciousness to the entire universe; as humanity has evolved from the minutest life form into the species that has filled and dominated the planet, so the next phase of humanity's evolutionary journey is to fill the entire universe and to merge our consciousness with it. Transhumanism is the belief that humanity is destined to evolve beyond our current definitions of humanity.

In the original vision of Julian Huxley, transhumanism is a process solely of biological evolution. In recent decades, new enthusiasm has sprung up around the movement as scientists and popular authors have speculated about how "Moore's law" may map out a pathway for the transhumanist vision of human destiny. "Moore's law" is at the core of what makes transhumanism seem possible in the imagination of some today. In 1965, Gordan Moore, who would later cofound Intel, published a paper titled "Cramming More Components onto Integrated Circuits," postulating that the number of transistors in computer chips would double every year for the next ten years. In 1975, Moore revised his estimate to conclude that transistors would double every two years, and this iteration of Moore's prediction has proven remarkably prescient for the past five decades. This principle has become known as "Moore's law."

In nontechnical terms, "Moore's law" forecasts that every two years, computers will become twice as powerful as current models while remaining at the same price point. When this doubling effect continues on long enough, you arrive at really astronomical amounts of computing power. The story of the king and the inventor of the game of chess is sometimes invoked to explain how Moore's law relates to the explosive growth of computing power.[13] The king was so enthralled with the game of chess that he asked the inventor to name any reward. The inventor said that he wished simply to receive one grain of rice on the first square of the chess board, and then double that amount on the second square of the chessboard, and so on. Since there are sixty-four small squares on a chess board, the inventor effectively asked for one grain of rice doubled sixty-four times.

The king laughed at the puny reward requested by the inventor and commanded that his palace officials begin immediately to grant the reward. The first row of squares on the chessboard filled with rice quickly. To fill the sixteenth square on the chessboard, the palace officials had to lay aside thirty-two thousand grains (or, a couple of pounds) of rice. But soon things got out of hand. To fill the sixty-fourth square would have required over eighteen quintillion grains of rice, or hundreds of times more rice than exists in the entire world! This is what exponential growth looks like, and this is the kind of growth that Moore's law predicts will continue on into the future for computing power. When I (Jonathan) was a child, our first family computer was an Apple II (1983); the first family computer my children know is the iMac (2015). The iMac's internal storage is equivalent to about one million of the Apple II's 5-inch floppy disks. If this story plays out another human generation or ten, what will life look like here on planet Earth?

Ray Kurzweil is probably the most influential visionary behind transhumanism as a philosophy and cultural force today. In 2005, Kurzweil published, *The Singularity Is Near: When Humans Transcend Biology*, and this book was met with tremendous acclaim as well as vigorous skepticism.[14] An accomplished inventor with patents in computer programing for text recognition and speech synthesis, Kurzweil received the National Medal of Technology and Innovation from Bill Clinton in 1999. Transhumanism, as Kurzweil exposits the movement, is the philosophy that humanity and superintelligent computers will merge and then explode outward to become one with the rest of the visible universe. Referring to this vision of the future, Kurzweil stated: "Does God exist? Well, not yet."[15] If we understand Kurzweil's exposition of transhumanism to be what the movement is, then Christian theology about God, creation, and new creation is radically opposed to transhumanism.

Many of the calculations that Kurzweil presents in his book

as arguments for his conclusions are based on Moore's law, which Kurzweil refers to as "The Law of Accelerating Returns." It is this principle that leads Kurzweil to what would otherwise seem to be completely unjustifiable and absurd conclusions. In 2001, Kurzweil prognosticated: "We won't experience 100 years of progress in the 21st century—it will be more like 20,000 years of progress (at today's rate)."[16] But already we can begin to detect a breakdown in Kurzweil's argument, even at a distance of only a few years after he set his predictions. For example, in 2005, Kurzweil predicted that "supercomputers will match human brain capability by the end of this decade."[17]

It is anticipated that the Frontier supercomputer, which will open at the Oak Ridge National Laboratory in early 2021 at a cost of $600 million, should deliver exascale computing power, which according to current estimates is equivalent to the processing power of the human brain.[18] Kurzweil stated that, by 2020, personal computers at a cost of $1,000 would possess computational power "sufficient to re-create human powers of pattern recognition, intellect, and emotional intelligence."[19] Since I am writing this book in 2020 on a computer that cost approximately $1,000, it seems to me that Kurzweil must have desperately miscalculated something.

From these initial projections, Kurzweil steps outward to the conclusion that, by 2045, computer intelligence will be approximately one billion times more powerful than the sum of biological intelligence in the universe.[20] It is this moment that Kurzweil calls the "singularity." The term "singularity" is borrowed here from physics, in which context it refers to a moment when the known laws of space and time do not apply, such as when attempting to model the Big Bang. When applied to technology, the "singularity" refers to an era in which technology advances so rapidly that human intelligence cannot begin to comprehend the changes. William Gibson, the science fiction author who coined the term "cyberspace," unflatteringly called the singularity the "Geek rapture."[21]

Newer voices in the transhumanist movement are sometimes explicit in their quest for godhood. Amy Webb argues that philosophers and theologians used to explain the soul by appealing to God, but now scientists know that consciousness arose through eons of evolution and is a process that computers can emulate. The creators of these thinking machines are "the new gods of AI," Webb declares.[22] Transhumanist authors today sometimes announce that the process of biological evolution itself is coming to a close, and we are now entering a period of cosmological history where humans and their creations will exercise absolute control over the destiny of the universe.[23] What can this possibly mean except that humanity is becoming god?

In *Homo Deus: A Brief History of Tomorrow*, Yuval Noah Harari, professor at the Hebrew University of Jerusalem, proposes a new religion that gives voice to this epiphany. He calls the new religion "dataism," and his founding doctrine is the conclusion that "*homo sapiens* is an obsolete algorithm."[24] Humanity's only purpose (from the perspective of evolutionary biology) was to process data in order to propagate the species, and now humanity has created machines that, by their superior capacities at data processing and replication, have made human beings obsolete. Before being sentenced to prison for stealing trade secrets from Google, Anthony Levandowski, the brilliant computer scientist known for his contributions to the technology behind self-driving cars, submitted legal papers in the state of California to found his own religion, which worships artificial intelligence as a god.[25]

The apostle Paul would not be too worried. The apostle could write: "For although there may be so-called gods in heaven or on earth—as indeed there are many 'gods' and many 'lords'—yet for us there is one God" (1 Cor. 8:5–6 ESV). The age-old problem with becoming your own god is that you are then responsible for your own salvation. We disagree with Kurzweil's vision of the future, not solely because his predictions have proven to require updating along the way. Far more fundamental is the problem that Kurzweil's philosophy maintains that human consciousness and the meaning of life itself can be reduced to information. If one believes in materialism—that is, that matter or the visible universe is the totality of that which exists—then it might be possible to argue compellingly that all of reality can be reduced to information.[26]

However, the Christian worldview holds up for us hope that is beyond materialism. In the Christian tradition, God created matter. God, who is ultimate reality, stands outside of matter and the visible universe. The Christian message is that the redeemed will not be confined to the limits of material existence but will experience abundant new life as "partakers of the divine nature" (2 Peter 1:4; see also John 10:10). And in fact, it is only the Christian perspective that there is something beyond matter that allows for us to understand the true significance of material realities. Transhumanism can arrive at the opinion that "matter doesn't matter,"[27] but the Christian teaching that God pronounced His creation "very good" (Gen. 1:31) and the promise of the resurrection after death assure us that matter does very much matter to God. Matter is part of God's good creation, which He lovingly fashioned and will marvelously restore.

Jason Thacker notes that, if you get the beginning of the story of humanity wrong, you are bound to get the ending wrong.[28] The transhumanist vision of the future that man will merge with machine is plausible only to those who already believe that man is essentially a machine. In the Christian view, human consciousness is not merely a function of brainwaves or physical processes, which means that there is a hope for the resurrection beyond the reach of active brainwaves or perfect digital copies of ourselves uploaded to the internet. At the very beginning of the Bible, we read that God created humankind in His image, and this assures us that we are not merely a unique set of particles or ingeniously concocted chemicals. Christianity is not compatible with transhumanism because Christianity and transhumanism disagree in their viewpoints on the ultimate nature of reality and concerning whether there is anything beyond the visible universe.

Technological Depravity

In the conversation about technology, the church, and education, we tend to hear dichotomized opinions on the subject. Is technology good or bad for Christian education? Are churches that congregate in VR real churches or not? This way of thinking misses the whole point. The Christian vision of reality is that God created the world good, but that the fall has allowed sin to enter into all aspects of life. This means that evil realities like selfishness, violence, disregard for the other, and pride easily creep into any human endeavor, whether this be the most primary of human activities (such as tending a garden or procreation) or the most abstruse (such as devising a system of government or discovering the secrets of the atom).

Rapturous good and unspeakable evil are, in the human experience, never more than a hairbreadth apart. Choices abound in our creativity. Some we make are good and others are less so; some are heroic, and some are catastrophic. The world which God declared "very good" has become a mixed bag that requires judgment and discernment to live well and flourish. The same challenge applies to our use of technology. It would therefore be futile for us to imagine that God's will for the human use of technology could be articulated in a few blanket statements such as "churches can meet legitimately only in person" or "technology is an effective way to communicate the gospel." We ought to know better than to seek such an approach. Our broader culture has a dichotomized view of technology, and the Christian community has absorbed this view unreflectively, without proper theological analysis, and has reproduced this type of thinking in the church.

The broader culture tends to conduct its thinking on technology from the perspective of either technological optimism or technological pessimism. Christian thinking on the subject is properly neither of these. Technological optimism is the premise that the advance of technology will fundamentally improve the human condition, and technological pessimism is the inverse of this hypothesis. Thus, we find many cultural commentators predicting a more enlightened, more virtuous society based on the apparently inevitable progress in technology. Technological pessimism is the inverse of this hypothesis.

This narrative is, arguably, little more than a twenty-first century rendition of the twentieth-century myth of progress. The twentieth-century version of this narrative viewed moral progress as inevitable. The disastrous unfolding of World Wars I and II left no doubt that the promise that industrial advancements and the playing out of political processes would translate into advances in virtue and human happiness were utterly hollow. In the current moment, the broader cultural narrative concerning where technology is going tends to be utopian (that is, concluding that progress in computer technology can only lead to the betterment of society) or dystopian (that is, concluding that the increased power that computer technology will attain will be given to a few who will abuse this power to reinforce their own privilege at everyone else's expense). The Christian approach to technology should be neither one of optimism nor pessimism.

Christians are not technological optimists or pessimists because they believe that salvation comes from God. Few have exposed more poignantly the misplaced hopes of humanity in technology as a version of secular salvation than Quentin J. Schultze. In his 2002 book, *Habits of the High-Tech Heart: Living Virtuously in the Information Age*, Schultze argues that we are asking all the wrong questions concerning our technology. "We have naively convinced ourselves that cyber-innovations will automatically improve society and make us better people, regardless of how we use them. The benefits of information technologies depend on how responsibly we understand, develop, and employ them in the service of venerable notions of the meaning and purpose of life."[29] He continues: "Unless we focus as much on the quality of our character as we do on technological innovation, potentially good informational techniques will ultimately reduce our capacity to love one another."[30]

Schultze calls this faith that technology will save us from our desperate moral condition "informationism," and he warns that this misplaced hope will render us unable to make moral sense of the world.[31] His message is clear and penetrating: If we misconceive of the problem from which we need salvation, then we will certainly misdirect our hope for the salvation from that problem. The Bible tells us that humanity's problem is a spiritual problem, not a problem of tools or technique. As in every age, so in the present, the real problem is that we do not recognize our nature as created in the image of God, designed to reflect the glory of God. We have been created as spiritual beings designed to know and love God, and our failure to reflect God's glory makes us sinful—quite literally, self-interested to a fault. We can make no real progress until we recognize that the nature of our need is not for faster computers or for more data but for a restored relationship with our Creator.

Christians are neither technological optimists nor technological pessimists but rather believe that salvation can come only through Jesus. The paradigmatic space where the themes of God's creation and the fall come together in Scripture is in the gospel itself. When the apostle Paul sought words to express the gospel, the greatest theme of all his writings, he turned to the language of creation and new creation. The theme of God as Creator and of redeemed humanity as restored creation is the whole arc of the message that Paul spent his life proclaiming. In 2 Corinthians 5:17, Paul writes: "Therefore, if anyone is in Christ, he is a new creation. The old has passed away; behold, the new has come" (ESV). Paul restates this theme again and again in some of his most powerful and luminous articulations of the gospel message (see Rom. 6:4; 2 Cor. 4:16; Gal. 2:20; 6:15; Col. 3:10).

The advances of technology have done nothing to alter the fundamental need of humanity for salvation or the uniqueness of the salvation which is in Jesus Christ. As wise stewards of the resources entrusted to us, our churches will seek to apply VR and related technologies to introduce those within reach to the life-transforming message of the gospel. Technology is set to its proper utility neither when it acts as a mechanism to escape reality nor when we apply technology without reflection in order to pursue our basic needs. The question is not whether technology is good or bad. The question is how we choose to use it. Here as everywhere, the question is how we can live out our identity as God's image bearers through our use of technology and align ourselves with God's redemptive purposes.

Chapter 6

THE INCARNATION AND PENTECOST

"THE SELF-REVEALING OF THE WORD IS IN EVERY
DIMENSION—ABOVE, IN CREATION; BELOW, IN
THE INCARNATION; IN THE DEPTH, IN HADES; IN THE
BREADTH, THROUGHOUT THE WORLD. ALL THINGS
HAVE BEEN FILLED WITH THE KNOWLEDGE OF GOD."[1]

✦ Saint Athanasius

When God became man in Jesus Christ, He became every bit as human as you or me. The Scripture tells us that Jesus knew every aspect of human weakness, and yet He did not yield to sin (Heb. 4:15). When we think of the incarnation, we remember the earthy scenes from the Gospels. Jesus experienced extreme hunger after forty days of fasting in the wilderness (Matt. 4:2). Jesus restored lepers, touching their diseased bodies compassionately with His healing hands (Matt. 8:2). Jesus became so exhausted from ministry that He fell asleep on a cushion in the back of the disciples' boat during a fierce storm (Mark 4:38). Jesus dabbed mud on the eyelids of the man born blind, mud that He had mixed from His own spit and the dirt on the ground (John 9:6). Jesus was truly man, and He was truly God.

How does the doctrine of the incarnation inform our question about the practice of the church assembling in VR? How does the doctrine that Jesus came to earth as God incarnate—entering His creation as a human being to interact with His creatures in His creation—shape and refine our applications of VR technology for ministry purposes? From His first night on earth as a baby in the manger to His suffering and crucifixion under Pontius Pilate, everything about Jesus' life and ministry was real, enfleshed.

But Jesus' sojourn among humanity during His years of earthly ministry is not the entirety of the Christian story. We know Jesus today exclusively through the written record in the Scriptures and in prayer and devotion through the presence of the Holy Spirit. We have never seen the incarnate Jesus, and yet we know Him through the Holy Spirit. How does Pentecost inform our theological analysis of VR churches? After Jesus had been resurrected and before He ascended to the right hand of the Father in glory, He instructed His disciples to wait in Jerusalem for the power of the Holy Spirit (Luke 24:49). While the disciples were "all together in one place" praying in the upper room, the presence of God came upon them "like a mighty rushing wind, and it filled the entire house" (Acts 2:1–2 ESV). Tongues of fire rested on each one of the apostles as the Holy Spirit filled them, empowering them to communicate the gospel in new languages and through miracles. This, too, was the presence of God, new and surprising, but unmistakably evidencing the reality of Christ's redemption, sanctification, and mission (John 15:26–27; 16:8; 2 Cor. 3:18). What does Pentecost and the coming of the Holy Spirit mean for our evaluation of virtual reality churches?

Over the past two millennia, the Christian church has exhibited an amazing capacity to adapt to different situations and cultural contexts. Whether in Berlin or Beijing, whether in the rural spaces of the Netherlands or in the capital of Nigeria, the church is there, and the church ministers and worships in ways that appear as vastly different as the surrounding cultures. This adaptability should give us pause to reflect. In his 1989 classic text, *Translating the Message*, Gambian-born convert from Islam to Christianity and later professor of World Christianity at Yale Divinity School, Lamin Sanneh (1942–2019), argues that Christianity is unique among world religions for its ability to adapt to any culture. The incarnation and Pentecost have been the church's map and guideposts along this journey.

The doctrines of Christology and Pneumatology have been the church's blueprint for proclaiming the unchanging message of salvation in an ever-changing world. The gospel is anchored in the unique, historical events of the life of Jesus Christ, who was born of the Virgin Mary, crucified under Pontius Pilate, and raised to life again on the third day, and it is through the faithful confession of these events that we can identify the church wherever we may find it and in whatever form we may find it in the world. But it is through the power of the Holy Spirit, whom Jesus said moves like the wind, which we can hear but not see (John 3:8), that the church is now represented in every country on planet Earth and expressed in literally thousands of cultures and languages.

The Word Became Flesh

When the subject of VR church arises, many Christians ask how the doctrine of the incarnation should inform our perspectives.

Many rightly perceive that the incarnation is somehow key to this theological discussion, but discerning what conclusions exactly can be deduced from this doctrine requires careful reflection. Scot McKnight puts his finger on the gist of the matter when he writes: "For some people Christianity is digital: God sent a message to us and we pick it up somehow, either believe it or not, and then either live according to it or not. But God didn't send a message. God sent his Son."[2] How does the doctrine of the incarnation—that God sent His Son into the world for our redemption—inform our theology of VR churches? In order to answer this question, we will examine three classic articulations of the doctrine of the incarnation.

First, let's look at the doctrine as formulated by Athanasius (ca. 295–373) in the treatise *On the Incarnation*. In Athanasius's exposition, it is important to remember that the doctrine of the incarnation presupposes the doctrine of creation. What God brings about in the redemption of the world through sending His Son is in perfect alignment with what God did in the creation of the world through His Word (Gen. 1:3). Christian salvation is therefore not an exit from material reality to a spiritual realm beyond but is rather a restoration of God's purposes for the physical order. As the one "who fills all in all" (Eph. 1:23), God had never been distant from the world at any time, but in the incarnation He entered into His creation in a unique way (see Phil. 2:5–11). God did not come to us in order to communicate information, as God could have accomplished this through angels and prophets (see Heb. 1:1–4). Instead, Athanasius argues, Jesus came into the world for the very specific reason of assuming a human body: "This He did that He might turn again to incorruption men who had turned back to corruption, and make them alive through death by the appropriation of His body and by the grace of His resurrection."[3] Jesus could not die in our place unless He had a real human body, one that could absorb the suffering and death of all of us. For Athanasius, the doctrine of the incarnation teaches us that God took on human nature so that He could save human nature, thus restoring our nature to God's own perfect design.

Anselm of Canterbury (1033–1109) works out an additional aspect of the theology of the incarnation in his treatise titled *Cur Deus Homo*, alternatively translated "Why the God-Man?" or "Why God Became Man?"[4] In Anselm's analysis, the logic of the incarnation is grounded in the analogy of sin as a debt to be paid. The depiction of sin as a financial debt is not the only way that the Bible portrays the problem of human sinfulness, but this analogy does appear, for example in the Lord's Prayer (Matt. 6:12; Luke 11:4) and in Paul's exposition of justification (Rom. 6:23). In Jesus' parable of the unforgiving servant (Matt. 18:23–35), the Bible speaks of forgiveness as the repayment of a mammoth debt. The amount owed by the unforgiving servant is almost beyond calculation, comprising some ten million weeks of labor on a six-day calendar! Only humanity owed this debt, and only God could repay this debt, Anselm argues, and so the atonement could become possible only because God became man.[5] Any other arrangement could not have fulfilled God's perfect justice. Anselm shows us again that the incarnation was the only possible way for God to offer salvation to humankind.

The third and final milestone in the development of the doctrine of the incarnation that we will review is the Council of Chalcedon in AD 451. The more famous Council of Nicaea, convened by Emperor Constantine in AD 325, had confessed

Jesus to be "eternally begotten of the Father, God from God, Light from Light, true God from true God."[6] While the Nicene Creed establishes the deity of Christ, the Chalcedonian Creed defines Jesus' human and divine natures. The Chalcedonian Creed affirms that Jesus possesses both a divine nature and a human nature, and that these two natures come together in the one person of Jesus Christ without confusion, change, division, or separation. That is to say, Jesus' humanity does not in any way diminish His divinity, and His divinity does not in any way dilute His humanity. We sometimes paraphrase this definition when we say that Jesus is both fully God and fully man. The apostle Paul points toward this doctrine when he writes: "For in him the whole fullness of deity dwells bodily" (Col. 2:9 ESV).

In concluding that Jesus possesses both a divine and human nature, the Council Fathers concluded that Jesus also possesses a human soul.[7] The doctrine of the incarnation does not teach that Jesus became man in body alone but that Jesus became man in body and soul—everything that a human being is physically and spiritually.

The relationship that God experiences with His creation in the incarnation is fundamentally different from the relationship that we experience as physical and spiritual beings when we interact with digital technology. Let's explore this for a moment. What are we saying when we say that something is "digital," anyway? The terminology of "digital" and "analog" came into currency in our culture way back in the 1980s and 90s, when CDs became the medium of choice for listening to music, overtaking vinyl records in terms of sales. Since sound is vibration—waves that register on the tiny bones in your inner ear, which are then converted to electrical impulses by the acoustic nerve and interpreted as sound by your brain—it can be recorded and played back by any device capable of inscribing and reproducing sequences of vibrations. Vinyl records recreate sound by running a diamond needle through the grooves of the spinning record, and the friction between the needle and the ridges of the grooves create a sequence of vibrations that can then be amplified and experienced as music by listeners.

By way of contrast, digital music, along with any form of digital media, is recorded as a series of "bits" (short for "binary digits") of 0s and 1s. Rather than recording sound by impressing a representation of it into a physical object, as is the case for vinyl records, digital music is encoded as a series of 0s and 1s. When you load a CD into a compact disk player, you insert the CD so that the shiny, silvery side faces downward. If you examined this shiny side of the CD under a microscope, you would discover a series of tiny spots, some light and some dark, arranged in a tightly woven spiral that covered the entire face of the CD. These light and dark spots convey the bits (the data interpreted as 0s and 1s) that your digital media player then reads and plays back as sound.

When you press the play button, the CD player starts to spin the disk, shining a laser beam into a single ring of the spiral of spots. When the laser beam encounters a light spot, the laser reflects back to the CD player, and the device reads this reflected laser as a 1. When the laser beam encounters a dark spot, the laser beam is dispersed, and no laser reflects back to the CD player, which the device then reads as a 0. The CD player then interprets this string of 1s and 0s as a set of computer instructions describing an exact blueprint for the sounds to be reproduced. All digital media is encoded as a series of 0s and 1s, whether the media is a piece of music, a video file, a Bible storybook app, or a VR experience.

The fact that digital media is recorded as a series of bits sets up a paradox at the heart of digital technology. On the one hand, digital media is pure information and absolutely immaterial, since 0s and 1s have no physical properties. But on the other hand, unless these 0s and 1s are recorded in a retrievable form and delivered to a device that is capable of reading the data, there is no possibility that this information can be known or experienced. This paradox affects the way that we think and speak about our experiences with digital media. For example, we speak of "the cloud" as though it were light and fluffy, but the datacenters that make cloud computing function are housed in gigantic warehouses, with some surpassing the size of one hundred American football fields. These datacenters are unbelievably resource-hungry, consuming a measurable percentage of the entire world's electricity supply and giving off colossal amounts of heat. The "cloud" simply would not work at all without these massive and incredibly costly datacenters. Yet, we tend to think of the data that we stream as pure information. When we write an email or upload a picture to a social media platform, we sometimes assume that these communications belong to us because we conceive of them in terms of pure information. But when we remember that this data could not leave our computers or our smartphones without a global infrastructure costing untold trillions of dollars, presumably none of which we own, discerning ownership of the digital media we transfer to others becomes far more complicated.

There are two key properties of digital technology that have allowed it to become so influential in our world today. First, because digital media can be represented as pure information, it can be communicated between computers that use different mechanisms to store, retrieve, and process information. Imagine that you and a group of ten of your friends play a game of telephone in which you literally pick up your telephones and pass a message from one person to the next. Let's say the message is a short paragraph from Shakespeare. Because the message can be represented as pure information, it would not matter at all how each friend documented the message (whether by ink on legal pad, dry erase marker on whiteboard, pencil on sticky note, or sidewalk chalk on the front driveway), so long as everyone could accurately read and recite the message to the next person.

Computers work the same way. Whether it is the punched cards (with their opened or closed holes) or the latest solid-state hard drives (with their charged and uncharged memory cells), the mechanisms used to store, retrieve, and process information continue to change. But digital media can theoretically be played across any number of digital computing platforms, and this property is partly the reason that the digital revolution has swept the entire world in such a short span of time. If it were not for this property of digital technology, copying software from one computer to another would be as difficult as keeping grandfather clocks in perfect synchronization.

There is a second key property that contributes to the phenomenal success of digital media in our world today, and that is this: because digital technology can be represented as pure information, it can be communicated over distances at the speed of light. Imagine that you are sailing in the ocean on a dark night, and on the horizon you see the light of another ship signaling a message to you in Morse code. If you were practiced in receiving messages in Morse code, you could interpret the short and long flashes of the light as the dots and dashes of a message. As long as you had a clear line of sight to the other ship, it would not matter at all whether the ship were one mile away or ten miles away. The message would seem to reach you in no time at all. Because digital media is stored as bits, it can be communicated as electrical impulses virtually instantly anywhere in the world via the fiber optic cables of the internet.

These two properties—that, because digital media can be represented as pure information, it can be played back across any number of computing devices, and it can be communicated across distances at the speed of light—are at the heart of what the digital revolution is all about. It seems as though every company on earth is in the process of exploiting these principles in the attempt to improve their services. The church finds itself in the middle of this storm.

The mystery of the incarnation is that Jesus is fully God and fully man. This sets up a relationship that is completely unique, ultimately incomparable to any other relationship experienced within creation. Regardless of how human knowledge may expand as the digital revolution progresses, God will continue to stand outside of His creation, and therefore God's relationship to creation in the incarnation will remain something that cannot be modeled perfectly from within creation. Whether it be the discovery of gravitational waves or graphene computer processors, no technological advancement will allow humanity to model the incarnation in this way. The church is certainly called to reflect the reality of the incarnation, but we do this in imitating the humility and sacrifice of Jesus, not by adopting or resisting particular technologies and protocols.

Do we continue the mission of Jesus when we "incarnate" ourselves as avatars in VR worlds in order to bring the good news to those with whom we may otherwise never come into contact? Or, on the contrary, does the precedent that Jesus became flesh mean that the church can properly assemble only in an enfleshed form? Does the incarnation of Jesus and the promise of the bodily resurrection so sanctify physicality that it would be theologically incorrect for the church to appeal to VR and related technologies in order to facilitate its community life and pursue its mission? The incarnation, as a point of Christian doctrine, does not definitively resolve for us the question of whether and in what constellations churches should appeal to VR for the purposes of assembly. Properly modeling the incarnation in the church is a matter of following the humility and selflessness of Jesus, who assumed the form of a servant (Phil. 2:5–8), washed the feet of the disciples (John 13:1–20), resisted temptation under extreme physical deprivation (Matt. 4:1–11), and remained submitted to the will of God even to the end (Matt. 26:39).

While the doctrine of the incarnation neither affirms nor denies in a once-and-for-all fashion whether it is theologically correct for churches to congregate in VR, the doctrine can correct and refine the presuppositions that we bring to questions about specific applications of technology. One aspect of the doctrine that is perhaps particularly relevant today is the observation that human beings are more than their material bodies. When God became man in Jesus Christ, He assumed not only a human body but also a human soul.

In the present time, when some philosophers and public intellectuals are beginning to ask whether ultimate reality consists of nothing but bits and bytes of information, the Christian tradition reminds us that we are spiritual beings. In 2001, it cost about $100,000,000 to sequence the human genome, but today people can have their genetic data mapped out in a laboratory for as little as $1,000.[8] We are discovering that more and more of the visible universe can be coherently described as information, but does this mean that there is no difference between physical reality and digital simulations of physical reality? What is the difference between a person and a computer simulation of that person's genetic code?

In confronting the materialism of his own time, C. S. Lewis would speak of the fallacy of "nothing buttery." Lewis thereby refers to the tendency he observed to conclude that, because man can be described as matter, man must be "nothing but" matter. By this logic, human emotion becomes "nothing but" chemical reactions in the brain, and human thought itself becomes "nothing but" the firing of neurons and synapses. Lewis aptly named this reductionist fallacy "nothing buttery." The digital revolution will surely continue to uncover amazing new insights as scientists and people from all walks of life explore the hypothesis that all of reality can be digitized and represented as information, but we would be wise to remember Lewis's warnings about the reductionist fallacy of "nothing buttery."

The doctrine of the incarnation teaches us that God became man, not that man is nothing but molecules in motion. If God can enter the world as a man, then we dare not regard anything as mundane or devoid of spiritual significance and possibility. The Word that created Adam and Eve did not become in Jesus nothing but atoms and electrons. Rather, the incarnation teaches us that reality as we know it can overflow with spiritual significance. If ever there was an instant in the history of the universe where there was more going on than met the eye, it would be in the person of the incarnate Christ. In contradistinction to the worldview of materialism, C. S. Lewis calls the worldview that the doctrine of the incarnation gives us "sacramental":

> The suns and lamps in pictures seem to shine only because real suns or lamps shine on them; that is, they seem to shine a great deal because they really shine a little in reflecting their archetypes. The sunlight in a picture is therefore not related to real sunlight simply as written words are to spoken. It is a sign, but also something more than a sign: and only a sign because it is also more than a sign, because in it the thing signified is really in a certain mode present. If I had to name the relation I should call it not symbolical but sacramental.[9]

To conclude that human beings are nothing but information, and therefore that there is no essential difference between human beings as we exist in the real world and as we may someday exist in virtual worlds, is to fall prey to the "nothing buttery" of our times. There are undeniable differences between actual reality and virtual reality, and the best way to discover these differences is sustained reflection on our experiences in the medium. But, on the other hand, to insist that, because God became man in the incarnation, so churches can assemble properly only in person is in a strange way to yield to a materialistic worldview. In essence, this is concluding that God in Jesus Christ had become matter and nothing but matter, and so a particular material arrangement was necessary in order to be in God's presence. God became man, who is not only a physical being but also a spiritual being, and we can worship God and experience communion with Him as truly when we are assembled as a church in VR as when we are assembled in a building.[10]

To the woman at the well, who was concerned over the debate between the Samaritans and the Jews whether Gerizim or Jerusalem represented the legitimate place of worship, Jesus delivered the shocking teaching: "Believe me, the hour is coming when neither on this mountain nor in Jerusalem will you worship the Father. . . . But the hour is coming, and is now here, when the true worshipers will worship the Father in spirit and truth, for the Father is seeking such people to worship him" (John 4:21, 23 ESV). Jesus tells us that true worship is not a matter of location but a matter of the heart.

What about Avatars of Jesus?

In 2009, the term "avatar" became a household word, following the phenomenal success of James Cameron's film by the same name. Borrowed from the ancient mythologies of India, the word has come to mean a virtual representation of a person. Avatars are predicted to be a major part of VR experiences in the future. Avatars will not only be the way that real people interact with others in VR, but avatars will also give expression to an array of artificially intelligent assistants. When we speak with another person on the telephone, we accept what we hear as the other person's voice, and the person on the other end of the call accepts what they hear as our voice. Of course, what we really hear is a digital reproduction of the other person's voice and vice versa. The digital reproductions of voices in telephone conversations are so instantaneous and so accurate that we seldom reflect on the fact that what we hear is not really the voice of the other person but a digital reproduction. VR promises to allow us to see other people in the form of avatars just like the telephones of today allow us to hear other people's voices.

In March of 2018, "Siren" made her debut at the Game Developers Conference in San Francisco. Siren was one of the first avatars to be—at least as portrayed from a screen across the showroom floor—more or less indistinguishable from a living human being. The physical likeness of Siren was modeled from Chinese actress Bingjie Jiang, and UK-based actress Alexa Lee animated Siren during the demonstrations at the convention.[11] Siren was played in real time by a live actor, but some predict that artificial intelligence will someday drive lifelike avatars. Will artificially intelligent personal assistants like Apple's "Siri" and Amazon's "Alexa" (released in 2011 and 2014, respectively) greet us in the future as VR avatars?

What about avatars of Jesus in VR? Images of Christ abound in every artistic medium known to the church through every era of Christian history. At the present time, the art form of creating VR avatars is still poorly understood, so we may be waiting some time before we see any masterpieces portraying the Savior in this medium. Even when powered by the world's most advanced computers, today's artificially intelligent avatars or AIs are still far from credible. Their performance can prove to be underwhelming at best and nothing short of a travesty at worst. On March 23, 2016, Microsoft introduced "Tay" (which stood for the acronym, "Thinking About You"), an AI chatbot who was meant to present itself in the persona of a nineteen-year-old girl, communicating to the world through Twitter. Microsoft shut down the operation after just sixteen inglorious hours, however, and Tay's brief life became a major publicity fiasco for Microsoft. As an AI, Tay was programmed to learn from her interactions with people. "The more Humans share with me, the more I learn," tweeted Tay cheerfully as she came into existence, like a robotic Eve on the first day of creation. Unfortunately, this also meant that she could be taught to mimic socially unacceptable behavior. Tweeting about one hundred Tweets per minute, Tay fell victim to a coordinated attack and was soon spewing a continuous stream of sexist and racist tirades. "Chill im a nice person! i just hate everybody," Tay finally exclaimed in exasperation.[12]

There are serious theological obstacles to ever allowing Jesus to be played in VR by an AI. It ought not be done, because Jesus is inimitable. His words surprised His first hearers, and they continue to surprise every subsequent generation of readers. Again and again in Scripture, we read that Jesus' hearers were amazed and perplexed by His words: "And they were astonished at his teaching, for he taught them as one who had authority, and not as the scribes" (Mark 1:22 ESV). Jesus' teachings and miracles are not a specimen of human thought and behavior or a particular category of philosophy. Attempting to make a completely automated, artificially intelligent avatar of Jesus would be a perilous and problematic project.

However, there may be another, more correct way to portray Jesus in VR. From antiquity the church has argued that, because Jesus is the image of God, it is theologically correct to portray Jesus in art (see Col. 1:15; 1 Cor. 11:3). It can be appropriate for people to model Jesus in art because people are made in the image of God. Human actors who portray Jesus in passion plays or in cinematic portraits of Jesus know the burden of standing in for the Son of God on set. And yet, this tradition has been done well with good effect for many centuries. From the Passion Play of Oberammergau (ongoing since 1634) to *The Passion of the Christ* (2004), actors have overcome the considerable artistic and spiritual challenges of portraying Jesus in theater and film, and such will be possible to do in VR as well.

The Presence of the Holy Spirit and Telepresence

We know that God is present everywhere, but how is God present? God is present through the Holy Spirit—the sanctifying presence of God, who is coequal and coeternal with the Father and the Son. In the words of the creed: "We believe in the Holy Spirit, the Lord, the giver of life, who proceeds from the Father [and the Son], who with the Father and the Son is worshiped and glorified, who has spoken through the prophets."[13]

As we enter this new age where we commonly experience "virtual presence" in our relationships, we should ask what the theological significance of presence is. What is the significance of our own presence? What is the significance of God's presence? How is it that God is present with His people? As one author observes, the primary promise from God in the Scriptures is that He will be present with us.[14] The Lord's promise to His people, "Fear not, for I am with you" (Isa. 41:10), is repeated many times throughout Scripture (see, for example, Gen. 26:24; Isa. 43:5; Jer. 1:8, 42:11; Hag. 1:13; Matt. 28:20; Acts 18:10).

When God chose a name for His virgin-born Son, He called Him "Immanuel," which means "God is with us" (Isa. 7:14). When Jesus promised the coming of the Holy Spirit, He explained that it would be for the advantage of the disciples that He depart because He would then send the Holy Spirit to be present with them (John 16:7), and the Holy Spirit will remain with us forever (John 14:16). Jesus instructed His disciples that the Holy Spirit would give them the most intimate kind of knowledge of God, because the Holy Spirit would indwell them (John 14:17).

It is a foundational principle of Christian spirituality that God is everywhere all the time. It is we who forget God and so experience an absence of God's presence. Christian devotional disciplines are developed and practiced not to summon God to where He is not but to remember God, to bring ourselves into alignment with Him so we can be truly aware of His presence and authority. In Jeremiah 29:13, God promises, "You will seek me and find me, when you seek me with all your heart" (ESV). God has been present in the world, even from the beginning in creation, when the Spirit of God brooded over the face of the waters (Gen. 1:2).

In the Bible, the terms used for God's Spirit can also mean "breath" (*ruach* in Hebrew and *pneuma* in Greek). God's breath is the medium that conveys His word in the creation narrative. In Psalm 104:29–30, we read that God's Spirit continues to play an active role in the renewal of creation: "When you hide your face, they are terrified; when you take away their breath, they die and return to the dust. When you send your Spirit, they are created, and you renew the face of the ground" (ESV). God's breath is the medium for divine revelation. God speaks creation into existence, and so His speech and action are one and the same.

The Holy Spirit is called "holy" because He is God's sanctifying presence. The Holy Spirit sanctifies and makes holy that which His presence rests on or those whom He indwells (see, for example, Rom. 15:16; 2 Thess. 2:13; 1 Peter. 1:2). In the Old Testament, the Spirit of the Lord is seen to come upon people (see Judg. 3:10; 2 Chron. 20:14; Isa. 61:1), to rush upon or fall upon people (see Judg. 14:6; 1 Sam. 16:3; Ezek. 11:5), to depart from people (see 1 Sam. 16:14), to carry people along (1 Kings 18:12; 2 Kings 2:16; Ezek. 37:1), and to rest on people (see Isa. 11:2). In Isaiah 42:1, the Lord says of His servant, "I have put my Spirit upon him; he will bring forth justice to the nations" (esv, see also Isa. 11:2). In the early history of Israel, the Bible often speaks of the Spirit of the Lord coming upon one of the leaders of the people for a special mission—for example, on King Saul (1 Sam. 10:9–10), who prophesied when the Spirit was on him. David had confidence that the Spirit of the Lord had inspired him when he delivered his departing words to the people of Israel (2 Sam. 23:2), and Jesus ascribes David's words in Psalm 110 to the inspiration of the Holy Spirit (see Matt. 22:43). Countless times in the Bible, the Spirit of the Lord is associated with the ministry of the prophets. The Holy Spirit is the breath of God who sanctifies, inspires, illumines, strengthens, empowers, and reveals. It is the Holy Spirit who convicts the world of sin (John 16:8–11). It is the Spirit who discerns our thoughts from afar (see Ps. 139:2).

In our daily interactions by telecommunication, we extend a form of our presence when in online meetings we make decisions with other people, provide counsel, and identify agenda items for further deliberation. Is our presence as communicated by VR analogous to the way that God is present with us in the Holy Spirit? Reference to such an analogy may perhaps be useful in some contexts, but this analogy, like all analogies for the Trinity, quickly breaks down. The principal difference is that the Holy

Spirit is not an attribute of God but God Himself. The Holy Spirit is more than the sum of His activity. The Holy Spirit is a divine person who is to be worshiped and glorified with the Father and the Son. When we say that the Holy Spirit is a person, we mean that He Himself is God—the one for whom we were formed to share relationship. We do not define God's personhood according to ours but rather our personhood is defined by God's. Stating that the Holy Spirit is a person is another way of saying that our relational capacities as human beings were created in order to know and love the God who is the Holy Spirit.

While the presence of God in the Holy Spirit is not properly analogous to our presence via telecommunication, the Holy Spirit can and does empower real spiritual communion between a person and God everywhere. This includes experiences of spiritual community facilitated on the internet and in VR. Paul claimed to be spiritually present with several congregations although physically absent (see Col. 2:5; 1 Cor. 5:3), and so Paul can truly be spiritually present with several congregations by letter, and so the Holy Spirit can empower spiritual communion between believers in telecommunicated forms. Even participating in significant issues of church discipline by letter in the case of the Corinthian correspondence, Paul not only communicated information to churches abroad but participated in the spiritual life of the community. It was possible for Paul to do this because it is the Holy Spirit who empowers our spiritual communion with God and with other believers.

Regardless of the medium of our communication with one another, it is the Holy Spirit who ushers us as a community into the presence of God. It is the Holy Spirit who gives unity to the body of believers (Eph. 4:3), not a technological apparatus or a particular mode of assembling. When the Holy Spirit first came on the apostles at Pentecost, we read that the apostles were "all together in one place" (Acts 2:1). It was the Holy Spirit who empowered the early church to scatter across Judea, Samaria, and outward to the ends of the earth, yet remaining united as the body of Christ on earth.

Patrick Dixon noted that prayer translates surprisingly well to virtual platforms. Because prayer is an exercise in focusing one's mind on God, the technical troubles that currently assail virtual telecommunication (such as jittery audio or video streams) tend to interfere with online prayer only in a minor way. The primary discipline of prayer is to focus one's interior reflection on God and His presence, regardless of where one is situated physically. When attempting to pray with others via virtual technology, even moments of complete silence (for example, in the case of total internet failure or the loss of electricity) are not counterproductive. Prayer can be sustained in an uncompromised state through any imaginable technical failure. The audio and video signals streaming across the internet during an online prayer service are never more than an aid to prayer in the first place, since prayer is practiced in the heart through the Holy Spirit, and it is there that one experiences an unmediated relationship with God. To lead another person in prayer is to encourage by example another to pray in his or her inner being (see Eph. 3:16), and in many cases this can be done with equal effectiveness via virtual technology as in person.

It is noteworthy that the apostle Paul mentions that he is praying for the churches to which he writes in many of his epistles (see Rom. 1:8–10; Phil. 1:3–4; Col. 1:3; 1 Thess. 1:2–4; 2 Thess. 1:3; 2 Tim. 1:3). On several occasions, Paul takes the time to write out his prayer specifically for the believers to whom he writes (see 1 Cor. 1:4–9; Eph. 1:15–2:10; 3:14–21; Col. 1:9–13; 1 Thess. 3:9–13). For example, in Philippians 1:9–11, Paul pens these words: "And it is my prayer that your love may abound more and more, with knowledge and all discernment, so that you may approve what is excellent, and so be pure and blameless for the day of Christ, filled with the fruit of righteousness that comes through Jesus Christ, to the glory and praise of God." Paul's point in this practice is that he anticipates his prayer will be read aloud in the congregation and that everyone will pray along, all the believers participating in his own prayer and learning to pattern their prayers after his example.

When the Holy Spirit descended on the apostles at Pentecost, God reversed the confusion of languages that He had placed over the peoples of the earth ever since the Tower of Babel.[15] Filled with the Holy Spirit, whose presence came in the sound of a rushing wind and the appearance of tongues of fire, the apostles began to preach in languages that they had never learned, communicating the good news with passion and persuasion. In the power of the Holy Spirit, fishermen from Galilee became eloquent heralds of God's reign on earth.

The Holy Spirit continues to turn the ordinary into the extraordinary by bringing our everyday lives into the light of God's presence. A storefront in an abandoned strip mall can become a center for community transformation, offering hope in the name of Jesus in an undesirable part of town. A segment of our daily commute can become a sanctuary where we encounter God, learning to walk with Him and discern His voice. And a teleconference call can become the context for the most profound spiritual breakthrough. The Holy Spirit continues to open new possibilities for the communication of the gospel that may seem to us today as miraculous as Pentecost.

Loving God and Loving Our Neighbors in the Digital Age

In response to the lawyer's question, "Who is my neighbor?" (Luke 10:29), Jesus tells the parable of the good Samaritan. The lawyer's motivation in asking this question, the Bible tells us, was to evade moral responsibility, but Jesus patiently unpacked the question and the lawyer's motivation, delivering one of His best remembered teachings in response. The question we are still asking today is: "Who is my neighbor?" Do Christians have a moral obligation to love those with whom we come in contact via the internet and VR? Is it possible to express Christian love to someone whom we know only through virtual reality and whom we have never met in person? In Jesus' parable of the good Samaritan, we learn that it was not the one who was physically nearby but the one who showed love who proved to be a neighbor (Luke 10:36–37). Jesus' concluding words to the lawyer and to us are: "You go, and do likewise."

Are we loving God and loving one another through our use of technology? Saint Augustine (AD 354–430) introduces to us the concept of rightly ordered loves.[16] This is the principle that we are to love God first, bringing all other loves into a subordinate relationship to our love for God. This is the only way that we can properly love anyone or anything. Augustine reminds us that we ought to love God through all other relationships, including our relationships with people and our relationship with technology. When we begin by loving technology as an end in itself, we are bound to experience the impoverishment of soul that wrongly ordered loves inevitably produce. We will experience the disorientation of self-deception and the pain of disintegrated relationships if our loves are for anything but God first. This method of evaluating our use of technology calls for soul searching, but it really is the best way to discern whether our use of technology is spiritually beneficial or self-destructive.

To evaluate our use of technology, we can ask ourselves: "Am I loving God through this or that specific application of technology?" We love God first when we love something or do something for His sake. We can use technology to extend ourselves to other people and to foster relationships of love, or we can use technology as a weapon to pursue our own interests at the expense of others. Technology can be a bridge for us to extend ourselves to others in love, or it can be a barricade we hide behind in selfishness. Technology continues to change, but God's call to love Him first is eternal.

What does it mean to love God and to love one's neighbor in a world where Christians have the option of congregating for church services in VR? Proper use of VR will require checks and balances to compensate for the limitations of the technology. Reflecting on the limitations of VR as a medium, Craig Detweiler stated: "I think the thing that I don't want us to lose in a VR church is that we are an embodied people. If I'm sick, I might need somebody to actually come to my house and bring me a cup of soup." He continued: "I might need someone to sit with me and be present—somebody that's not a robot, that's not a virtual friend. It's maybe not enough on Facebook to say, 'I'll pray for you,' or to send a heart emoji. It maybe takes us to actually get in the car and show what that heart emoji means."[17] The spiritual difficulty of following Jesus in the way of sacrifice is not a problem created or solved by digital technologies, but perhaps more than others, churches that assemble in VR will need to be especially exercised in developing practical ways to minister to one another and to the world around them.

Sometimes the neighbor to whom Jesus calls us to show love is not yet a believer. VR churches show promise in opening avenues to reach new communities. Sean Dunn says that his ministry's strategy starts by interrupting people.[18] The internet operates on the principle that anyone can search for whatever they want to find, but the people who need Jesus are not necessarily searching for Him in Google. "They're not asking the right questions, and so that's why interruption is so important," Dunn contends. "They're not coming online for the most part saying, 'I need Jesus,' they're coming online and saying, 'I need something. I'm messed up.' And so it's really meeting them in their point of crisis. They're not waking up in the middle of the night and saying, 'Oh no, I'm going to hell.' They wake up in the morning and say, 'Oh no, I'm going through hell.'" The internet and VR are making everyone in the world digital neighbors. Through creativity and persistence, Dunn and others are discovering ways to use digital tools to empower evangelism and to reach these new neighbors with the gospel.

Jesus taught that the authentic love of His disciples would be the definitive witness of the church (John 13:35). So we should ask the question: "Can we love someone with whom our relationship is conducted exclusively by technology?" The answer to this question is probably "yes, in some circumstances," but relationships of real love will seek in-person exchange where such exchange is possible. If a relationship that purports to be one of mutual love does not ever seek in-person encounters when such interaction is possible, then it is probably right to question the legitimacy of the love that this relationship allegedly represents. The Bible would surely challenge this notion of love, calling us to express Christian love in tangible ways. As the apostle John reminds us: "He who does not love his brother whom he has seen cannot love God whom he has not seen" (1 John 4:20 ESV).[19] If we use technology not as an avenue to show love to those whom we cannot see physically but as an excuse to avoid encountering those whom we could have met in person, then it is right to question the faithfulness and fervency of our love for God.

Chapter 7

THE NEW PEOPLE OF GOD AND VISIBLE SIGNS OF INVISIBLE GRACE

"I WILL BUILD MY CHURCH, AND THE GATES OF HELL
SHALL NOT PREVAIL AGAINST IT."

✦ Jesus Christ (Matt. 16:18 ESV)

"IF 'CHURCH' IS WHAT HAPPENS WHEN PEOPLE
ENCOUNTER THE RISEN JESUS AND COMMIT THEMSELVES
TO SUSTAINING AND DEEPENING THAT ENCOUNTER IN
THEIR ENCOUNTER WITH EACH OTHER, THERE IS PLENTY
OF THEOLOGICAL ROOM FOR DIVERSITY OF RHYTHM AND
STYLE, SO LONG AS WE HAVE WAYS OF IDENTIFYING THE
SAME LIVING CHRIST AT THE HEART OF EVERY EXPRESSION
OF CHRISTIAN LIFE IN COMMON."[1]

✦ Rowan Williams

We live in a time of transition. We rely on technology countless times each day, frequently with little awareness of the digital processes that make our daily activities possible. And yet, we live with a certain reticence about our own use of technology. We are sometimes amazed by the possibilities opening up before us, and we sometimes experience serious doubt whether these possibilities will bring about a better future. On March 10, 2020, as the coronavirus crisis was beginning to unfold in the US, Pastor Andy Huette published a blog post on the Gospel Coalition website titled, "You Can't Livestream Church."[2] Huette confesses that his church produces a livestream, and he confirms that the livestream represents a clear benefit to the church, but also he remarks tellingly: "Church shouldn't be something we consume but something we participate in." The recent emergence of VR technology and the coronavirus crisis present us with an opportunity to reexamine theological questions about the nature of the church.

It is important to remember that the church is a mystery (Eph. 5:32). While we may assume that the technological challenges that the church faces at the moment are our primary concern, these are secondary to the challenges that the church will continue to face because we live between the "already" and the "not yet" of the coming of the kingdom of God. Jesus explained that the kingdom of God had already arrived in seed form when He said, "The kingdom of God is in the midst of you" (Luke 17:21 ESV). But after His resurrection, Jesus confirmed to His disciples that the time for the coming of the kingdom of God in fullness had not yet arrived (see Acts 1:6–8). The challenge of gaining a firm grasp on the concept of "the VR church," from a theological point of view, may turn out to be no more nor less problematic than defining "the church." Our institutions, forms of worship, and modes of assembly will continue to be in a pilgrim state until the coming of the King, until the church is presented to Christ in splendor (Eph. 5:27).

In the contemporary conversation about the VR church, many of us presume that the focus of the discussion should be on what virtual reality is and what it can do for us. There is an appropriateness to discussing these questions, especially in light of recent milestones in the development of VR technology and in the wake of the coronavirus crisis. But what is likely to keep us productively engaged for far longer is not the "virtual reality" part but the "church" part. Long after VR technology settles and becomes the foundation for whatever new forms of culture may arise, what will remain mysterious and ever new, what will remain ever worthy of our focus, is the discussion about the nature of the church. The massive hype around VR tends to capture the lion's share of our imagination about the future, leaving intact the dangerous assumption that we all share common experiences of worship and church life. We can sometimes give in to the fear that the church will be won by those who "get the tech right" and lost by those who do not. But this is not true. The future of the church is for those who "get the church right." In this final chapter of the book, we will reflect on what the doctrine of the church means in the age of VR and the question of whether the church can practice the sacraments via virtual technologies.

What Is the Church According to the Bible?

In the Bible, we encounter no abstract definition of the church. The Bible's approach to teaching us about the church is neither to deliver a definition of what the church is nor to lay down a list of rules about what the church does. Rather, the Bible paints a series of word pictures. From this set of analogies, we may discern a way forward in determining what it means to be the church faithfully and boldly in every context. In fact, the word "church" (*ecclesia*) occurs only three times in the four Gospels, appearing only in Matthew 16:18 and 18:17. Given that the Gospels are an accurate report of Jesus' teaching, it is clear that Jesus did not give specific guidelines outlining how the church should conduct its business, even though the disciples and first-century Christians surely would have been interested in such questions. Instead, Jesus taught His disciples that He Himself was the way to the Father and promised the coming of the Holy Spirit (see John 13:16; 14:6).

When we casually use the word "church" to refer to a reoccurring meeting of Christians at a particular location, we are not out of step with the customary biblical usage of the term. The word "church" often carries this everyday sense in the New Testament, basically acting as the equivalent to a mailing address. In fact, the word "church" is used literally in the mailing addresses of many of the New Testament epistles (see 1 Cor. 1:2; 2 Cor. 1:1; Gal. 1:2; 1 Thess. 1:1; 2 Thess. 1:1; Rev. 1:11).[3] This use of the word "church" as shorthand for a community of believers who assemble in a particular place on a regular basis is not necessarily untrue to the biblical sense of the word. The rest of the New Testament contains over a hundred references to the word "church," and the most common use of the word is simply to refer to a congregation of Christian believers in a particular city or locality.[4]

But there are also instances in the New Testament where the

word "church" refers to a universal, cosmic community of the redeemed who could never be assembled within the four walls of an ancient or contemporary structure.[5] Remember that in Jerusalem, for example, the church was made up of thousands of community members, but there was not any place of worship except the temple large enough to accommodate them all at once. And so even the church in Jerusalem was made up of several distinct "churches" or congregations that would meet in different locations, but this practical reality did not prevent each congregation from representing the larger church. There are times when the biblical author will simply refer to "the church," and it is clear that the author intends to speak of the entire community of the redeemed. We may call this the "universal church."

The word *ecclesia* preexisted Christian usage of the term. In pre-Christian Greek, the noun *ecclesia* simply means "an assembly," and the verb form *ecclesiazo* means "to hold an assembly."[6] The word *ecclesia* therefore refers to a smaller part of a larger community. The concept of an *ecclesia* is sometimes explained as a community that is "called out." In this sense, *ecclesia* does not refer to those who are "called out" from a heterogeneous group (for example, Christians called out from the unbelieving world). Rather, *ecclesia* refers to those who are "called out" or summoned from the larger community in order to represent the larger community (for example, an assembly of citizens who are gathered in order to represent the entire Greek city-state). The church is a body of members gathered together in a particular place and at a particular time who represent the body of Christ. Our local congregations are gatherings of believers who are called out to represent the new people of God.

Inherent in this sense of the church as a particular

community summoned in order to represent the larger community is the relationship between the particular and the universal church. The identity of the particular church is predicated on the identity of the universal church. This is to say that the church cannot be complete in and of itself as a local community. No Christian congregation would claim to be the complete fulfillment of God's redeeming purposes. Every single church carries with it this identity of belonging to and bearing witness to the larger work of God in salvation.

This relationship between the particular and the universal is at the heart of what the word "church" means in the Bible. We see this dynamic surface again and again in the New Testament record. The closest the Bible comes to defining the church is to declare it to be a mystery, analogous to God's intention for the unity of the marriage relationship (Eph. 5:32). What does it mean that the church is a mystery? It means that the church is the visible reality of the kingdom of God on earth now. The building on the corner of Charles and York Street that I (Jonathan) drive to on a Sunday morning is not the fulfillment of God's promise "to reconcile to himself all things, whether on earth or in heaven" (Col. 1:20 ESV). Nor are the people who congregate there the consummation of God's vision for "a great multitude that no one could number, from every nation, from all tribes and peoples and languages" (Rev. 7:9 ESV). The particular church is identified in the universal church, and the universal church is witnessed in particular churches. The visible church assembling in any locale and at any time points toward the larger reality of the body of Christ.

In *Images of the Church in the New Testament* (1960), Paul Minear identifies ninety-six specific word pictures that the New

Testament uses to describe what the church is. The church is like a body, says the apostle Paul. In some ways, this is the archetypical analogy for the church. The church is the body of Christ (Rom. 12:5; 1 Cor. 12:12, 26–27; see also 1 Cor. 10:17; Eph. 4:12; Col. 1:24). We are members of Christ's body, and Christ is the head of the church (Eph. 1:22–23; 4:15–16; 5:23). The church is like a temple, built up from living stones (Eph. 2:21–22; 1 Peter 2:5), or like a holy nation (1 Peter 2:9). The church is like a flock, whose shepherd is Christ (Matt. 25:32; Luke 12:32; John 10:16; 21:15–17; Heb. 13:20; 1 Peter 2:25). In all of these word pictures, the relationship of part and whole, particular and universal is central to the analogy, whether member to body, stone to temple, citizen to nation, or sheep to flock.

In some of the word pictures the Bible uses to describe the church, the analogy is to one or more personal relationships. In this way, the church is like a bride (Eph. 5:32; see also Matt. 25:1; John 3:29; 2 Cor. 11:2; Rev. 21:2; 22:17), but a bride cannot be a bride unless there is a larger relationship—a marriage—to which the bride is related. So, too, the church cannot be the church unless it is situated within the greater relationship of the universal church, the cosmic redemption of the world in Christ. Christ is connected to each particular church, just as individual church members are also connected to each other through Christ. The church is likened to a community of citizens (Eph. 2:19; see also Phil. 3:20), exiles (1 Peter 1:1; 1:17; 2:11; Heb. 11:13), and ambassadors (2 Cor. 5:20; see also Eph. 6:20). The church is said to be the family of God (1 John 3:1–2; see also John 1:12; Gal. 6:10; 1 Tim. 3:16), and we are brothers and sisters to one another (Matt. 12:50). We have been adopted into God's family and can now address Him as "Abba" (Rom.

8:15, 23; Gal. 4:5; Eph. 1:23). We can therefore also call Jesus our brother (Heb. 2:11).

Each of these word pictures is configured such that the group of individuals is in relationship with an assumed, larger collective (a marriage, city, fatherland, kingdom, and family). We should observe that, when taken on their own, some of these word pictures in fact seem contradictory. For example, the word pictures of citizens and exiles would seem to speak of opposite realities. Citizens enjoy the privileges of belonging to a certain political body, while exiles identify themselves by the loss of these privileges. The point is not that the church has any particular political composition or structure but that the church is composed of individual members who are spiritually bound up in the new identity of Christ. Whether the specific members of the church are assembled in the same location or whether they are assembled at the same time, they are united to God and to one another. This can be because God, who is Father, Son and Spirit, is everywhere at all times.

The church is a mystery. Its identity is defined not by what it is presently but by what it will become. We can therefore say that the church is an eschatological community. Each individual congregation is a picture in microcosm of what the church is in a fuller, spiritual sense—the new people of God who await the kingdom of God, the community who prays, "your will be done, on earth as it is in heaven" (Matt. 6:10). In the New Testament, the church is both a local congregation (a set of individuals who meet in a particular place and at a particular time) as well as an eschatological reality—the fulfillment of God's redemptive purposes.

In whatever constellation we consider churches—whether

at the level of a ministry team within a particular congregation, or a congregation within a denomination, or a denomination within a historic Christian tradition, or all historic Christian traditions within the universal church—we can conclude incorrectly that the particular part of the church that we participate in would be of increased validity or effectiveness if it were a greater proportion of the larger body to which it relates. But God has made the individual parts diverse for His own purposes. "If the foot should say, 'Because I am not a hand, I do not belong to the body,' that would not make it any less a part of the body," Paul reminds the church in Corinth and the church across the ages (1 Cor. 12:15 ESV). Particular churches are not—in fact, cannot be and will abandon their proper role if they attempt to be—the universal church. If the local church pours all of its resources into global service projects, where will the community be? "The eye cannot say to the hand, 'I have no need of you,'" Paul says, reminding us that certain groups of Christians are not to be disregarded as somehow not a part of the body of Christ simply because they have a different role to play (1 Cor. 12:21 ESV).

If there was ever a time when the lines between the local church and the global church became difficult to discern, it would be now. If the members of your local congregation have internet access, then your local church is a global reality. The local church now has the opportunity to pray with believers in all countries of the globe, to listen to and be edified by preaching pouring in from churches in all countries on earth, to participate in colloquia and spiritual enrichment experiences in perpetual array. It is not that the local church is in a particular locality and the global church is somewhere else "out there."

Our local churches are active participants in the global

church, as real Christians join with other real Christians from other parts of the real world, in VR and by the power of the Holy Spirit. It would be incorrect to conclude that because there is endless opportunity to listen to preaching online there is no longer any need for the local church to foster the discipline of preaching. But it would also be a tragedy for the local church to pretend that Christianity did not exist outside the four walls of its sanctuary. Discovering ways for local churches to participate in the ministries of the global church and for the global church to participate in the ministries of the local church will prove essential for pursuing spiritual health in the future.

How Can We Stir Up One
Another to Love and Good Works?

The most famous text in all of the Bible concerning church attendance reads: "And let us consider how to stir up one another to love and good works, not neglecting to meet together, as is the habit of some, but encouraging one another, and all the more as you see the Day drawing near" (Heb. 10:24–25 ESV). When we contemplate the differences between assembling as a church virtually and assembling as a church in person, this passage has something to teach us. Online communications are of inestimable value in their ability to overcome the boundaries of space and time, to cross geographical, economic, cultural, and linguistic divides. But gathering with other Christians in person will always allow us to draw out faith from one another to a degree not possible through any mode of virtual telecommunication. We may be able to absorb information equally well online as in person, and we may be able to appreciate theatrical or musical performances equally well in VR as in person. But we cannot inspire, encourage, and sharpen one another with equal effectiveness via virtual telecommunication as when we assemble in person.

In his classic *The Four Loves*, C. S. Lewis writes about the richness of friendship, which is the calling of the Christian: "In each of my friends there is something that only some other friend can fully bring out. By myself I am not large enough to call the whole man into activity; I want other lights than my own to show all his facets."[7] We could adapt Lewis's observation to note that the church is meant to be the context for spiritual friendships. Church attendance is not merely an opportunity to listen to preaching or experience worship or even to receive the sacraments. For all of these activities, we are primarily in the position of recipients of the grace of God, and it may be that these activities can be transferred partially or entirely to VR platforms. But it is clear that deep, enduring friendships will always be best lived person to person. Friendship will always seek unmediated contact. We will never be able to draw out the spiritual gifts in others or help others clarify their own vision and calling to the same extent that we will be able to do when present in person. Opportunities for person-to-person encounters that are left unexplored are gifts left unopened.

For many who begin studying the phenomenon of VR churches, the presumption is that churches will assemble either exclusively in person or exclusively via virtual technologies. But neither of these scenarios seem likely to us. About twenty years ago, there was a debate about whether e-books or paper books would win the market. What we have learned in the intervening period of time is that neither format possesses all the advantages and that people read e-books and paper books for different reasons. Probably this is what is going to happen with brick-and-mortar churches and VR churches.

Douglas Estes concludes: "One thing that I strongly believe is that in the far future, there won't really be virtual churches (end stop) and then brick-and-mortar churches (end stop). But that every church will be a brick-and-mortar church to some degree, and every church will be a virtual church to some degree."[8] For the present time, it turns out that almost no church leaders recommend that Christians assemble exclusively in VR. Walt Wilson, the visionary behind the pioneering ministry Global Media Outreach, could write: "The local church will never be replaced by the Internet."[9] It would be a misstep for churches to disavow opportunities to foster in-person interaction merely because the means to meet virtually are also available.

The question is not whether churches should meet exclusively in person or exclusively in VR. Probably the real question for many of us at this time is whether we should conceive of our churches as networks of interconnected ministries or "everyone we see in the sanctuary on a Sunday morning." VR and virtual telecommunication tools offer an incredible opportunity for people from anywhere to convene at any time, and if churches begin applying the strengths of these tools, then our presumed definitions of the church as "everyone we see in the sanctuary on a Sunday morning" will begin to be dismantled. But aiming for a new model of the church as a network of interconnected ministries could also connect us in a new way to what it means to be the body of Christ.

As our churches begin to be restructured from institutions to networks, churches will be able to reevaluate their needs for physical space. This transition to virtual churches—churches that take seriously the convening potential of virtual technologies—will allow churches to begin to reevaluate their needs for physical space. If our model of church remains "everybody sitting in the sanctuary pews on a Sunday morning," then a three-hundred-person church will require seating for three hundred people. If our model of church is open to appealing to VR for the purposes of assembly, then a church building which seats three hundred might be able to serve a congregation of one thousand members or more.

At the same time, it would be unwise of us not to cultivate the opportunities for ministry and spiritual enrichment all around us in person. Simon Jenkins said, "I think, ideally, churches are physical meeting places. They always have been, and there is no reason for them not to be, unless there really is a reason for them not to be due to persecution."[10] At a distance of nearly a quarter of a century, Patrick Dixon's reflection on this question still measures out the right amount of openness while clearly pointing to the responsibility of Christian leaders to steward the possibilities of in-person assembly: "It is extremely difficult to square a biblical view of Christianity with any teaching that suggests it is tolerable to encourage Christians that they do not need to meet together 'in the flesh' (albeit in the Spirit too!). One could go further and say that any group which promoted such an idea was likely to lead people astray and weaken a fundamental teaching of the church."[11]

When asked whether he believed Christians should attend church services in VR exclusively, Jay Kranda, who has served as the first full-time Online Campus Pastor at Saddleback Church since 2012, affirmed that VR churches are a plausible and biblical expression of the church. But he added: "I still hold to a view where I don't want to make the exception normative."[12] Kranda said that the problem of building community in VR is not unlike the problem of building community in mega-churches. The purpose of a megachurch is "not so you can slip in and out and not be known," Kranda urged, but so that one can find real community. But Kranda also expressed concern about catering to the convenience of church attenders: "There are unintended consequences, and I think we should be honest about those." For Kranda, VR church is real church, but virtual churches belong in association with in-person churches: "I want to be an advocate that face-to-face community is probably the best expression [of church]. . . . I ultimately want people who are part of my community to know that that is the expression [of church] that I am living out."

Kranda is acutely aware of the fact that virtual technologies allow the church to extend its ministries to those who would otherwise not have a source of Christian encouragement and spiritual nourishment. If someone cannot go to church "because of sickness, security, season of life, I think God honors that," Kranda explained. "Let's just say physical [church attendance] is the best, and let's lean into that."[13] Kranda points to the story of the thief on the cross (Luke 23:39–43). Jesus assured the thief that he would be with Him in paradise that very day. The thief's faith was sufficient, Kranda explained, but this does not mean that we should conclude that we should seek to emulate the thief's minimum expression of faith.

Virtual participation in church services and Christian com-munity can be real participation, but this does not mean that we should aim for our participation in church life to be solely virtual, never meeting in-person with other Christians for the purposes of fellowship and discipleship.[14] Nona Jones, leader of Global Faith-Based Partnerships at Facebook, can write: "I think we can all agree that in-person, face-to-face, eyeball-to-eyeball ministry is essential. Some have suggested that the format for ministry is an either/or proposition, but I believe it's a both/and opportunity."[15] As members of the church, Christians are called "to stir up one another to love and good works" (Heb. 10:24). Such a calling can be fulfilled only in a diminished form in exclusively virtual relationships.

Is Christ Spiritually Present in a Virtual Eucharist?

The Bible presents the church to us as individual congregations as well as the universal body of Christ. God is truly present with His people, whether they assemble by the thousands in cathedrals or whether they gather in twos and threes online. There is no sanctuary so grand that it can accommodate the universal church, which is the entire company of the redeemed across all ages, and there is no meeting space so lowly that Jesus does not promise to be in the midst of those who gather in His name, even when they number only two or three (see Matt. 18:20). But does this mean that there are no clear boundary lines demarcating one local church from another?

In the majority of Christian traditions, the identity of the local congregation as a legitimate expression of the universal church is tied to the administration of the sacraments of baptism and communion. In order to perform the sacraments of baptism and communion validly, most Christian traditions require that the minister of the congregation be ordained, and this establishes a relationship between the local congregation and some form of ecclesiastical authority. If a particular congregation can welcome new members and assure the good standing of its current members (and these functions are the practical significance of the rites of baptism and communion), then many Christians are content to conclude that this congregation represents a legitimate expression of the universal church.

Questions about whether and how Christians who are assembled in VR can celebrate the sacraments will almost assuredly be controversial, and yet the controversy these questions elicit will be in many cases indicative of preexisting disagreements. These questions may not bring about new disagreements so much as expose unresolved discord among Christian churches. Mark Howe writes perceptively: "Online church is likely to have trouble pleasing everyone in terms of the sacraments, but this is hardly an unusual problem in post-Reformation church history."[16] In the immortal words of Billy Joel, VR didn't start the fire! For this reason, we plead with the reader to exercise patience and Christian charity especially when considering the questions in this section.

In the analysis below, we consider whether churches may practice the sacraments (or, "ordinances") of the Eucharist (or, "communion," or, "the Lord's Supper") and baptism in VR. We will consider the administration of these rites from the perspective of many different Christian churches, and therefore to any of our particular Christian readers, the following discussion may seem unspecific or even uncommitted. Please be assured of our commitment to baptism and the Lord's Supper, as we believe these practices are taught in Scripture. Nevertheless, any analysis of sacramental life that does not demonstrate an awareness of a latitude of Christian positions would overlook vital clues concerning the meaning of the sacraments for any Christian tradition.

Despite the bewildering diversity of protocols for the celebration of the Eucharist and baptism in churches around the world, Christians of all traditions look to these rites as expressions of the unity of the church. In the practice of the sacraments, Christians partake of the symbols of Christian unity. We experience in our hearts a longing for Christian unity at the Eucharistic table and the baptismal font. God has given these rites to the church as gifts precisely to point toward the unity that the church will experience in fullness in eternity. Only in a few instances are Christians proud of the fact that they celebrate the sacraments in a way that is unique to their particular tradition. Perhaps Baptists are proud to be the champions of adult baptism by immersion; perhaps Roman Catholics are proud to be the champions of the doctrine of transubstantiation. In the majority of cases, however, Christians are encouraged and strengthened to know that, in practicing communion and baptism by whatever form they may, they are identifying with a tradition that is more ancient and broader than their particular denominational affiliation.

The theological positions concerning the Eucharist can be articulated as four: memorialism, spiritual presence, real presence, and transubstantiation.[17] In fact, even among professional theologians, it is extremely difficult to establish agreement on the precise delineation of these positions. Each of these traditions has unique terminology and metaphors to express their respective positions, but establishing exact boundary lines between these positions and finding common language to express these differences is problematic. Memorialism and transubstantiation are the most obviously distinct positions. In memorialism, the Lord's Supper is all about the act of remembering the Lord's death; nothing mysterious transpires in the bread or in the grape juice. Memorialists focus their interpretation of the Lord's Supper on Jesus' words to His disciples, "Do this in remembrance of me" (Luke 22:19b). In transubstantiation, on the other hand, the substance of the bread and the wine are replaced with the actual body and blood of the Lord. The elements literally become the body and blood of the Lord, and so to witness the Eucharist is to witness a miracle. Those who hold to transubstantiation focus their interpretation on Jesus' words: "This is my body" (Matt. 26:26b; Mark 14:22b; Luke 22:19b).

Sifting through the shades of meaning between the real presence and spiritual presence positions introduces greater challenges. Positions that maintain the real presence of Christ affirm that the actual body and blood of the Lord are present in the Eucharistic elements, but these positions differ from transubstantiation in one way or another in the language used to describe how Christ is present in the bread and in the wine. The doctrine of consubstantiation, for example, affirms that the substance of the bread and the wine are not replaced by the substance of the body and blood of the Lord but are present alongside the body and blood of the Lord. Some Anglican churches subscribe to the doctrine of consubstantiation.

Martin Luther's position is nearly but not quite identical to consubstantiation and is sometimes referred to as "sacramental union." In his own words, Luther explained: "It is the true body and blood of our Lord Jesus Christ under the bread and wine."[18] Lutheran theologians have traditionally expanded this definition and affirmed that Jesus' body and blood are received "in, with, and under" the communion elements.[19] John Calvin, whose view is representative of the spiritual presence position, followed Saint Augustine in defining a sacrament as a "visible sign of an invisible grace."[20] As such, the sacraments seal the antecedent promises of God, and so the sacraments are inseparable from the word of God.[21] Calvin rejected the memorialism of Ulrich Zwingli as well as Martin Luther's teaching on the sacrament. For John Calvin, Christ is spiritually present in the sacrament when it is received in faith.

Drawing up these boundary lines will not accurately describe the way that every Christian celebrates the Eucharist, but identifying these positions is the first step in seeking a way forward. We now pose three questions that we recommend every church reflect through before celebrating the sacraments in VR. We speak predominantly of "VR" in our presentation of these questions, but readers may substitute "virtual telecommunication technology" for any of these references in order to reflect more accurately their present situation.

1. What Constitutes the Assembly of the Church in VR?

For Christians of all traditions, the Eucharist is not a private meal but is to be celebrated only in the context of the assembled church. In his instructions in 1 Corinthians 11:17–34, the apostle Paul uses the verb "to come together" (*sunerchomai*) no fewer than five times, and it is clear that the frame of reference for Paul's teaching on the Lord's Supper is the assembled church. In 1 Corinthians 10:17, Paul writes: "Because there is one loaf, we, who are many, are one body, for we all share the one loaf" (NIV). Paul teaches that the church demonstrates its unity in sharing the bread, and so the celebration of communion is clearly depicted as a corporate act of the church.

In the chaos of the coronavirus crisis, churches began asking questions about whether the sacraments could be administered by virtual telecommunication technology before clear answers had been established concerning what constitutes the assembly of the church in online venues. On March 8, 2020, as the world watched in horror as the numbers of those diagnosed with the coronavirus skyrocketed into the tens of thousands and then hundreds of thousands, the Catholic bishops of Italy announced the suspension of all public celebrations of the Eucharist. And it was not only the Roman Catholic Church. Technology companies across the board were busy trying to figure out how their scheduled conventions could migrate to virtual platforms as well.[22] For the Roman Catholic Church, the decision to suspend the celebration of the Eucharist was monumental, because as the catechism explains, the Eucharist is "the source and summit of the Christian life."[23] To suspend the public gathering of the faithful to partake in the Eucharist was effectively to suspend the spiritual life of the church.

More than theology was at play in the response of the Roman Catholic Church. As a church with its administrative apparatus in Italy—a country that the media had identified as a hotspot for the outbreak of the coronavirus and one with a notably aged population—the Roman Catholic Church was one of the first churches to communicate its standards on whether communion could be practiced via virtual telecommunication technology, and the answer returned in the negative. Catholic churches celebrate the Eucharist every week, and some celebrate the Eucharist every day. Although some Protestant churches also celebrate communion every week, the majority of evangelical churches practice communion less frequently, usually once per month or once per quarter. The question of whether to celebrate the Eucharist via virtual technology was therefore one that required immediate response in Roman Catholic circles, but Protestant churches by and large had other questions at the top of their agendas at the outbreak of the coronavirus crisis.

While some evangelical churches had already established protocols for celebrating communion online—notably including Saddleback Church in California, as early as 2014—the vast majority had not.[24] Spurred on by John Wesley's sermon, "The Duty of Constant Communion," in which Wesley argued that "it is the duty of every Christian to receive the Lord's Supper as often as he can," the Methodist church demonstrated itself to be remarkably progressive on the issue. Even as early as 1938, the Methodist Bishop Garfield Bromley Oxnam had conducted Holy Communion by radio broadcast. This radio broadcast from Omaha, Nebraska, was part of a coordinated effort across fifteen hundred Methodist churches throughout Nebraska and Iowa, whose pastors were not ordained and therefore could not preside over communion according to Methodist protocols. The communion service made national news.[25]

In 2010, the Methodist minister, Tim Ross, announced that he planned to conduct a communion service via Twitter.[26] The service was never conducted, as his church authorities requested that he cancel the service, but his proposal became the centerpiece of deliberations at the denominational level concerning the use of virtual telecommunication technologies in administering the sacraments. In 2013, the Methodist Church determined to suspend the practice of partaking in Holy Communion online until further study could be dedicated to the issue.[27] Early in the unfolding of the coronavirus crisis, the Methodist Church announced its decision to stand with bishops who permitted local ministers to lead Holy Communion services online as well as with bishops who did not permit this practice in the congregations under their supervision.[28]

Some churches issued emergency protocols allowing for communion to be celebrated online, even in cases when this had not been done previously and presumably would not be permitted afterwards. On March 24, 2020, the Presbyterian Church USA issued an advisory notice stating that a congregation may "celebrate the Lord's Supper within an electronic worship service during an emergency or pandemic."[29] There is a Christian tradition of bringing the elements of communion to those who were sick and could not be part of a regular church service, and this tradition dates back at least to the second century.[30] Based on this tradition, some churches permitted the Eucharist to be celebrated via virtual technology as an emergency measure during the coronavirus crisis.

Responses began pinging in from the evangelical blogosphere. On March 25, 2020, the Gospel Coalition website published two articles on the subject, one by Bill Riedel ("Practicing the Ordinances in a Pandemic"), arguing for the affirmative position, and another article by Bobby Jamieson ("Can Baptism and the Lord's Supper Go Online?"), defending the negative position. On March 27, 2020, *Christianity Today* weighed in with an opinion piece by Chris Ridgeway titled, "Online Communion Can Still Be Sacramental." In the article, Ridgeway contends that "human presence is not synonymous to physicality," and concludes: "There is nothing inherently

Gnostic—disembodied—here. Real bodies. Read bread. And the real presence of the Triune God, on Zoom this weekend and joyfully gathered back together in person once this too has passed."[31] Scott Swain responded by reminding his readers that the assembly of the church is prerequisite to the celebration of the Eucharist.[32]

In the early weeks of the coronavirus crisis, churches were forced to respond without extensive consultation even within their own denominational circles. Church leaders found themselves suddenly shut off from in-person contact with their colleagues, and decisions had to be made quickly and in the context of novel self-quarantine measures. In all of this, questions about what constitutes the assembly of the church when convening via virtual telecommunication technology were typically not addressed.

As we contemplate the administration of the sacraments in VR in the future, it will be important for churches to define first what constitutes the assembly of the church for their communities. Can church committees conduct meetings online? What about the annual business meeting? Should Sunday morning Bible classes be offered online? Are the online prayer meetings on Wednesday nights an official service of the church? Is the Sunday morning livestream edition of the church service an emergency protocol to be repealed as soon as assembling in person is legally permissible again or part of the "new normal" of what it means to be the church in the present moment? Different churches will answer these questions differently, but before churches can determine whether they can and should practice the ordinances in VR, they will first need to define what constitutes the assembly of the church.

2. What Is the Church's Liturgical Tradition?

The doctrinal position of a church is only one part of the formula that determines how the sacraments are actually celebrated in a particular congregation. In addition to subscribing to a certain doctrinal position, all churches also bring an array of liturgical traditions to the administration of the rite, and these liturgical traditions are an integral part of the spiritual significance of the sacrament in the life of the community. Does the church use grape juice or wine? Do church members come forward to the front of the church in order to partake of the elements, or are the elements passed from person to person? Does the minister recite a particular phrase when distributing the elements ("the body of Christ, given for you")? If members of the congregation come forward to the front of the church in order to receive the elements, is there an option to kneel? Is there an option to receive prayer? Does one receive the bread as a wafer, cracker, or table bread? What styles of music and singing accompany the Lord's Supper? Who prays prior to the partaking of the elements? Is this prayer scripted or extemporaneous? The answers to all of these questions and countless others represent liturgical tradition and cannot be derived solely from the doctrinal position of the church.

In the majority of cases, it will not be possible for churches to replicate in VR the administration of the sacraments precisely as they are performed in the sanctuary. Liturgical creativity will be required to exposit the meaning of the sacraments in the new context. In fact, this type of creativity is required whenever churches celebrate the sacraments in new contexts, whether this new context is a building that is unfamiliar to the congregation (such as a rented space in a local high school) or a new social situation (such as celebrating the Eucharist at a pilgrim site in Israel while on tour with the congregation). Liturgical creativity has always been required in some measure. The apostle Paul assumed that a single loaf of bread would be used for the celebration of the Lord's Supper (see 1 Cor. 10:17), but the rite can be properly celebrated if two or more loaves are used, for example, when serving a large congregation. When celebrating the Last Supper in the Upper Room, Jesus instructed His disciples to all drink from a common cup (see Matt. 26:27), but it is, of course, permissible for reasons of public health to serve the communion wine or grape juice in individual cups.

Any administration of the sacraments entails creativity in translating the biblical and theological significance of the rite into the particular context. Before celebrating communion in VR, we recommend that churches review carefully the liturgical tradition explicit and implicit in the way that they have historically practiced the sacrament. Only when the priorities of the particular liturgical tradition are clearly articulated will it be possible for this tradition to be faithfully and expediently translated into VR.

3. How Can the Sacraments Be Celebrated as Fully as Possible?

We speak of "celebrating" the Eucharist, but a celebration that minimally commemorates an occasion can hardly be said to be a celebration. When we "celebrate" a friend's birthday or anniversary by liking someone else's Facebook post, it probably appears from the perspective of our friend that we have not celebrated the occasion at all. VR as a medium possesses many strengths which will enable communities to pursue convenience and increased efficiency, but the significance of certain spiritual practices is diminished as the efficiency of its administration increases. We can thank God for the many time-saving devices available to our church offices, but when it comes to the celebration of the sacraments, our aim should not be to practice them as efficiently as possible but as fully as possible. We believe that one way to safeguard the spiritual significance of communion will be to continue to use real bread and real wine or grape juice rather than virtual elements.

Some churches have already begun to respond formally to the question of whether the Eucharist can be celebrated with virtual bread and wine. The Vatican has clarified its position on some of these issues. While the popular understanding of many non-Catholics is that the doctrine of transubstantiation teaches that the bread and wine become the body and blood of the Lord physically, this is not quite correct. The Roman Catholic Church does not appeal to the categories of "physical" and "non-physical" in explaining its position. The Catholic catechism defines transubstantiation as the position that "by the consecration of the bread and wine there takes place a change of the whole substance of the bread into the substance of the body of Christ our Lord and of the whole substance of the wine into the substance of his blood."[33] Here, "substance" refers not to physical substance (that is, the material reality of atomic and subatomic particles) but to the innermost reality of a thing that makes it what it is. While the physical reality (also referred to as the "accidents") of the bread and wine remain unchanged, Christ is so completely present in the consecrated bread and the wine that the elements can properly be identified only as Christ's body and blood.

For transubstantiation to take place, the substance of the bread and wine must be present prior to consecration so that the substance of Christ's body and blood can be exchanged in the element of the Eucharist. Therefore, the doctrine of transubstantiation cannot be upheld in a celebration of communion in which there is no actual bread and wine. The Vatican arrived at this conclusion already in 2002 when it declared: "Virtual reality is no substitute for the Real Presence of Christ in the Eucharist. . . . There are no sacraments on the Internet."[34] From a Roman Catholic point of view, this closes off definitively the possibility that one could validly partake in the Eucharist solely by partaking in virtual bread and wine. The most that could be accomplished in an entirely VR environment without recourse to actual bread and wine would seem to be the practice of "spiritual communion."

When church buildings across Italy were closed during the early weeks of the coronavirus crisis, Pope Francis was among the first church leaders to respond with clarity concerning the question of whether and how to celebrate the Eucharist online. Pope Francis explained that the Eucharist could not be celebrated until churches reopened, but he exhorted the faithful to practice something called "spiritual communion." In explaining this practice, Pope Francis cited Alphonsus Liguori (1696–1787), whose prayer of adoration reads: "Since I cannot at this moment receive you sacramentally, come at least spiritually into my heart."[35] To practice spiritual communion is not to partake in the communion *per se* but is rather the meditative exercise, declared to be spiritually beneficial, in which one longs to participate in the Eucharist. In *He Leadeth Me*, the Polish-American Catholic Priest, Walter Ciszek, describes how the practice of spiritual communion kept him connected to God, even while suffering for two decades in communist prison camps under the most inhumane conditions. Spiritual communion is practiced among Roman Catholics, as well as among some Anglican, Lutheran, and Methodist churches, and the practice of spiritual communion would seem to translate quite well to VR environments.

While the doctrine of transubstantiation will require that actual bread and actual wine be used in the administration of the sacrament, the question remains whether the priest or officiating minister must be within physical proximity to the bread that he consecrates. Although not permitted at the present time, it is conceivable that the Vatican would allow priests to consecrate Eucharistic elements by virtual telecommunication technology in the future. Roman Catholic theologian, Antonio Spadaro, correctly reminds us that the introduction of the microphone altered the liturgical context such that some members of the congregation could no longer hear the minister's voice except by electronic reproduction.[36]

The situation in many Roman Catholic churches which use microphones for audio amplification is therefore already fundamentally not dissimilar from the proposed practice of consecrating actual bread and actual wine in VR. If Roman Catholics were to practice the celebration of the Eucharist in VR at some point in the future, real bread and wine would have to be present, and an ordained priest would have to consecrate the elements. But the doctrine of transubstantiation, with its emphasis on the metaphysical, is notably nonrestrictive concerning the range of physical situations in which it might be validly practiced.

If the doctrine of transubstantiation is the least open to celebrating communion via VR, then the memorialist position is probably the most open. Memorialisism emphasizes that the bread and grape juice are not actually the body and blood of the Lord but are only symbols of His body and blood. As such, memorialism resists notions of consecrating the bread and the grape juice. It seems that there is almost no theological obstacle, from the memorialist position, to practicing the Lord's Supper in VR. The spiritual significance of the Lord's Supper pivots on the communal act of remembering, and commemoration certainly can be transacted to some degree in VR.

Does memorialism require physical bread and wine for the celebration of the Lord's Supper, or could a memorialist position be properly fulfilled when church members partake of virtual bread and grape juice as avatars in a virtual world? What has been said above about the spiritual dangers of pursuing a minimal expression of one's Christian faith could be repeated here. Why would a church that assembles in VR not encourage its members to partake in eating real bread and drinking real grape juice? It is exceedingly difficult to imagine a scenario in which it would be unreasonable to ask members of a church to procure the elements of bread and wine (or saltine crackers and grape juice) for the purposes of communion.

While there is no obvious theological principle in memorialism that prohibits churches from practicing the Lord's Supper in VR without recourse to actual bread and wine, it seems that doing so would minimize and therefore misconstrue the spiritual significance of the rite. We could also argue that physical bread and grape juice are aids to memory. Sense experience aids in the formation of memories, and so using actual bread and wine in a communion service would certainly imprint a fuller memory on participants than simply looking at virtual bread and wine. But we should note that there is probably nothing in the theology of the memorialist position itself that, once and for all, closes the door to partaking of the Lord's Supper in VR without recourse to actual bread and wine. We should also note that, in the discussion above, we have considered "actual" and "virtual" as mutually exclusive categories, although it is possible that someday the technology would exist whereby one could ingest bread that is simultaneously actual and virtual—that is, bread that is both real as well as represented graphically in the VR environment. However, until such time as eating and drinking in VR is a common and culturally understood experience, practicing communion in VR without actual bread and wine is likely to be a spiritually confusing proposal rather than an edifying expression of the unity of the Christian church.[37]

What about Immersion by Immersive Media?

The same three questions that we have recommended above for churches contemplating the celebration of the Eucharist in VR can also serve as guideposts for discussions about VR baptisms. As with communion, baptisms are not to be performed as private ceremonies but rather are to be conducted in the assembly of the church.

According to some definitions, virtual baptisms have been performed in the Christian church for some time. In countries where religious liberty is restricted, it is not uncommon for ministers to baptize converts in the bathtubs of obliging church members. Because only a small percentage of the congregation can fit into the bathroom to witness this baptism, the service is recorded or broadcast live for the rest of the community to witness. Reports are that churches in the Middle East and in other areas where there is persecution have conducted baptisms in this fashion for some time.[38]

There are real differences in the practical administration of communion and baptism that require parsing out. In the case of the Eucharist, some churches anticipate participants to be far more active than others. In some churches, people receiving the bread and the wine are expected to come forward and perhaps even kneel at the altar rail, whereas, in other churches, the congregation remains seated and passes the elements one to another. In the case of baptism, the person being baptized is basically passive in all Christian traditions. Regardless of the mode of baptism (whether adult baptism or infant baptism, whether baptism by immersion or sprinkling), the person being baptized is intended to be in a passive role, and this passivity is not incidental but gives expression to the biblical imagery that the new Christian is brought from death into life.

This also means that the minister has an active role to play and, in the case of adult baptism by immersion, it is not uncommon to witness the minister evidence physical strain in performing the rite. Because only the minister and the person being baptized are directly involved in the performance of the ritual, baptism is fairly easy to conceptualize as part of a recorded or broadcasted church service. The theatrical elements of the performance of baptism are theologically significant symbols and can translate well to the format of a livestreamed church service.

If the Eucharist would be disfigured by partaking in the rite without actual bread and water, then so, too, baptism would be deformed in rites that did not use actual water. Is it possible that the technology would someday exist which would allow for the administration of baptisms that are simultaneously actual and virtual? From the way that we experience VR today, it would seem that this is pure science fiction. The technical difficulties in creating VR equipment that delivers credible simulations of sensory experience even while submersed in real water seem insurmountable. Still more problematic are questions of how and why churches that practice infant baptism would apply VR to the administration of the rite.

The wide variety in the theology and liturgical tradition of churches in regard to the sacraments means that, invariably, different churches will begin applying virtual telecommunication technology to the practice of the sacraments at different paces and to greater or lesser extents. Invariably Christians from one tradition will find fault with Christians of other traditions whose practice of the sacraments seems misshapen or lacking in reverence or power from the other's perspective. This would be, in fact, to describe a situation that already exists in the church, and the advent of VR and the possibility of administering communion and baptism by a variety of virtual telecommunication technologies will require more, not less, Christian charity.

Conclusion

The church has been called many things through the centuries but, so far as we are aware, it has never been given the very appropriate title of "undisruptable." *Ecclesia triumphans* ("the church triumphant"), *Ecclesia poenitens* ("the church penitent"), or *Ecclesia militans* ("the church militant") are all titles that have been used to describe the church in various eras of church history. *Ecclesia semper reformanda* ("the church ever being reformed") is a title that theologians have used in recent decades to describe the life of the church. We propose a new title for the church— "the Church Undisruptable." The church will not finally be disrupted or replaced by technology. The church may struggle to learn how to use new technology effectively, but the church will not be conquered or defeated by technology.

Harvard Business School professor Clay Christenson has made a career of speaking of disruptive innovation. Disruptive innovation arises when a new product—which at first cannot compete with the established market, either because its price is too high or because its performance is too low—finally is improved to the point that it poses real competition. The automobile, for example, at first posed no threat to sales for horse-drawn carriages, because automobiles were fiercely expensive and unreliable. However, as the price of automobiles dropped and as their performance improved, there came a "disruption" or a tipping point in the market when people rapidly adopted the new model of transportation. Are we at a tipping point when virtual technologies are finally becoming inexpensive enough and convenient enough that our whole model of church may shift?

Church models come and go; certainly our pastors know this best. But the church itself cannot be disrupted. Medical schools are some of the places where virtual reality is being used first for education. At the time of the writing of this book, the medical community is proving itself to be a leader in applying VR and AR to learning. It is now possible for doctors to perform surgeries remotely, virtually controlling robots that perform the surgery on patients many miles away. But there is no outcry; no one is anxiously claiming that, if hospitals adopt virtual reality, people will abandon the medical system.

There may be challenges in reconfiguring our hospitals for optimal use in a world where VR is a common communication option, but no one fears that people will finally no longer need medicine simply because we have VR headsets. Why? People will still have bodies, which will still need physical care. We can draw an analogy here to the church. In the same way, even if VR becomes commonplace, people will still have souls and will still need spiritual care. Churches should be no more concerned than hospitals that VR will render them obsolete. The adoption of VR in the medical school will not make the medical industry obsolete because people have real bodies, and the adoption of VR will not make the church obsolete because people will still have real souls. The church is undisruptable, because Jesus has promised to fulfill His purposes of redemption in and through the church.

Bob Pierce, the president of World Vision, could see as early as 1966 that computers would play a leading role in advancing the mission of the church.[39] "Is it too much to believe," Pierce asked provocatively, "that the tools now being used to put man on the moon could have their ultimate purpose in bringing the gospel to every creature?"[40] Jesus promised us: "I will build my church, and the gates of hell shall not prevail against it" (Matt. 16:18b ESV). Virtual reality is not the one cultural phenomenon that Jesus failed to account for. The one who created the universe will supply His church with sufficient creativity and guidance to figure out how to use the emerging technology of VR for His kingdom purposes. And Jesus adds to this His promise—no less to be treasured in our day than in previous generations of pioneers—"And behold, I am with you always, to the end of the age" (Matt. 28:20b ESV).

EPILOGUE

I (Jonathan) attended only one Billy Graham crusade in my life, and it happened to be the very last day of Billy Graham's very last crusade—June 26, 2005, at Flushing Meadows–Corona Park in New York City. As I anticipated attending the crusade, I had in the back of my mind the conversion story of my father, who placed his faith in Christ while watching a live television broadcast of one of Billy Graham's crusades. As the broadcast drew to a close, Graham called forward to the stage in the arena where he was preaching all who had decided to follow Christ, and Graham also directed an invitation to those who were watching via television. While in front of his bedroom television set in the tiny town of Dafter, Michigan, my father surrendered his life to Christ one night in the spring of 1967.

In the months leading up to what proved to be Graham's last crusade in 2005, giant billboards across New York City announced the evangelist's arrival. I was excited to witness Graham's preaching in person. I lived in the Bronx at the time as a PhD student in theology at Fordham University, and so I was a local attendee, traveling only some twenty miles to the crusade. Although a relatively straightforward journey, it nonetheless required a series of subway rides, first on the orange "D" train from the Bronx to downtown Manhattan near Times Square, and then on to Flushing Meadows–Corona Park in Queens via the purple "7" train. This was a two-hour, one-way commute in any case. Attendees from out of town or out of state had to make substantially deeper sacrifices in order to attend the Graham crusade live.

Once I had arrived at Flushing Meadows–Corona Park (an outdoor venue of nearly nine hundred acres that had proudly hosted the 1964 New York World's Fair), I exited the sweltering subway train and commenced the march alongside the endless sea of other visitors who were in search of seating. I was determined to sit as close as possible to the famed evangelist, but what I quickly discovered as I walked from the subway station to the event grounds was that there was not a single seating area but many seating areas set up all over the park, each equipped to present a video relay of the program. It seemed that I was trapped in some sort of hall of mirrors, searching for the real Billy Graham among the electronic copies of his voice and image all around me. I finally succeeded in locating the mainstage and in securing a seat that had providentially opened up at the very back of the venue, many hundreds of feet away from the front but in line of sight with Billy Graham. Incredibly, George Beverly Shea stood up at ninety-six years of age and sang—with detectibly quivering yet ever majestic voice—"How Great Thou Art."

When Billy Graham gave the altar call after his sermon on Noah and the flood, I felt compelled to come forward. I had been a believer for almost all of my life at that time, but something urged me irresistibly to come as close as I could to the man whom God had touched to reshape history in the twentieth century. A swell of humanity came forward, like a wave washing up on the ocean shore. In an era before smartphones, everyone had their cameras raised high in the air, and I heard the perpetual snapping of hundreds of pictures simultaneously. Graham commented that he hoped that people had come forward not to get close to him but to meet with God. God was surely at work among those who had come forward that day, but viewing the crusade from the quietness of one's bedroom might have been a more likely place to hear God's voice.

There is an axiom that futurists are farsighted concerning the speed of change but shortsighted concerning the depth of change. That is, we tend to expect that change will happen faster than it actually does, and at the same time we tend to fail to appreciate fully how these changes will affect us once they arrive. In my brief career as a futurist, I can see that this principle has proven true in the case of my understanding of how the advent of VR will affect churches. On the one hand, if you had asked me a few years ago what VR would be like in 2021, I would have predicted that the technology would have advanced further than it actually has. I would have said that the resolution of the VR headsets would be higher, that the processing power of these devices would be greater, and that far more people would have adopted VR by 2021. On the other hand, not in my most imaginative moments would I have predicted that, by Easter of 2020, nearly every church on the planet would have considered conducting at least one virtual church service.

Maybe in another twenty years we will have seen less change than we might think. Maybe in twenty years people will still be able to buy an iMac computer. Maybe by then the jury will have returned on augmented reality, only to announce that no one actually wants holograms interlaced constantly into their vision of the real world through their glasses or contact lenses. Maybe in twenty years virtual assistants like Siri and Alexa will still be basically annoying. But I think Simon Jenkins, the founder of the Church of Fools, probably had some very wise words to say when he commented that we can expect wartime advancement in virtual communication technology in the years ahead.[1]

Just as World War I ushered in the radio as a household device, so the coronavirus crisis is likely to significantly advance VR development and adoption. The church has always pursued the mission to communicate the unchanging message of God's love and redemption to a constantly changing world. The task at hand is to present Christ to a generation that not only has never known a world without the internet or a world without smartphones and social media but now to a generation whose memories of VR will be almost as old as their earliest memories from the real world. The church today is called to disciple a rising wave of new Christians whose relationship with Jesus began not when they came to the front of a church building but when they clicked on an internet ad that promised them hope and led them to a gospel-proclaiming website.

We sometimes speak of "digital natives" and "digital immigrants," referring to the generation whose formative years were prior to the rise of digital technology and the generation who were already adults when digital technology arrived. The analogy resonates with us in some circumstances, but it can also be misleading. The analogy sets up the expectation that one can settle down with a technology or learn to call technology home. But just about the time that we have grown comfortable with one technology, we discover that it has already been discontinued by the manufacturer. This is partly due to the aggressive marketing of the tech companies, but it is also partly due to the nature of technology itself. Technology will continue to change at a rapid pace in the years ahead, maybe for the better, but we can be sure that it will change. When speaking about the future, Kevin Kelly, founder of *Wired,* averred: "All of us—every one of us—will be endless newbies in the future simply trying to keep up. . . . Endless Newbie is the new default for everyone, no matter your age or experience."[2] In the epoch unfolding before us, the church needs to develop a theology of innovation, learning to learn in what sometimes feels like a technology supernova.

In the fall semester of 2014, I (Jonathan) served as the professor of record for an experimental class offered at Moody Bible Institute's branch campus in Spokane, Washington. I teach a class on Global Theology which would host live presentations and panel discussions with professors from all over the world. Google Hangouts had been released in the spring of 2013, and this was the first free internet broadcasting platform of which we became aware. Google Hangouts facilitated video conference calling for up to eight people at a time, or at least, this was the theoretical capacity. In our experience, the quality of the call deteriorated to a level where actual communication became difficult after about the fourth or fifth caller joined. Beginning in the fall of 2013, I worked alongside a small team of students to line up an all-star cast of professors and panelists. By the close of the semester in the fall of 2014, fifty-six professors from sixteen different countries had participated in the course as either lecturers or panelists, all assembled in real time via virtual technology. To us it felt like a miracle.

In fact, we had confirmed arrangements with over eighty professors to speak at one point or another during the class, but about three in ten were not able to join the broadcast on the day of the class, usually due to internet failure on their end. Some were not able to join the broadcast because of the complexity that joining an internet broadcast entailed at that time. In order to guide presenters and panelists through the process of joining the conference call, four students operated phone lines during the class broadcast and provided step-by-step instructions. Even with knowledgeable students providing technical assistance by telephone, not a few professors gave up in despair after about an hour of attempting to connect to the class broadcast.

Looking back from the perspective of 2020, when it is commonplace for classes of sometimes hundreds of students to join together via Zoom, it is stunning to think of how far the technology of conference calling has advanced in the span of a few years. One of the professors whose travel schedule did not permit him to join us live in the fall of 2014 but who agreed to allow us to prerecord his lecture was Darrell Bock. We prerecorded Darrell's lecture in the summer prior to the launch of the class, and it became clear to me that the technology then emerging would forever change education.

On the first morning of this experimental Global Theology class, the technology melted down almost completely. Some of our technical team had started working at two o'clock that morning in order to ensure smooth operation, and everything had been in place. But as we fired up the systems and the presenters began to come online from all corners of the globe, internet speeds proved too slow to make any sort of reasonable communication possible. Suddenly I was struck with a sense of dread—if internet speeds were insufficient to make our teleconferencing model of class possible, then our project would inevitably fail. In the testing that we had conducted prior to the launch of the class, Google Hangouts had performed up to the benchmarks that we required, but our testing had been done on relatively new computers with high-speed internet connections, and not all of our speakers from all parts of the world had access to up-to-date technology.

As I stood on the podium in front of the class, looking back at the quizzical expressions of the students, I realized that the experiment might completely fail. Just then, one of the twenty-three students enrolled in the course, James Robinson, came up on the stage with me and put his hand on my shoulder and started praying. I didn't resist. I knew we needed prayer in that moment. It was no more than a few seconds after James started praying that the screens flickered on, internet connections restored, and our technical team excitedly announced that we were "on" again. "Praise the Lord," James said, taking his seat.

In the months and years ahead, James introduced me to the faith community whom I am convinced will lead in the application of emerging technology for the purposes of Christian ministry—global prayer networks. In January of 2020, at the GO2020 conference in Orlando, I had the opportunity to meet in person with John Robb and ask him about his views on the application of virtual technologies for the purposes of prayer. Robb had been instrumental in convening the World Prayer Assembly in Jakarta, Indonesia, in May of 2012, an event that drew over one hundred thousand people to the national stadium for a prayer service. The prayer service was relayed by simulcast to 378 cities throughout Indonesia, with an estimated reach of over two million people. Robb was a leader who knew well that technology could serve to further the spiritual work of prayer networks. But now Robb and a network of other Christian leaders associated with GO2020 were envisioning something far larger. Founded by German evangelist, Werner Nachtigal, the stated ambition of GO2020 is to mobilize five hundred million Christians to pray for one hundred million Christians to share the gospel with one billion people on planet Earth. Nachtigal had lined up stadium events across the world as part of this initiative.

And then the coronavirus crisis began to break in ominous news stories. By March of 2020, it was clear that conducting evangelistic events in stadiums was totally out of the question. What could be done in order to continue pursuing the Great Commission? Global prayer calls within the GO2020 network and everywhere started popping up like mushrooms. The GO2020 network announced that it would conduct its first prayer call on May 1, 2020. This prayer call was to be facilitated by Zoom and then broadcast live to YouTube, translated simultaneously into 26 languages. The morning of the prayer call was one of the first beautiful spring days after several days of rain in Chicago.

The rising sun made the drops of water on the tips of the new, spring grass glisten. I planned to join the prayer call from my noise-canceling headphones while walking the neighborhood. I pushed a few buttons on my iPhone, and I started receiving a stream of clear sound. While I walked up and down my neighborhood in the suburbs of Chicago, prayer leaders from around the world began leading this massive but invisible assembly in prayer. After weeks of not being able to attend regular church services, it was an incredibly joyful experience to be united with other Christians in this way. John Robb came on the call and proclaimed: "Isn't it awesome, that with this technology, we are here in the presence of the Lord of eternity? He is on the call with us, as He promised! He said: 'Even where two or three gather, I am there with you.' And He is here on the call. He is online with us!" There were over 650,000 people watching the call live that morning, several times more people than could have assembled even in the largest stadiums in the world.[3]

I returned to my home later that morning, refreshed by the awareness that God was working in new ways despite the tragedy of the coronavirus crisis. As I set aside my headphones and prepared to sit down with my family for a hot, oatmeal breakfast, I said to my three little girls: "God is doing something new! While I was taking a walk around our neighborhood, I was praying with people from all over the world! There were people from Egypt and Canada and India! There were musicians playing worship songs from Tennessee. They were playing from their living room in Tennessee, but I was singing with them in my heart here in Chicago. Isn't that weird?" My eight-year old daughter looked at me, head half-cocked. At first, I thought her curious expression concerned the technological marvel that I had newly become convinced would reshape the practice of Christianity within a generation. Then I realized that her difficulty in understanding had not been to grasp the technological possibility that I described but the reason why I should be amazed in the first place. "No," she responded, "it's not that weird."

As I have pondered the changes now underway and gone back to the drawing board countless times to start all over again with a new idea on what VR churches could look like in the future, one image has come to me again and again: the aircraft carrier. I have never stepped foot on an operational aircraft carrier, but I know that an aircraft carrier exists to keep a fleet of fighter planes aloft and ready for action. The USS Gerald R. Ford can carry about 75 aircraft, and the Navy's F18 fighter fleet has a flight range of about 1,500 miles. But for aircraft that can fly at top-speeds of almost 1,200 mph, this means that the fighter fleet is never more than a few minutes' flight time from the mothership.

What would happen if a new kind of fuel were discovered that allowed these aircraft to stay aloft not for an hour or two but for a couple of days at a time? Entirely different responsibilities could be assigned to individual aircraft, and the relationship between carriers would change as well, as aircraft might relate to two or more carriers in running a particular mission. This would require a complete overhaul of the Navy's strategy for aircraft carriers. I believe this is what is happening to our churches in the age of virtual reality. Our churches are the aircraft carriers, and our ministry teams are the aircraft, and the emerging technology of VR is the new kind of fuel that is allowing people to extend relationships vastly further than previous social structures have known. People are still going to need dedicated church buildings for certain purposes, but the way that these on-the-ground churches equip and supply ministry teams, and the way that these churches relate to one another, is about to change.

ACKNOWLEDGMENTS

As one who has hosted a podcast for years and has seen technology make a ministry more accessible and efficient, I (Darrell) appreciate all that digital technology can accomplish through getting the Word out, discussing issues, and engaging people with ideas. None of that happens without competent IT and media specialists who handle cables and connections with skill, putting out fires as they go. The recent coronavirus crisis has only reinforced their value. In a way, this book is a tribute to their long hours of labor, often unseen and often accompanied by a panicked emergency call or a need to plan for what lies ahead. My heartfelt thanks come with deep appreciation for their faithful work. Much of what I have written in this book is a direct result of their contribution to my own work and ministry. So, I thank the IT and media departments at Dallas Theological Seminary for making my experience on campus and with the Table podcasts such a joy. I name a few who have been most helpful in one way or another: John Dyer, Ryan Holmes, Jayme Hightower, Jonathan Galloway, Elijah Misigaro, Jim Hoover, Samira Khalid, and Dave Largent, but there are entire teams whose help has been immense.

Thank you also goes to the staff at the Hendricks Center, including Table podcast co-hosts, Bill Hendricks, Kymberli Cook, Mikel Del Rosario, and other present or past core team members, including Pam Cole, Amanda Stidham and Amy Leigh Bamberg. The administration at Dallas Theological Seminary also has been so supportive of our efforts to extend the reach of the school through technological means. Appreciation here goes to Mark Bailey and Mark Yarbrough for the partnership of reaching out with the hope that is so central to our shared faith and mission. I wish to thank Jonathan J. Armstrong for the invitation to join this project that really was his brainchild and who did most of the work. Finally, my wife, Sally, also needs acknowledgment for having to cope with constant book writing, podcasting, and Zoom work that takes me out of the loop, leaving her to pick up the pieces left undone.

For me (Jonathan), the beginnings of this book project trace back to the Global Proclamation Congress, convened by Ramesh Richard in Bangkok, Thailand, in the summer of 2016. This congress assembled some 2,500 pastoral trainers from 101 countries. From the conversations in Bangkok and from the online dialogues following the congress, several of which were chaired by Darrell Bock, I and the administration at Moody Bible Institute became aware in a new way of the demand for pastoral training for Christian leaders worldwide. The majority of my work in researching VR for educational purposes has been done in response to the challenges outlined at this global congress.

I would like to thank my students who extended to me patience and openness as I experimented with VR in the classroom. I would like to thank especially the students who served as assistants in the VR Lab at Moody Bible Institute from 2016–2020: Alden Wright, Chase Baxter, Sean Pierce, Isaac Iverson, and Jordan Calendar. Without their expertise and willingness to learn a never-ending stream of new platforms and processes, none of our technical work would have been possible. I would like to express appreciation to Bryan O'Neal, who championed this project at Moody and created the necessary latitude for me to engage in genuine exploration. Fr. Timothy Clancy, S. J., graciously invited me to present on VR applications for Christian ministry at "Seeking the Sacred in the Digital Age," a conference he convened at Gonzaga University in the spring of 2019. I owe a debt of gratitude to legendary game designer, Rand Miller, whose *Myst* and *Riven* enlivened my adolescence and whose accessibility and sage musings provided immense encouragement along the way. My fellow traveler in the pilgrimage of serving in Christian education, Bryan M. Litfin, pointed me faithfully to the trinitarian God, whose nature is unchanging even while all else around us changes. I could always count on Dan Churchwell to help me separate reality from nonreality, virtual, or otherwise. Thank you, Dan, for being my Morpheus—keep giving me the red pill! I owe my deepest thanks to the love of my life, Gerlinde, without whose shared life experiences and endless support, I would never have been able to ask the questions in this book, let alone make any real progress in discovering answers.

NOTES

Chapter 1: New Media and the Good News

1. *The Journal of John Wesley*, ed., Percy Livingstone Parker (Chicago: Moody Press, 1951), 74 (June 11, 1739).

2. Billy Graham, *Just as I Am: The Autobiography of Billy Graham* (Grand Rapids: Zondervan, 1997), 97.

3. Ibid., 210.

4. Grant Wacker, *America's Pastor: Billy Graham and the Shaping of a Nation* (Cambridge, MA: The Belknap Press of Harvard University Press, 2014), 20.

5. Idem., "The Legacy of Billy Graham," *First Things* (February 22, 2018), https://www.firstthings.com/web-exclusives/2018/02/the-legacy-of-billy-graham.

6. Walter P. Wilson, *The Internet Church: The Local Church Can't Be Just Local Any More* (Nashville: Word Publishing, 2000), xi.

7. Interview with Jeff Gowler (CEO of Global Media Outreach), conducted by Jonathan J. Armstrong on April 22, 2020.

8. "The Bible App," *YouVersion*, https://www.youversion.com/the-bible-app/.

9. "The Bible App for Kids," *YouVersion*, https://www.youversion.com/the-bible-app-for-kids/.

10. Interview with Sean Dunn (Founder and President of Groundwire), conducted by Jonathan J. Armstrong on April 23, 2020.

11. Interview with Ken Cochrum (Vice President of Global Digital Strategies at Cru), conducted by Jonathan J. Armstrong on April 21, 2020.

12. Wilson, *The Internet Church*, 13. See also Tom Wheeler, *From Gutenberg to Google: The History of Our Future* (Washington, DC: Brookings Institution Press, 2019), 148–52.

13. Wilson, *The Internet Church*, 13.

14. Tom Goodwin, "The Battle Is for the Customer Interface," TechCrunch, March 3, 2015, https://techcrunch.com/2015/03/03/in-the-age-of-disintermediation-the-battle-is-all-for-the-customer-interface/.

15. Stephen D. O'Leary, "Cyberspace as Sacred Space: Communicating Religion on Computer Networks," *Journal of the American Academy of Religion* 64 (1996): 787.

16. For example, Klaus Schwab writes: "The spindle (the hallmark of the first industrial revolution) took almost 120 years to spread outside of Europe. By contrast, the internet permeated across the globe in less than

a decade" (*The Fourth Industrial Revolution* [New York: World Economic Forum, 2016], 8).

17. "World Internet Users and 2020 Population Stats," Internet World Stats: Usage and Population Statistics, https://internetworldstats.com/stats.htm.

18. See Erik Brynjolfsson and Andrew McAfee, *The Second Machine Age* (New York: W. W. Norton, 2014), 14–20.

19. IBM, "IBM Watson: Final Jeopardy! and the Future of Watson," February 16, 2011, https://www.youtube.com/watch?v=lI-M7O_bRNg.

20. Paul Mozur, "Google's AlphaGo Defeats Chinese Go in Win for A.I." *The New York Times*, May 23, 2017, https://www.nytimes.com/2017/05/23/business/google-deepmind-alphago-go-champion-defeat.html.

21. Christof Koch, "How the Computer Beat the Go Master," *Scientific American*, March 19, 2016, https://www.scientificamerican.com/article/how-the-computer-beat-the-go-master/.

22. "Now comes the second machine age. Computers and other digital advances are doing for mental power—the ability to use our brains to understand and shape our environments—what the steam engine and its descendants did for muscle power" (Brynjolfsson and McAfee, *The Second Machine Age*, 7–8).

23. Schwab writes, "The premise of this book is that technology and digitization will revolutionize everything, making the overused and often ill-used adage, 'this time is different' apt. Simply put, major technological innovations are on the brink of fueling momentous change throughout the world—inevitably so" (*The Fourth Industrial Revolution*, 9).

24. See Thomas L. Friedman, *Thank You for Being Late: An Optimist's Guide to Thriving in the Age of Accelerations* (New York: Farrar, Straus and Giroux, 2016), 93–95.

25. Ibid., 44–52. See also Wheeler, *From Gutenberg to Google*, 187–88.

26. Jack Dongarra and Piotr Luszczek, "Anatomy of a Globally Recursive Embedded LINPACK Benchmark," paper presented in September 2012 at the IEEE Conference on High Performance Extreme Computing. Brynjolfsson and McAfee also note that the ACSI Red, which was the world's fastest supercomputer in 1996, achieved a top speed of 1.8 teraflops, which is the same peak performance benchmark as Sony's PlayStation 3, which was released in 2006 (*The Second Machine Age*, 49–50).

27. James Vincent, "The World's Fastest Supercomputer Will Be Built by AMD and Cray for US Government," The Verge, May 7, 2019, https://www.theverge.com/2019/5/7/18535078/worlds-fastest-exascale-supercomputer-frontier-amd-cray-doe-oak-ridge-national-laboratory.

28. Jeremy Bailenson, *Experience on Demand: What Virtual Reality Is, How It Works, and What It Can Do* (New York: W. W. Norton, 2018), 174.

29. Joel Stein, "The Surprising Joy of Virtual Reality: And Why It's about to Change the World," *Time*, August 17, 2015, https://time.com/3987059/

in-the-latest-issue-41/. Stein can summarize: "Virtual reality has been promised for decades, but . . . never before have so much money and talent bet on its imminent arrival."

30. Jeremy Hsu, "Virtual Reality Pioneer Looks beyond Entertainment," *Spectrum*, April 30, 2015, https://spectrum.ieee.org/tech-talk/consumer-electronics/portable-devices/virtual-reality-pioneer-looks-beyond-entertainment.

31. See Jaron Lanier, *The Dawn of the New Everything: Encounters with Reality and Virtual Reality* (New York: Henry Holt, 2017).

32. Katelyn Beaty, "Geek Theologian," *Christianity Today*, July 15, 2011, https://www.christianitytoday.com/ct/2011/julyweb-only/geektheologian.html.

33. Kelly continues: "At its most fundamental level this machine copies every action, every character, every thought we make while we ride upon it" (*The Inevitable: Understanding the 12 Technological Forces That Will Shape Our Future* [New York: Viking, 2016], 61).

34. Caitlin Dewey, "If You Could Print Out the Whole Internet, How Many Pages Would It Be?" *The Washington Post* (May 28, 2015), https://www.washingtonpost.com/news/the-intersect/wp/2015/05/18/if-you-could-print-out-the-whole-internet-how-many-pages-would-it-be/.

35. Interview with Heidi Campbell (Professor of Communication at Texas A&M University), conducted by Jonathan J. Armstrong on December 11, 2018. See also Heidi A. Campbell and Stephen Garner, "New Media Theory 101: Understanding New Media and the Network Society," in *Networked Theology: Negotiating Faith in Digital Culture* (Grand Rapids: Baker Academic, 2016), 39–59. In a statement titled, "The Church Must Learn to Cope with the Computer Culture," which he delivered in connection with World Communications Day on May 27, 1989, Pope John Paul II noted: "Today, for example, one no longer thinks or speaks of social communications as mere instruments or technologies. Rather they are now seen as part of a still unfolding culture whose full implications are as yet imperfectly understood and whose potentialities remain for the moment only partially exploited."

36. McLuhan refined and furthered his thinking in these matters in his 1964 book, *Understanding Media: The Extensions of Man*.

37. "The Future of Man in the Electric Age," https://web.archive.org/web/20200129141024/http://www.marshallmcluhanspeaks.com/interview/1965-the-future-of-man-in-the-electric-age/.

38. In a 1966 interview with Robert Fulford broadcast on the Canadian Broadcasting Corporation, McLuhan states, "Instead of going out to buy a book that has had five thousand copies printed, you will go to the telephone and describe your interests, your needs and your problems. You might say that you are working on a history of Egyptian arithmetic. You know a bit of Sanscrit. You are qualified in German and you are a good mathematician. In reply you will be told that what you need will

be right over. Then, with the help of computers from the libraries of the world, all the latest material is xeroxed just for you personally—not as something to be put out on a bookshelf. Instead, the package is sent to you as a direct personal service. This is where we are heading under electronic information conditions. Products are increasingly becoming services," "Predicting Interactive Communication via the Internet," Marshall McLuhan Speaks Special Collection, 1966 (https://web .archive.org/web/20201106035001/http://www.marshallmcluhanspeaks .com/prophecies/1966-communication-via-the-internet/index.html).

39. "The global village is not created by the motorcar or even by the airplane; it is created by instant electronic information movement," "This Is Marshall McLuhan: The Medium Is the Message," Marshall McLuhan Speaks Special Collection, 1967 (https://web.archive.org/ web/20200116125911/http://www.marshallmcluhanspeaks.com/ sayings/1967-global-village/index.html).

40. Neil Postman, *Technopoly: The Surrender of Culture to Technology* (New York: Vintage, 1992), 18.

41. "Neil Postman Talk in LA 1993/7/28 (VRI-0131)," YouTube, April 19, 2016, https://www.youtube.com/watch?v=QqxgCoHv_aE&t=5707s.

42. Wheeler, *From Gutenberg to Google*, 41.

43. Plato, *Euthyphro, Apology, Crito, Phaedo, Phaedrus*, trans. Harold North Fowler, in *Loeb Classical Library*, 36 (Cambridge: Harvard University Press, 1914), 563. See also Neil Postman, *Technopoly*, 3–4.

44. "Barth in Retirement," *Time* (Friday, May 31, 1963), 63.

45. In 1975, Pope Paul VI declared in the encyclical *Evangelii Nuntiandi* ("On the New Evangelization"): "Our century is characterized by the mass media or means of social communication. . . . When they are put at the service of the Gospel, they are capable of increasing almost indefinitely the area in which the Word of God is heard; they enable the Good News to reach millions of people. The Church would feel guilty before the Lord if she did not utilize these powerful means that human skill is daily rendering more perfect. It is through them that she proclaims 'from the housetops' the message of which she is the depositary. In them she finds a modern and effective version of the pulpit. Thanks to them she succeeds in speaking to the multitudes" ("Evangelii Nuntiandi: Apostolic Exhortation of His Holiness Pope Paul VI," December 8, 1975, http://www.vatican.va/content/paul-vi/en/apost_exhortations/ documents/hf_p-vi_exh_19751208_evangelii-nuntiandi.html).

46. For information on those who have never heard the gospel, see https:// joshuaproject.net/people_groups/statistics.

47. Ash Turner, "How Many Smartphones Are in the World?," BankMyCell, https://www.bankmycell.com/blog/how-many-phones-are-in-the-world.

48. Some of these predictions simply misidentified the operating principles of future technology ("Have you ever renewed your driver's license at a cash machine?" or "[Have you ever] carried your medical history in your

wallet?"). Some of these commercials predicted inventions that are still in development and that are not sufficiently reliable to be serviceable as consumer products in 2020 ("Have you ever opened doors with the sound of your voice?" or "[Have you ever] conducted business in a language you don't understand?"). And some of these commercials were correct in part of their prediction but incorrectly framed how the technology would actually be applied (the commercials correctly anticipated video calling but presumed that video calling would be conducted from phone booths). "AT&T 'You Will' Commercials (High Quality)," YouTube, April 22, 2016, https://www.youtube.com/watch?v=a2EgfkhC1eo.
49. Wilson, *The Internet Church*, 19.

Chapter 2: The Only Constant Is Change

1. "Measures to Promote Revivals," in *Revivals of Religion* (New York: Revell, 1960), 311.
2. Wheeler, *From Gutenberg to Google*, 232.
3. "What a Revival of Religion Is," in *Revivals of Religion* (New York: Revell, 1960), 5.
4. Benjamin B. Warfield, *Perfectionism* (Philadelpia: Presbyterian and Reformed Publishing Company, 1958), 193; quoted in James E. Johnson, "Charles G. Finney and a Theology of Revivalism," *Church History* 38 (1969), 351.
5. "Measures to Promote Revivals," 284.
6. Ibid., 284–85.
7. Ibid., 306.
8. In 1920, only 35 percent of Americans had electricity in their homes. By 1930, this number had increased to 70 percent, leaving only those in rural areas without electricity.
9. Christopher H. Sterling and John Michael Kittross, *Stay Tuned: A History of American Broadcasting*, third edition (Mahwah: Lawrence Erlbaum, 2002), 66.
10. Spencer Miller Jr., "Radio and Religion," *The Annals of the American Academy of Political and Social Science* 177 (1935): 135.
11. Ibid., 135–36.
12. Ibid., 66–67.
13. Quentin J. Schultze, "Evangelical Radio and the Rise of the Electronic Church, 1921–1948," *Journal of Broadcasting and Electronic Media* 32 (1988): 291.
14. Mark Rogers, "End Times Innovator: Paul Rader and Evangelical Missions," *International Bulletin of Missionary Research* 37 (2013): 18.
15. Quoted in Lois Neely, *Come Up to This Mountain: The Miracle of Clarence W. Jones and HCJB* (Wheaton, IL: Tyndale House, 1980), 80.
16. Ralph L. Power, "Angelus Temple Is Unique Among Broadcasters," *Radio in the Home* (January 1925): 44. In the days when religious broadcasting was new and Aimee was a starlet celebrity, Power writes: "This,

friends, is the story of a radio station with a soul. . . . This is a personal narrative of a church that not only brings the people to it by the thousands but it also goes to the people by the hundreds of thousands in their homes" (ibid., 24).

17. Daniel Mark Epstein, *Sister Aimee: The Life of Aimee Semple McPherson* (New York: Harcourt Brace Jovanovich, 1993), 74.

18. Edith L. Blumhofer, *Aimee Semple McPherson: Everybody's Sister* (Grand Rapids: Eerdmans, 1993), 268–69.

19. Quoted in Tona J. Hangen, *Redeeming the Dial: Radio, Religion, and Popular Culture in America* (Chapel Hill: The University of North Carolina Press, 2002), 21. Schultze observes: "Evangelicals were far more optimistic about radio than were their mainline Protestant counterparts. Even the liberal rector of the Calvary Church, which sponsored the legendary first religious broadcast on KDKA in January 1921, later expressed publicly his misgivings about religious radio, comparing the temptation to air religious programs with King Jeroboam's desire to lord over the early nation of Israel by making sacred calves for the people to worship" ("Evangelical Radio and the Rise of the Electronic Church, 1921–1948," 290).

20. Miller, "Radio and Religion," 140.

21. Billy Graham recalled his first encounter with television at the New York World's Fair: "My first excursion north was when I finished Bible school in 1939. I was invited to hold some meetings in York, Pennsylvania. After that I went to the New York World's Fair for a few days. We didn't have enough money to stay very long. . . . That's when I first heard of television. They had a camera and you could walk in front of it and see your picture a few yards away. They said this was going to come to the whole country. Of course, nobody believed it. It was too impossible to think about" ("This Date in History – The 75th Anniversary of Television," Billy Graham Library, April 20, 2014, https://billygrahamlibrary.org/this-date-in-history-the-75th-anniversary-of-television/).

22. "First Television Broadcast of Easter Services," *The Gazette and Daily* (York, Pennsylvania, March 25, 1940), 5. The midnight Mass celebrated in Notre Dame Cathedral in Paris on Christmas of 1948 is also celebrated as an early televised church service and reached far greater numbers of viewers than Sheen's 1940 broadcast.

23. Ben Armstrong, *The Electric Church* (Nashville: Thomas Nelson, 1979), 87.

24. Oral Roberts, *My Story* (Tulsa: Summit, 1961), 161. See also David Edwin Harrell Jr., *Oral Roberts: An American Life* (Bloomington, IN: Indiana University Press, 1985), 129–30.

25. J. Thomas Bisset, "Religious Broadcasting: Assessing the State of the Art," *Christianity Today*, December 12, 1980, 29.

26. William F. Fore could ask: "Has the electronic church become captive to commercial broadcasting?" ("Beyond the Electronic Church," *The Christian Century* 98 [January 7–14, 1981], 29).

27. See William Hendricks, "The Theology of the Electronic Church," *Review and Expositor* 81 (1984): 59–75. Several of the articles in this special issue are dedicated to researching the "Electric Church."

28. See Jeffrey K. Hadden and Charles E. Swann, *Prime Time Preachers: The Rising Power of Televangelism* (Reading, PA: Addison-Wesley, 1981), 159–74. Hadden and Swann argue that the claimed reach of the Moral Majority, as well as the claimed audiences of most televangelistic ministries, was greatly inflated.

29. Quentin J. Schultze, "Electronic Church," in *Dictionary of Christianity in America* (Downers Grove, IL: InterVarsity Press, 1990), 386.

30. See idem., "Redeeming the Electronic Church," in *Televangelism and American Culture: The Business of Popular Religion* (Grand Rapids: Baker, 1991), 225–48; Mark Ward, Sr., *Air of Salvation: The Story of Christian Broadcasting* (Grand Rapids: Baker, 1994).

31. Roberts, *My Story*, 158.

32. See Peter Malone, *Screen Jesus: Portrayals of Christ in Television and Film* (Plymouth: Scarecrow Press, 2012).

33. Franklin Foer, "Baptism by Celluloid," *New York Times* (February 8, 2004), https://www.nytimes.com/2004/02/08/movies/baptism-by-celluloid.html. See also Bill Bright's introduction to Paul Eshleman, *I Just Saw Jesus* (San Bernardino: Campus Crusade for Christ, 1991).

34. Eleanor Blau, "A Movie Translation of Entire Bible Begun to Transmit Faith to Today's Nonreaders," *New York Times* (January 26, 1976), 25.

35. Ibid.

36. "The History of Jesus Film Project," Jesus Film Project, https://www.jesusfilm.org/about/history.html.

37. Masterworks, "Jesus Film Project: Measuring Global Impact" (January 2017), 59; https://www.jesusfilm.org/content/dam/jesusfilm/pdf/Masterworks-Jesus-Film-Final-Presentation.pdf.

38. https://www.jesusfilm.org/watch/jesus.html/english.html.

39. Interview with Irv Klaschus (producer at The Jesus Film Project), conducted by Jonathan J. Armstrong on April 20, 2020.

40. Power, "Angelus Temple Is Unique Among Broadcasters," 44.

41. As it appears in print, the quote reads: "Tradition is the living faith of the dead, traditionalism is the dead faith of the living. And, I suppose I should add, it is traditionalism that gives tradition such a bad name" (*The Vindication of Tradition: The 1983 Jefferson Lecture in the Humanities* [New Haven: Yale University Press, 1984], 65).

42. See George M. Marsden, *Jonathan Edwards: A Life* (New Haven: Yale University Press, 2003), 54–55.

Chapter 3: The Church Steps into Virtual Reality

1. Tim Hutchings, *Creating Church Online: Ritual, Community and New Media* (London: Routledge, 2017), 244.

2. Rhoda Thomas Tripp, *The International Thesaurus of Quotations* (New York: T. Y. Crowell, 1970), 280.
3. See Randall J. Stephens, *The Devil's Music: How Christians Inspired, Condemned, and Embraced Rock 'N' Roll* (Cambridge: Harvard University Press, 2018).
4. See Andrew R. Chow, "'Come As You Are in the Family Car.' Drive-in Church Services Are Taking off During the Coronavirus Pandemic," *Time Magazine* (March 28, 2020), https://time.com/5811387/drive-in-church-coronavirus/.
5. Caitlin Dewey, "A Complete History of the Rise and Fall—and Reincarnation!—of the Beloved '90s Chatroom," *The Washington Post*, October 30, 2014, https://www.washingtonpost.com/news/the-intersect/wp/2014/10/30/a-complete-history-of-the-rise-and-fall-and-reincarnation-of-the-beloved-90s-chatroom/.
6. "Cyberspace as Sacred Space," 794. O'Leary was raised a Roman Catholic and died prior to the outbreak of the coronavirus crisis on February 4, 2020.
7. See Heidi Campbell's account of "The Great Anglican Online Listmeet" in *Exploring Religious Community Online: We Are One in the Network* (New York: Peter Lang, 2005), xi–xii. Campbell discusses the use of email in religious networks extensively in this monograph.
8. Erik Davis, "Technopagans: May the Astral Plane Be Reborn in Cyberspace," *Wired*, July 1995, 126–33, 174–81.
9. Joshua Cooper Ramo, "Finding God on the Web: Across the Internet, Believers Are Re-Examining Their Ideas of Faith, Religion and Spirituality," *Time*, December 16, 1996, http://content.time.com/time/magazine/article/0,9171,985700,00.html. Some things have clearly changed since 1996, such as when the author of the article expresses surprise and amazement that even sacred Scripture is being rendered into hypertext. The article exults, "Just as the first illuminated manuscripts exposed readers to early theological debates, these hypertexts open up thousands of interpretations of God's words to anyone curious enough to click a mouse."
10. The Barna Group determined that, by 2000, still only 34 percent of Protestant churches had websites; by 2005, this number had jumped up to 57 percent ("New Research Describes Use of Technology in Churches," [April 28, 2008], https://www.barna.com/research/new-research-describes-use-of-technology-in-churches/). By 2010, email had become more or less ubiquitous, with about 90 percent of Christians having email addresses (Scott Thumma, "Virtually Religious: Technology and Internet Use in American Congregations" [Hartford: Hartford Institute for Religious Research, 2012]: 2). See Walt Wilson's account of a church staff learning to use email for the first time (*The Internet Church*, 94–95).
11. Nina Flourney, "Welcome to Worship: Click Here," *The Dallas Morning News* (May 20, 2000), https://www.godweb.org/dallas.htm.

12. Interview with Douglas Estes (Associate Professor of New Testament and Practical Theology at South University – Columbia), conducted by Jonathan J. Armstrong on October 4, 2019.
13. Douglas Estes, *SimChurch: Being the Church in the Virtual World* (Grand Rapids: Zondervan, 2009), 94.
14. Ibid., 96.
15. Patrick Dixon, *Cyberchurch: Christianity and the Internet* (Eastbourne: Kingsway, 1997).
16. Ibid., 55–56.
17. Ibid., 86.
18. Ibid., 177.
19. Ibid., 39.
20. Ibid., 94.
21. Dixon writes, "We might conclude then that while the Internet can fulfill the condition of two or three gathering together in prayer, it is unlikely to fulfill the conditions for an assembly. But are we being too rigid here? If Jesus is present with two believers talking to each other and praying on the telephone, and therefore in the midst of an Internet voice call or video link for similar purposes, and also in an Internet Relay Chat prayer link, then what is the situation with a larger electronic gathering?" (ibid., 91).
22. Ibid., 153. Dixon notes that Paul, too, faced the possibility of miscommunication in the application of technology: "The technology he used, pen and ink, was not universally understood, for many were illiterate. It was state-of-the-art in his day."
23. Barna Research Group, "The Cyberchurch Is Coming: National Survey of Teenagers Shows Expectation of Substituting Internet for Corner Church," April 20, 1998.
24. Ibid.
25. The conclusions Barna reached indeed seem puzzling when one reviews the actual data cited. For example, Barna reported that only 12 percent of the adult population of the US used the internet each month for religious purposes, stating, "The most common of those purposes is to interact with others via chat rooms or e-mail about religious ideas, beliefs or experiences." Further, only 9 percent of teenagers reported using the internet every day, and only 4 percent of teenagers reported using the internet to pursue religious or spiritual experiences. Barna's conclusions seem not to have been based on current practice but rather based on what those who participated in the study reported as their expectation for the future: "One out of six teens (16%) said that within the next five years they expect to use the Internet as a substitute for their current church-based religious experience" (ibid.).
26. "But in the case of internet, web and net, a change in our house style was necessary to put into perspective what the internet is: another medium for delivering and receiving information. That it transformed

human communication is beyond dispute. But no more so than moveable type did in its day. Or the radio. Or television" (Tony Long, "It's Just the 'internet' Now," *Wired*, August 16, 2004, https://www.wired.com/2004/08/its-just-the-internet-now.

27. Interview with Tim Hutchings (Assistant Professor of Religious Ethics at the University of Nottingham), conducted by Jonathan J. Armstrong on October 1, 2019.

28. The Archbishop's Council on Mission and Public Affairs, *Mission-Shaped Church: Church Planting and Fresh Expressions of Church in a Changing Context* (London: Church House Publishing, 2004), 7.

29. Ibid., vii.

30. In the official report issued following the initial launch of the church, i-church (https://www.i-church.org/gatehouse/) is described as "an online Christian Community" and "a Christian community of the Church of England based in the Diocese of Oxford." The report states: "The original vision was to use the internet to create a new spiritual community; a network church for people who do not wish, or are not able, to join a local church. It was also hoped that it would be available as 'added value' to existing church members who travel or who are otherwise unable to be part of their local church" (Angie Paterson, "Cutting Edge Ministries: The Journey: 2002–2008" [Diocese of Oxford, 2008], 26). See also Pam Smith, *Online Mission and Ministry: A Theological and Practical Guide* (London: SPCK Publishing, 2015), 96–97; Mark Howe, *Online Church? First Steps Towards Virtual Incarnation* (Cambridge: Ridley Hall, 2007), 3.

31. Rebecca Paveley, "Click Your Way to Church," *Church Times* (August 12, 2009), https://www.churchtimes.co.uk/articles/2009/14-august/features/click-your-way-to-church.

32. "First Web-Pastor Appointed," BBC News, last updated May 11, 2004, http://news.bbc.co.uk/2/hi/uk_news/magazine/3704205.stm.

33. Smith, *Online Mission and Ministry*, 1.

34. Ibid., 2.

35. Ibid., 56–57.

36. Ibid., 57.

37. Blog post by Matt Rees titled "Still at the Cutting Edge" at the Diocese of Oxford's website: https://www.oxford.anglican.org/tag/i-church/

38. Personal email from Pam Smith to Jonathan J. Armstrong on January 22, 2020.

39. Hutchings, *Creating Church Online*, 67.

40. Barnaby J. Feder, "The First Church of Cyberspace: Services Tomorrow," *The New York Times* (May 15, 2004). See also the report by Giles Wilson, the BBC journalist, who experienced and reported on one of these services: "In Cyberspace, Can Anyone Hear You Pray?," http://news.bbc.co.uk/2/hi/uk_news/magazine/3706897.stm.

41. Simon Jenkins, "Rituals and Pixels: Experiments in Online Church," *Heidelberg Journal of Religions on the Internet* (2008): 95. Jenkins gives a detailed account of the technical and psychological aspects of the project.

42. Interview with Simon Jenkins (founder of the Church of Fools), conducted by Jonathan J. Armstrong on April 22, 2020.

43. Jenkins published print editions of the magazine until 1983, when the project was discontinued. "The project died, partly because I got a good job and I needed to focus," Jenkins explained. He worked with the Scripture Union in London and then Lion Publishing, where he served as Commissioning Editor, finally transitioning to work as a freelance editor from 1988 until the present. "But I always missed it," Jenkins recalls: "It was a lovely project." Jenkins explained that he did not have internet access until 1997: "In '97 I finally got on the internet. I had a year when I couldn't get on the internet because the cable of my computer wouldn't reach the plug in the wall. But eventually in '97 I got on the internet, and as soon as I did I realized, talking to Steve [Goddard], that 'Ship of Fools' would be much better on the internet than it ever could have been in print."

44. Jenkins, "Rituals and Pixels," 100.

45. Ibid., 101.

46. Ibid., 108.

47. Ibid.

48. Howe, *Online Church?*, 19.

49. Ibid., 20.

50. "Hundreds Rely Entirely on Online Church for Christian Contact," *Christian Today*, October 20, 2007, https://christiantoday.com/article/ hundreds.rely.entirely.on.online.church.for.christian.contact/14082.htm.

51. Interview with Simon Jenkins (founder of the Church of Fools), conducted by Jonathan J. Armstrong on April 22, 2020.

52. Jenkins, "Rituals and Pixels," 109. Tim Hutchings noted that the Anglican liturgy transferred well to the online environment: "It was a style of worship that worked pretty effectively in the technology available in chatrooms. A text-based chatroom is a fantastic place for a traditional call-and-response liturgy" (interview conducted by Jonathan J. Armstrong on October 1, 2019).

53. "History," The Anglican Cathedral of Second Life, https://slangcath .wordpress.com/about/history/.

54. "What Is The Robloxian Christians?," The Robloxian Christians Online Church, https://www.therobloxianchristians.org/about.

55. See J. Clement, "Hours of Video Uploaded to YouTube Every Minute as of May 2019," Statista, August 25, 2020, https://www.statista.com/ statistics/259477/hours-of-video-uploaded-to-youtube-every-minute/.

56. BEME News, "Is Virtual Religion the New VR?," YouTube, May 7, 2018, https://www.youtube.com/watch?v=N0IImB0gItI&feature=youtu.be.

57. Jessica Chou, "This Pastor Is Putting His Faith in a Virtual Reality Church," *Wired*, February 2, 2018, https://www.wired.com/story/virtual-reality-church/.

58. Interview with D. J. Soto (founder of VR Church), conducted by Jonathan J. Armstrong on July 24, 2019.

59. Personal email with D. J. Soto, January 23, 2020.

60. Interview with D. J. Soto (founder of VR Church), conducted by Jonathan J. Armstrong on July 24, 2019.

61. 100 Huntley Street, "VR Church / DJ Soto", YouTube, October 28, 2019, https://www.youtube.com/watch?v=pdGC-xzIGEA&feature=youtu.be.

62. KPIX CBS SF Bay Area, "VR Church: Bay Area Pastor Gives Services a High Tech Twist, Delivering Using VR Technology," YouTube, September 2, 2018, https://www.youtube.com/watch?v=F6_dv-OUr1A&feature=youtu.be.

63. Interview with D. J. Soto (founder of VR Church), conducted by Jonathan J. Armstrong on July 24, 2019.

64. Chou, "This Pastor Is Putting His Faith in a Virtual Reality Church," https://www.wired.com/story/virtual-reality-church/.

65. Frank Newport, "Religion and the COVID-19 Virus in the U.S," Gallup, April 6, 2020, https://news.gallup.com/opinion/polling matters/307619/religion-covid-virus.aspx.

66. Interview with Tim Hutchings (Assistant Professor of Religious Ethics at the University of Nottingham), conducted by Jonathan J. Armstrong on October 1, 2019.

Chapter 4: The Nature of Virtuality

1. T. S. Eliot, *The Complete Poems and Plays: 1909–1950* (New York: Harcourt, Brace & World, 1962), 96.

2. Freeman J. Dyson, *Infinite in All Directions* (New York: Perennial, 2004), 270.

3. Cline writes, "I wrote a science fiction novel about virtual reality because I was fascinated by the concept and wanted to imagine its vast potential and limitless application. Where is this technology that I've been promised for decades? And what will it look like, if and when it actually becomes a reality?" (Blake J. Harris, foreword by Ernest Cline, *The History of the Future: Oculus, Facebook, and the Revolution that Swept Virtual Reality* [New York: HarperColins, 2019], xv). Harris concurs: "Really, the only 'limit' to the limitless possibilities of VR was the computing power. The faster computers got, the better the graphics would be and the more real virtual worlds could feel" (11). Harris paraphrases the conclusion of Palmer Luckey, the inventor of Oculus: "If technology existed that could allow *anyone* to be *anywhere* at *any time*, then not even the sky was the limit" (12).

4. Jacques Barzun, *From Dawn to Decadence: 1500 to the Present: 500 Years of Western Cultural Life* (New York: HarperCollins, 2000), 539.
5. For this observation, we are indebted to Jeremy Bailenson, who gained this insight through years of research as founding director of the Virtual Human Interaction Lab at Stanford University (see *Experience on Demand: What Virtual Reality Is, How It Works, and What It Can Do* [New York: W. W. Norton, 2018], 253).
6. In fact, the history of early VR intersects with the history of the flight simulator (Bailenson, *Experience on Demand*, 23–25).
7. TED, "Chris Milk: How Virtual Reality Can Create the Ultimate Empathy Machine," YouTube, April 22, 2015, https://www.youtube.com/watch?v=iXHil1TPxvA.
8. Bailenson, *Experience on Demand*, 215.
9. Interview with John Dyer (Dean of Enrollment Services and Distance Education at Dallas Theological Seminary), conducted by Jonathan J. Armstrong on July 22, 2019.
10. Tim Hutchings, *Creating Church Online: Ritual, Community and New Media* (London: Routledge, 2017), 1.
11. See "On the Apparel of Women," trans. S. Thelwall, in *Ante-Nicene Fathers*, eds., Alexander Roberts and James Donaldson (Peabody, MA: Hendrickson, 1995), 4:14–25.
12. Andrew Tarantola, "'Fortnite' Made a Historic 1.8 Billion in 2019," Engadget, January 4, 2020, https://www.engadget.com/2020-01-04-fortnite-made-historic-1-8-billion-in-2019.html.
13. Pam Smith, *Online Mission and Ministry: A Theological and Practical Guide* (London: Society for Promoting Christian Knowledge, 2015), 80–86.
14. Issie Lapowsky, "Mark Zuckerberg Answers to Congress for Facebook's Troubles," *Wired*, April 10, 2018, https://www.wired.com/story/mark-zuckerberg-congress-facebook-troubles/.
15. "Urbana 15 'Hackathon' Inspires Opportunities for Missions," CBN News, December 28, 2015, https://www1.cbn.com/cbnnews/us/2015/December/Urbana-15-Hackathon-Inspires-Opportunities-for-Missions.
16. Sherry Turkle, *Reclaiming Conversation: The Power of Talk in a Digital Age* (New York: Penguin, 2015), 307.
17. Shane Hipps, *Flickering Pixels: How Technology Shapes Your Faith* (Grand Rapids: Zondervan, 2009), 36–38.
18. "Virtual Reality Church - John Crist," YouTube, December 11, 2018, https://www.youtube.com/watch?v=R_bkNkrWdz8&t=1s.
19. Jeremy Bailenson writes, "But focusing on all the spectacular solo experiences that VR makes possible obscures what I believe is the truly groundbreaking promise of the technology. It's right there in the first literary journey through virtual reality, in William Gibson's 1984 cyberpunk thriller *Neuromancer*. . . . Gibson's virtual reality—what he calls 'cyberspace' and 'the matrix'—is defined in the novel as 'a *consensual*

hallucination' (my emphasis). What Gibson suggests is that it won't be the graphics or photorealistic avatars that will make these virtual worlds feel real—it will be the community of people interacting within them, bringing the world alive through their mutual acknowledgement of its reality" (*Experience on Demand*, 174).

20. See Gary Wilson, *Your Brain on Porn: Internet Pornography and the Emerging Science of Addiction* (Kent, UK: Commonwealth Publishing, 2015).

21. See Barna Group and Josh McDowell, "The Porn Phenomenon: The Impact of Pornography in the Digital Age" (2016).

22. "Seize the Net," Ship of Fools, http://www.ship-of-fools.com/features/2008/seize_net.html.

23. "The Internet places in the grasp of young people at an unusually early age an immense capacity for doing good and doing harm, to themselves and others. It can enrich their lives beyond the dreams of earlier generations and empower them to enrich others' lives in turn. It also can plunge them into consumerism, pornographic and violent fantasy, and pathological isolation" (John P. Foley, "The Church and Internet" [Rome: Pontifical Council for Social Communications, 2002], paragraph 11).

24. Interview with Alan Noble (Assistant Professor of English at Oklahoma Baptist University), conducted by Jonathan J. Armstrong on April 29, 2019.

25. Interview with Craig Detweiler (President of the Wedgewood Circle), conducted by Jonathan J. Armstrong on December 18, 2019.

26. Shoshana Zuboff, *The Age of Surveillance Capitalism: The Fight for a Human Future at the New Frontier of Power* (New York: PublicAffairs, 2019). See also George Guilder, *Life after Google: The Fall of Big Data and the Rise of the Blockchain Economy* (Washington DC: Regnery Publishing, 2018).

27. Wheeler, *From Gutenberg to Google*, 192.

28. J. Clement, "Social Media - Statistics & Facts," Statista, May 18, 2020, https://www.statista.com/topics/1164/social-networks/.

29. "Seize the Net," Ship of Fools, http://www.ship-of-fools.com/features/2008/seize_net.html.

Chapter 5: God, Creation, and New Creation

1. David G. Benner, *Opening to God: Lectio Divina and Life as Prayer* (Downers Grove: InterVarsity Press, 2010), 34; Benner attributes this insight to his reading of Thomas Merton's *New Seeds of Contemplation* (New York: New Directions, 1961).

2. Arthur F. Holmes, *All Truth Is God's Truth* (Grand Rapids: Eerdmans, 1977), 8.

3. A perennial research theme in her career, Sherry Turkle touches on these ideas in the introduction to her first book: "Technology catalyzes

change not only in what we do but in how we think. It changes people's awareness of themselves, of one another, of their relationship with the world. The new machine that stands behind the flashing digital signal, unlike the clock, the telescope, or the train, is a machine that 'thinks.' It challenges our notions not only of time and distance, but of mind" (*The Second Self: Computers and the Human Spirit*, twentieth anniversary edition [Cambridge: MIT Press, 2005], 19).

4. "The argument for the simulation [theory], I think, is quite strong. . . . If you assume any rate of improvement at all, then games will be indistinguishable from reality, or civilization will end, one of those two things will occur, although we are most likely in a simulation, because we exist." "Joe Rogan Experience #1169 Elon Musk (w/transcript)," YouTube, September 9, 2018, https://www.youtube.com/watch?v=VeIasZ6WbxA.

5. Anglican Church in North America, *The Book of Common Prayer* (Huntington Beach, CA: Anglican Liturgy Press, 2019), 109.

6. "Hence we may infer, that the human mind is, so to speak, a perpetual forge of idols" (John Calvin, *Institutes of the Christian Religion*, trans. Henry Beveridge [Peabody, MA: Hendrickson, 2008], 55 [I.11.8]).

7. Justin Martyr, *The First and Second Apologies*, trans. Leslie William Bernard (New York: Paulist Press, 1997), 84 [*Second Apology*, 13].

8. Augustine, *Teaching Christianity*, trans. Edmund Hill (Hyde Park, NY: New City Press, 1996), 144 [2.18].

9. Crouch concludes: "So how do we make sense of the world? The two senses turn out to be more intertwined than we might have thought. We *make sense* of the world by *making something* of the world.... Meaning and making go together—culture, you could say, is the activity of making meaning" (*Culture Making: Recovering our Creative Calling* [Downers Grove, IL: InterVarsity Press, 2008], 24).

10. See *The God Who Is There*, in *The Complete Works of Francis A. Schaeffer: A Christian Worldview*, 1–202 (Wheaton, IL: Crossway, 1982), 54.

11. For an introduction to the topic, see Jacob Shatzer, *Transhumanism and the Image of God: Today's Technology and the Future of Christian Discipleship* (Downers Grove, IL: IVP Academic, 2019). See also Jason Thacker, "Future: What's Coming Next?" in *The Age of AI* (Grand Rapids: Zondervan, 2020), 167–182.

12. Julian Huxley, "Transhumanism," in *New Bottles for New Wine* (London: Chatto and Windus, 1957), 13–17. Julian was the brother of Aldous Huxley, author of *Brave New World* (1932).

13. Brynjolfsson and McAfee, "Moore's Law and the Second Half of the Chessboard," in *The Second Machine Age*, 39–56. See also Friedman, *Thank You for Being Late*, 26.

14. Ray Kurzweil, *The Singularity Is Near: When Humans Transcend Biology* (London: Duckworth, 2005). Many of the same themes trace back to Hans Moravec's *Mind Children: The Future of Robot and Human Intelligence* (Cambridge, MA: Harvard University Press, 1988).

15. This is the concluding line of the documentary "Transcendent Man," directed by Barry Ptolemy, and released in the US in 2011.

16. Ray Kurzweil, "The Law of Accelerating Returns," KurzweilAI.net, March 7, 2001, https://www.kurzweilai.net/the-law-of-accelerating-returns.

17. Kurzweil, *The Singularity Is Near*, 70. Kurzweil then estimates the capability of the human brain to be equivalent to the computing power of ten-to-the-sixteenth power calculations per second (ibid., 124).

18. "U.S. Department of Energy and Cray to Deliver Record-Setting Frontier Supercomputer at ORNL," Department of Energy, May 7, 2019, https://www.energy.gov/articles/us-department-energy-and-cray-deliver-record-setting-frontier-supercomputer-ornl.

19. Kurzweil, *The Singularity Is Near*, 124. He concludes: "For these reasons, it is reasonable to expect human brain capacity, at least in terms of hardware computational capacity, for one thousand dollars by around 2020" (ibid., 126).

20. Ibid., 136. Kurzweil's final estimate in terms of chronology is that, by the year 2080, a personal computer that costs $1,000 will be able to "perform the equivalent of all human thought over the last ten thousand years (assumed at ten billion human brains for ten thousand years) in ten microseconds" (ibid., 135).

21. Malcolm MacIver, "The Geek Rapture and Other Musings of William Gibson," *Discover*, October 17, 2011, https://www.discovermagazine.com/mind/the-geek-rapture-and-other-musings-of-william-gibson.

22. Amy Webb, *The Big Nine: How the Tech Titans and Their Thinking Machines Could Warp Humanity* (New York: PublicAffairs, 2019), 50.

23. Max Tegmark writes: "Freed from its genetic shackles, humanity's combined knowledge has kept growing at an accelerating pace as each breakthrough enabled the next: language, writing, the printing press, modern science, computers, the internet, etc. This ever-faster cultural evolution of our shared software has emerged as the dominant force shaping our human future, rendering our glacially slow biological evolution almost irrelevant" (*Life 3.0: Being Human in the Age of Artificial Intelligence* [New York: Alfred A. Knopf, 2017], 28–29).

24. Yuval Noah Harari, *Homo Deus: A Brief History of Tomorrow* (New York: HarperCollins, 2017), 386–87.

25. https://www.wired.com/story/god-is-a-bot-and-anthony-levandowski-is-his-messenger/.

26. Max Tegmark does a commendable job in explaining his position of how this could be possible with the theory of "substrate independence" (see *Life 3.0: Being Human in the Age of Artificial Intelligence*, 49–81).

27. Tegmark, *Life 3.0*, 67.

28. Thacker, *The Age of AI*, 177.

29. Quentin J. Schultze, *Habits of the High-Tech Heart: Living Virtuously in the Information Age* (Grand Rapids: Baker Academic, 2002), 17.

30. Ibid., 19.

31. "We are succumbing to *informationism:* a non-discerning, vacuous faith in the collection and dissemination of information as a route to social progress and personal happiness" (ibid., 26).

Chapter 6: The Incarnation and Pentecost

1. Athanasius, *On the Incarnation* (Yonkers, NY: St Vladimir's Seminary Press, 2002), 44 [3.16].
2. Jay Y. Kim, *Analogue Church: Why We Need Real People, Places, and Things in the Digital Age* (Downers Grove, IL: InterVarsity Press, 2020), 2.
3. Athanasius, *On the Incarnation*, 34 [2.8].
4. Anselm of Canterbury, *The Major Works*, ed. Brian Davies and G. R. Evans, in *Oxford World's Classics* (Oxford: University Press, 2008), 260–356.
5. Ibid., 352 [2.19].
6. Anglican Church in North America, *The Book of Common Prayer* (Huntington Beach, CA: Anglican Liturgy Press, 2019), 109.
7. This conclusion was adopted from the Council of Ephesus in AD 431. See "The Epistle of Cyril to Nestorius," trans. H. R. Percival, in *Nicene and Post-Nicene Fathers*, second series (Peabody: Hendrickson, 1995), 14:197–198.
8. The Cost of Sequencing a Human Genome," National Human Genome Research Institute, August 25, 2020, https://www.genome.gov/about-genomics/fact-sheets/Sequencing-Human-Genome-cost.
9. C. S. Lewis, *The Weight of Glory and Other Addresses* (Grand Rapids: Eerdmans, 1965), 23–24.
10. Some have asked whether the very concept of a VR church is out of tune with the Bible's presuppositions about ultimate reality, perhaps even intrinsically Gnostic. One author remarks that some interpretations of VR do sound "reminiscent of the ancient heresy of Gnosticism, which taught that the material world was evil and salvation is achieved by transcending beyond the material to the spiritual" (C. T. Casberg, "The Surprising Theological Possibilities of Virtual Reality," *Christianity Today*, November 11, 2016, https://www.christianitytoday.com/ct/2016/november-web-only/surprising-theological-possibilities-of-virtual-reality.html); see also the blog post by Roger E. Olson on January 11, 2018, "How Much Change in Church Life Is Too Much?" (https://www.patheos.com/blogs/rogereolson/2018/01/much-change-church-life-much/). The Gnostics were a group of heretics in the early church who held the physical order in such contempt that they concluded that the god who created matter must be evil and not the true God. The Gnostics then proffered a knowledge (*gnosis*) of the true God, whom they claimed could not be known through creation or a common reading of the Bible. Certainly, wearing a VR headset does not prevent one from espousing a heretical worldview, but as a medium, VR technology no

more inclines one to a Gnostic worldview than does listening to music by CD player.

11. Dana Cowley, "Siren at FMX 2018: Crossing the Uncanny Valley in Real Time," Unreal Engine, April 18, 2018, https://www.unrealengine.com/en-US/events/siren-at-fmx-2018-crossing-the-uncanny-valley-in-real-time.

12. Samantha Masunaga, "Here Are Some of the Tweets That Got Microsoft's AI Tay in Trouble," *Los Angeles Times*, March 25, 2020, https://www.latimes.com/business/technology/la-fi-tn-microsoft-tay-tweets-20160325-htmlstory.html.

13. Anglican Church in North America, *The Book of Common Prayer*, 109.

14. John Ortberg, *God Is Closer Than You Think* (Grand Rapids: Zondervan, 2005), 15.

15. See John P. Foley, "The Church and the Internet" (Rome: Pontifical Council for Social Communication, 2002), paragraph 2.

16. See Augustine, *Teaching Christianity*, trans. Edmund Hill (Hyde Park, NY: New City Press, 1996), 18 [1.27.28].

17. Interview with Craig Detweiler (President of the Wedgewood Circle), conducted by Jonathan J. Armstrong on December 18, 2019.

18. Interview with Sean Dunn (Founder and President of Groundwire), conducted by Jonathan J. Armstrong on April 23, 2020.

19. In a paragraph titled "Cyberchurch is no substitute for real-life membership," Dixon argues: "After all, a fundamental command from Jesus to his disciples was that they must love each other. He told them that their love for each other would be a sign of the kingdom, an unmistakable demonstration that they were his followers (John 13:34–35). But love requires involvement. Jesus was not talking of sentimental love but of family *agape* love. To all who believed on his name, he gave the right to become children of God (John 1:12). We are brothers and sisters to each other, in close relationship, with eternal bonds of mutual commitment and self-sacrifice. The biblical picture of a church is of a gathered community, a royal priesthood, a holy nation, a people called by God out of darkness into his marvelous light (1 Peter 2:9). None of this can be fulfilled merely by virtual reality friendships, where people can unplug the modem every time they feel like giving up on people" (*Cyberchurch*, 94).

Chapter 7: The New People of God and Visible Signs of Invisible Grace

1. Rowan Williams, foreword to *Mission-Shaped Church: Church Planting and Fresh Expressions of Church in a Changing Context* (London: Church House Publishing, 2004), vii.

2. https://www.thegospelcoalition.org/article/cant-livestream-church/.

3. The use of the word "church" to refer to a local congregation of believers is also the customary usage in Acts. In one instance (Acts 8:3), we see that the church in one location is comprised of a network of houses. In several instances, the church is referred to as an intercity or regional

network (for example, Acts 14:23; 1 Cor. 16:1; 2 Cor. 8:1; Gal. 1:22; 1 Thess. 2:14). Sometimes the term is used to refer to a gathering in a particular house (Rom. 16:5; Col. 4:15; Phil. 1:2).

4. For example, "I commend to you our sister Phoebe, a servant of the church at Cenchreae" (Rom. 16:1 ESV; see also Col. 4:16). This is the way the word functions in every instance in Acts as well as the majority of instances in the Epistles.

5. See Eph. 1:22; 3:10; Col. 1:18. This includes references where Paul speaks of persecuting the church (see 1 Cor. 15:9; Gal. 1:13). When referring to the universal church, Paul generally uses the singular of the term "church," whereas when referring to networks of churches he almost always employs the plural (see, for example, 2 Cor. 11:28).

6. See Liddell, Scott, and Jones, *A Greek-English Lexicon* (Oxford: Clarendon Press, 1996).

7. C. S. Lewis, *The Four Loves: An Exploration of the Nature of Love* (New York: Mariner Books, 2012), 61.

8. Interview with Douglas Estes, conducted by Jonathan J. Armstrong on October 4, 2019.

9. Wilson, *The Internet Church*, 22.

10. Interview with Simon Jenkins (founder of the Church of Fools), conducted by Jonathan J. Armstrong on April 22, 2020.

11. Patrick Dixon, *Cyberchurch: Christianity and the Internet* (Eastbourne: Kingsway, 1997), 157.

12. Interview with Jay Kranda (Online Campus Pastor at Saddleback Church), conducted by Jonathan J. Armstrong on February 24, 2020.

13. Ibid.

14. Clyde Taber concurs. Although virtual participation is not the "end game" for Christian ministry, Taber affirms: "But if that's the starting point for people who can find faith, find relationships, find community, find nurturing, I'm all for it" (interview with Clyde Taber [Director of Visual Story Network], conducted by Jonathan J. Armstrong on July 24, 2019).

15. Nona Jones, *From Social Media to Social Ministry: A Guide to Digital Discipleship* (Grand Rapids: Zondervan, 2020), 32.

16. Mark Howe, *Online Church?*, 22.

17. See John Dyer's helpful analysis in "Digital Communion: History, Theology, and Practices" (March 23, 2020), https://j.hn/digital-communion-summary-of-theology-practices/.

18. "What Is the Sacrament of the Altar?," in *Luther's Small Catechism with Explanation* (St. Louis: Concordia Publishing House, 2017), 28.

19. Ibid., 323.

20. John Calvin, *Institutes of the Christian Religion*, 4.14.1; see Augustine, *Explanations of the Psalms*, 99.8.

21. Calvin, *Institutes of the Christian Religion*, 4.14.3.

22. Arielle Pardes, "Amid Coronavirus Fears, Startups Rethink the Virtual Conference," *Wired* (March 9, 2020), https://www.wired.com/story/amid-coronavirus-fears-startups-rethink-virtual-conference/. When it was announced on February 11, 2020, that the Mobil World Congress would be cancelled—the event, scheduled for the end of February and which sought to bring some 100,000 people at Barcelona—many gained their first glimpses of the crisis that would unfold. A whole series of high-profile tech conventions were then cancelled, like dominoes falling one after another.

23. *Catechism of the Catholic Church*, second edition (New York: Doubleday, 1995), 368 [1324]; see also *Lumen Gentium*, 11; *Ecclesia de Eucharistia*, 1.

24. "Take Communion Online with Us," Saddleback Church, January 24, 2014, https://saddleback.com/archive/blog/internet-campus/2014/01/24/take-communion-online-with-us.

25. See the June 6, 1938, article in *Time*, http://content.time.com/time/magazine/article/0,9171,771109,00.html.

26. Simon Jenkins, "Can Online Communion Be Real?," *Church Times*, August 25, 2020, https://www.churchtimes.co.uk/articles/2010/27-august/comment/can-online-communion-be-real.

27. Heather Hahn, "Moratorium, Study Urged on Online Communion," UM News, October 4, 2013, https://www.umnews.org/en/news/moratorium-study-urged-on-online-communion.

28. Sam Hodges, "Both Green Light, Red Light for Online Communion," UM News, April 30, 2020, https://www.umnews.org/en/news/both-green-light-red-light-for-online-communion-2.

29. "Advisory Opinion - Communion in an Emergency/Pandemic," PCUSA, edited March 24, 2020, https://www.pcusa.org/site_media/media/uploads/oga/pdf/advisory_opinion_communion_in_an_emergency_or_pandemic.pdf.

30. Justin Martyr's *First Apology* [65], dating to about the middle of the second century, contains the earliest reference to the tradition of carrying the consecrated elements to members of the church who had been absent for services.

31. Chris Ridgeway, "Online Communion Can Still Be Sacramental," *Christianity Today*, March 27, 2020, https://www.christianitytoday.com/ct/2020/march-web-only/online-communion-can-still-be-sacramental.html.

32. Scott Swain, "Should We Live Stream the Lord's Supper?," *Reformed Blogmatics*, March 30, 2020, https://www.scottrswain.com/2020/03/30/should-we-live-stream-the-lords-supper/.

33. *Catechism of the Catholic Church*, 384 [1376].

34. John P. Foley, "The Church and the Internet" (Rome: Pontifical Council for Social Communication, 2002), paragraph 9.

35. CNA Daily News, "Pope Francis Offers This Spiritual Communion Prayer during Coronavirus Pandemic," Catholic World Report, March 21, 2020, https://www.catholicworldreport.com/2020/03/21/pope-francis-offers-this-spiritual-communion-prayer-during-coronavirus-pandemic/.

36. Antonio Spadaro, *Cybertheology: Thinking Christianity in the Era of the Internet*, trans. Maria Way (New York: Fordham University Press, 2014), 72–73.

37. Almost no one proposes that avatars should partake in sacramental life, as though people should participate in the life of Christ vicariously through an avatar. This proposal is not completely unattested, however. In June 2009, Paul Fiddes, Professor of Theology at the University of Oxford, contributed a paper to a theology symposium titled "Sacraments in a Virtual World?" This paper proposes that avatars can participate in sacraments performed within a virtual world. Fiddes writes, "The key theological question is whether the triune God is present, and whether Christ is incarnate (in some form, including the church) within the virtual world. If the answer is yes, then one can conceive of the mediation of grace through the materials of that world, i.e., through digital representations." We would argue, on the contrary, that the virtual world in this sense is not a space at all. God's grace is present in the physical space from which real people access VR worlds, but VR is no more a space that God's grace inhabits than is an optical illusion.

38. See Justin Murff, and Ashley Staggs-Kay, eds., "A Primer on Digital Ecclesiology," The Institute of Digital Ecclesiology, 2020.

39. See "New Tools for World Evangelism," special issue of *World Vision Magazine* (October 1966).

40. "Computers for Christ," *Christianity Today*, October 14, 1966, 51; see also Edward R. Dayton, "Computerize Evangelism?," *World Vision Magazine* (March 1966): 4–5.

Epilogue

1. Interview with Simon Jenkins (founder of the Church of Fools), conducted by Jonathan J. Armstrong on April 22, 2020.

2. Kevin Kelly, *The Inevitable: Understanding the 12 Technological Forces That Will Shape Our Future* (New York: Viking, 2016), 11.

3. One set of global broadcast events hosted by Pastor Nick Hall (Pulse Ministries) over the Easter 2020 weekend is reported to have totaled 1.7 million viewers on YouTube and Facebook in 43 languages with over 100 nations represented. Over 117,000 people responded to the gospel invitation. Some online commentators referred to this event as "The Great Quarantine Revival," https://www.westernjournal.com/great-quarantine-revival-117000-new-confessions-faith-reported-one-ministry/.

COULD BRAIN SCIENCE BE THE KEY TO SPIRITUAL FORMATION?

WHAT IF, INSTEAD OF KEEPING UP WITH CHANGE, YOU COULD GET AHEAD OF IT?

MOODY
Publishers®

*From the Word **to** Life*®

In *What Comes Next?*, you'll develop the capacity to guide your organization by shaping the future so that it can thrive. Strategists and innovation experts Nick Skytland & Ali Llewellyn provide a framework for us to lead as futurists and grow our businesses and ministries.

978-0-8024-1966-8 | also available as an eBook